THE
ANATOMY OF LANGO RELIGION
AND GROUPS

THE
ANATOMY OF LANGO RELIGION AND GROUPS

BY

T. T. S. HAYLEY

M.A. (CANTAB.), M.A. (OXON.)

INDIAN CIVIL SERVICE

DIRECTOR OF PUBLICITY AND RURAL DEVELOPMENT
TO THE GOVERNMENT OF ASSAM

NEGRO UNIVERSITIES PRESS
NEW YORK

Originally published in 1947
by Cambridge University Press

Reprinted 1970 by
Negro Universities Press
A DIVISION OF GREENWOOD PRESS, INC.
NEW YORK

SBN 8371-2871-4

PRINTED IN UNITED STATES OF AMERICA

CONTENTS

ILLUSTRATIONS

FOREWORD

While taking the Economics Tripos at Cambridge, I became interested in psychology and decided that it was a subject best approached through social anthropology, which I read for two years. For it was the social aspect of psychology that seemed to me to be important. The platitude that the physical progress of the modern world has outstripped its moral progress becomes much clearer when restated in terms of the obvious fact that the physical sciences have advanced by leaps and bounds, while the social sciences are still in their infancy. The peace of the world depends upon a reconciliation of this discrepancy.

During visits to Germany, totalling eight months in all, I had been struck by the symbolisms under which the emotional life of National Socialist Germany was organised. From the lightning flash embossed on the belt of the Hitler Youth to the swastika of the national flag could be seen the conscious efforts of the rulers of Germany to unify the peoples within their frontiers. 'Ein Volk zu sein ist heute unsere Religion', and the swastika became the focus of all the aspirations of the young German.

Professor F. C. Bartlett has emphasised one of the lessons of history that a group when threatened will strive to withstand disintegration. On what bases are groups organised? What forces hold them together? What elements are combined in nationalism? It was to questions such as these that modern Germany suggested answers.

I had intended to do a study of culture change in Lango, but my old interest in groups and symbolisms was reawakened by the discovery that in a relatively simple society, such as that of the Lango, it was quite possible to isolate the forces that train the individual in loyalty to his group. My main interests then became focused on dissecting the structure of Lango society into its constituent groups and analysing the physical and emotional forces which kept each group in existence. The value of each group in the economy of the Tribe had also to be determined. I have given the results of this investigation in Chapter II.

I found that the religious ceremonies of the Lango provided the most important means of inculcating and maintaining group and inter-group loyalties. If the ceremonies were to be described in detail, then the religious premises that lay behind them had also to be stated. This I have done in Chapter I. And so I have tried to show how the Lango groups were organised and how their religious beliefs permeated the whole of their social system.

Great confusion and inaccuracy arise from the use of approximate English equivalents of vernacular terms. To avoid this I have always used the Lango word, which I explain carefully in the Glossary. All items of material culture have also been described in the Glossary.

I reached Lango in September 1936 and left in May 1937. I had letters to the old chiefs from J. H. Driberg, who had been their District Commissioner in the early days of British administration. The Lango accepted me as his classificatory son. As soon as I could speak their language and when they saw me living with them, dancing, hunting, eating and drinking with them, they eagerly invited me to see all their ceremonies so that I might record them in a book. Their children, they complained, were forgetting the old Lango customs. This immediate acceptance compensated me for the brevity of my stay among them.

On correcting the proofs some five years after completing the book, I find it heavy reading. I would suggest it be regarded primarily as a book of reference and that full use be made of the Index-Glossary for extracting from the body of the book whatever facts are required. The 'Conclusions' appended to each chapter may also be of use. Occasionally I have added an unitalicised 's' to a Lango term in order to avoid the confusion which might have been caused by use of correct plural and genitive forms.

The delay in publishing my results has been due chiefly to the second World War, but also to the fact that I first wrote a much larger book, from which the present volume has been extracted, stating certain theories of human groups deduced from the working of Lango society.

I had wished to show that Man was social only by necessity; that he had no natural weapons such as great strength, speed,

powers of scent and so on, which could enable him to predominate over other animals; that it was the excessively large
cerebral cortex of his brain which had made it possible for his
instinctive reactions to be subordinated to cultural needs by
training, thus making group life possible, and establishing his
predominance over the animal world; that his two main in-
stincts of self-preservation and reproduction, motivating as they
do his economic and sexual quests, had to be regulated by
custom, morality and law, if quarrels arising from them were
not to disrupt the group, on the integrity of which the existence
of the individual depended. From all this I wished to argue
that Man was separatist by nature and the progressive fusion
of small groups up to the size of the modern Nation State had
been occasioned, not by any wish for world-brotherhood, but
by conquest or for self-protection as communications developed;
that the machinery by which the Nation State ensures its integrity in the face of aggression—its administrative system and
the sentiments to which its members are conditioned—is such
as to make voluntary fusion into a stable world organisation
impossible in fact though apparently feasible. International
armed forces composed of units from Nation States would be as
useless as an unarmed League of Nations for the purpose of
preventing war. The maintenance of peace should be entrusted
to a super-national body of men, specially trained from birth
in loyalty to a non-national ideal.

These immature cerebrations were frowned upon by the
anthropologists and it seemed advisable to separate fact and
theory completely. The life of an administrator has left neither
time nor means for the research necessary to substantiate these
theoretical considerations. They must await another day.

T. T. S. HAYLEY

SHILLONG, ASSAM, INDIA

JUNE 1945

ACKNOWLEDGMENTS

J. H. Driberg suggested my visit to the Lango. He made my researches there easy, allowed me to quote from his book and gave me valuable advice on reading my results. I wish to thank the Rev. L. G. Amey and others of the C.M.S. Boroboro for their hospitality and help. The Government of Uganda were kind enough to allow me to carry out these researches and the local administrative officers, headed by F. H. Rogers, gave me every help. I must thank the Uganda Society for allowing me to re-publish chapter 1, which is practically identical with an article written in Vol. vii, No. 3, of *The Uganda Journal*. E. B. Musman drew Plate IV, and Miss Audrey Cantlie drew Plate V.

It would be difficult to thank sufficiently all my Lango friends, who willingly did whatever they could to make me comfortable and to enable me to collect the information I desired. I can, however, single out *Rwot* Ogwalajungu, without whose aid and friendship I could have achieved very little.

Financially I am indebted to Cambridge University for the following grants: A Bartle Frere Exhibition of £57, £50 from the Leaf Bequest of Peterhouse and £30 from the Worts Fund. The remainder was provided by my father and mother, to whom this book is dedicated. Finally I wish to thank the Government of Uganda and the Syndics of the Cambridge University Press for their help towards the cost of producing this book. T. T. S. H.

CHAPTER I

LANGO RELIGION AND MAGIC

The distinction between magic and religion is of theoretical rather than of practical importance. Some would reserve the term 'Religion' to designate that corpus of beliefs concerning the superphysical world and powers which forms the philosophic background to the pattern of culture of a given society. The term 'Magic' is then applied to the processes arising out of these beliefs, by which man strives to control those superphysical powers for his own or for his society's ends. As Driberg has put it, 'Magic is the practice of religion'. He has also pointed out that it would be better to avoid the term magic, for it suggests that magic is a phenomenon peculiar to primitive peoples, since it is not usual to refer to our own religious practices as magic. I consider that the anthropological distinction between religion and magic is useful when analysing a culture. Those who cannot see that the practices of their own religion are magic to the same extent as the magic of the primitive would surely not be persuaded of the similarity even were we to jettison the word magic when dealing with the religious performances of primitives. When describing the religious activities of the Lango, I will therefore attempt to distinguish between religion and magic.

It is difficult to understand fully the religious philosophy of a people after living with them for so short a time as I was able. It was particularly difficult where all those who had been to school wished to have as little to do as possible with the practices of their fathers. I did not find much desire for concealment among the old people once I had persuaded them of my good intentions. The lack of success of my endless quest for explanatory information was due not to reticence but to ignorance. The beliefs of the majority were not clear-cut, and when pressed they would say that only the *ajwaka* (medicine-men) understood these questions. But the *ajwaka* were no more sure, and on points of detail their replies rarely agreed. Certain beliefs are so obvious to the individual that it never occurs to him that there is anything requiring explanation. A good example of this was the amusement of the women at a hunt when I asked why one should not kill a roan antelope (*ochwil*). 'He asks why a roan should not be killed!' they said in amused amazement. 'Yet he must know that the roan will give a man the affliction of *jok orongo*.'

Successive generations have learnt the ceremonial forms and the emotional attitudes underlying them by imitation of their elders without intellectual explanations being desired, save for the broadest principles. The invariable answer to the question, 'Why do you do that?' asked during a ceremony, was, 'Because it is a custom of the ritual observance (*kite me kwer*)', or, 'Because the child will then become well'. I deemed myself lucky to receive an answer as detailed as 'Because then no one will steal the blood', which was given me during a birth ceremony (p. 131). Perhaps there are individual Lango who can interpret their religion, but I never found one. Interpretation, therefore, must be based on deduction from behaviour on all occasions, particularly at ceremonies. For this reason I have adopted the policy of recording ceremonies exactly as they occurred. My interpretation follows closely the interpretation of African religion given by Driberg. I went into the field fully critical of Driberg's theories, but I could find no hypothesis that fits the facts so nearly as his does.

The following three sections:

    I. The Premises of Lango Religion,
   II. The Practice of Lango Religion: White Magic,
  III. The Practice of Lango Religion: Black Magic,

are elaborations of eight cardinal assumptions round which the religious beliefs and practices of the Lango are organised.

I. The Premises of Lango Religion

Among the Lango *Jok* is the mainspring of all religion and magic. It may be considered as the Mana principle of the Lango. In pp. 216–25 of *The Lango* Driberg gives an account of *Jok*. For the sake of brevity I will merely give an analytical account of the principles underlying the term *Jok*. Most of the evidence from which my deductions are drawn is to be found in the records of the ceremonies that I witnessed; the rest is drawn from daily conversations and observations that cannot be recorded in the text.

A. *Jok* is a neutral power permeating the universe, neither well nor badly disposed towards mankind, unless made use of by man.

Under this premise fall all the religious and magical manifestations of the Lango. The conceptions of this *jok* power we may term Religion. The practices by which man tries to harness *jok* power we may term Magic—White Magic where the ends are for the good of society, and Black Magic or witchcraft where the ends are harmful to society.

B. Anything of an unusual and apparently causeless nature must be associated with some aspect of *jok* power.

Under this premise come:

1. *Abnormal births.* While *jok* power is considered to be responsible for all births, it is particularly in evidence at abnormal births and therefore must be controlled by special magical ceremonial. Where the abnormality is of a purposeless kind, such as a child born with teeth and abnormal deliveries, the event is unwelcomed and looked upon as ill-omened. Not surprisingly this is particularly so in the case of abnormal deliveries, where the death of the mother or baby is a common result. A child born in this way may even be called an *ajok* (sorcerer), so I was informed by a man at Anwongi near Nabieso. This man's wife had given birth to a child feet first. The child had died, much to his father's relief, for the abnormality of his birth showed them that the child must be an *ajok*. So they built an *ot rudi* (twin house) for the child and performed the ceremony of mixing the seed (*rubo koti*) at the next sowing (p. 123) in order to avert the danger that this manifestation of evil *jok* power might herald. The birth of twins, on the other hand, is a happy event in so far as two individuals arrive to strengthen the Clan. But again the presence of *jok* power thus manifested necessitates careful magical control by those affected. The elaborate twin ceremonies (*myel arut*, p. 97) serve to exercise this control.

2. *Abnormal natural objects.* These do not affect the life of the Lango much. There is no cult of fetish objects. But any peculiarly shaped stone, root or such like object, which as far as the people's knowledge goes is not the product of man's handiwork, is thought to be the outcome of *jok* power and may therefore be used for magical purposes. The best examples of this were the Bushman digging-stick weights termed *kide jok* (stones of *jok*) by the men of Amaich and used by them for rain-making purposes (p. 79). The fear of hills as associated with *jok* power may come under this category, since they are relatively abnormal protuberances in a flat country. The caves found in hills and used for rain-making as being *ot jok* (house of *jok*) must also come within this category (p. 79), as must bare patches of ground found in the bush and termed *laro jok* (*jok*'s threshing floor).

3. *Mystifying occurrences.* These denote the presence of *jok* power and are the means by which *ajwaka* (medicine-men) prove their worthiness as practitioners. Every *ajwaka* has a conjuring trick of some sort which is performed as the primary essential of his treatment of a case. Examples of this are very numerous: Odur's shillings that stuck to the wall (p. 154), the frog-spawn that came out of the cuts in a baby's stomach (p. 160), Oming, who spoke from under the ground (p. 164), stones that were sucked from the patient's body (p. 161), the bundle of sticks that balanced on end (p. 166), charcoal pulled from the patient's ear (p. 158). Two further examples concerned me. I was waiting in a village for an old man to arrive, and to amuse the other old men round me I performed that party trick by which a string is cut and then apparently joined together in the mouth without any knot being visible. Immediately one old man drew me aside and showed me an ulcer on his leg. He begged me to give him medicine, for if I could tie string together in my mouth like that I could certainly cure him. I told him to go to the dispensary for treatment. He laughed, saying that they merely gave one water to drink there, whereas by my string trick I had clearly shown that I had the power to cure him. The other occasion concerned a trick I had made out of two pieces of bamboo. The illusion is given that a piece of string pulled out of one stick is joined to the string hanging out of the other stick.

But the sticks can be held apart and still the drawing of one string causes the other to disappear. When I showed my boys how the trick worked, they told me to destroy it, for, 'Should anyone gain possession of it he would become a great *ajwaka* (medicine-man) and deceive the people'.

4. *Good and bad luck.* It is realised that in many quests there is an element of chance. This is particularly so in hunting, fighting and travelling. Some individuals seem to have better luck than others. The causeless nature of this luck marks it out as being associated with *jok* power. Reference may be made of a person that 'His *jok* is good' or 'bad' (*jokere ber, jokere rach*), though it is more usual to-day to say that his '*Obanga*' is good or bad, '*Obanga*' being the Christian God. A synonym for this expression is '*Winyo*', which means literally 'Bird'. It may be said of a person 'He has *winyo*' (*etye ki winyo*), meaning he has good luck. It seems as though this has become a specialised aspect of *jok* power. The bird envisaged when referring to *winyo* is the pennant-winged nightjar (*achulany*), which is usually seen at dusk. It is considered very fortunate should this bird fly round a person on the night before an undertaking, such as a hunt. [It is also considered good luck for a bat (*olik*) to knock against one. But I did not find anyone who thought of the bat when discussing *winyo* (see, however, *The Lango*, pp. 225–8).]

I do not think that Driberg is quite accurate in translating *winyo* as Guardian Spirit. I think that 'luck' is a more appropriate rendering. I was told that animals did not possess *winyo*. If on killing an animal in the hunt a man did not perform the magical rites (*gwelo*), his own *winyo* might desert him, so that he killed no more animals. But on killing a man (see *The Lango*, pp. 110 and 227) the head-dress (*tok*) was cut off and hung in the slayer's village on the tree by the fireplace (*otem*). In this way the slayer added the dead man's *winyo* to his own, which made him strong to kill other men. Moreover, people would see the number of head-dresses hanging in a man's village and would not dare to kill him or steal his cattle, for they would know what a strong man he was.

Winyo can be controlled to a certain extent, as with all manifestations of *jok* power. This is done by the old men. A father will give his son *winyo* before the son goes on a journey.

On the night before the hunt the *won arum* (guardian of the hunting ground) with the help of his *Etogo* group will invoke good luck (*gato winyo*). Beer is prepared and drunk and the *gato* chant and chorus are sung. The presence of the *Etogo* group on this occasion suggests that there is a close connection between *winyo* and *tipo* (spirit). I think that this can be explained in the light of the father being able to give his son *winyo*, which is always conferred by the older on the younger generation. The *tipo* of the dead will be able to give *winyo* to their descendants, and therefore the *Etogo*, which can exercise control over the *tipo* (p. 111), will be the most effective group for obtaining *winyo*.

It is my tentative view that the causelessness of good and bad luck is of such a special nature as to merit a specialised manifestation of *jok* power. The vague personification of this quality in the shape of a bird probably has an historical origin impossible to discover now. It has been suggested to me that the eagle of the Baganda kings may be linked up with it in some way. Seligman is of the opinion that this eagle is connected with the falcon of the Egyptian kings. So that the *winyo* of the Lango might be traced back to Egypt by those who find interest in such connections.

C. Phenomena affecting society, the vicissitudes of which, while familiar, cannot be predicted or controlled empirically, are associated with *jok* power.

Under this premise come:

1. *Natural phenomena, such as rain, hail, locusts and lightning.* The failure of the rains or the destructions caused by hail, locusts and lightning can only be explained as manifestations of *jok* power. This uncontrolled or evilly controlled *jok* power must be brought under control by the appropriate magical ritual, which is the way in which the Lango express that universal desire of man to control his own destiny.

2. *Sickness and disease.* In his chapter on religion and magic (*The Lango*, pp. 216–40) Driberg gives a series of 'Manifestations of *jok*', such as *Jok Atida, Jok Adongo, Jok Lango, Jok Orongo, Jok Nam, Jok Omarari*. My short stay in Lango does not justify me in questioning any of his assertions, and my evidence on the

jok manifestations is particularly poor. However, since my interpretation of the little evidence I obtained differs from that of Driberg to some extent, I will record my views here for what they are worth.

An *ajwaka* (medicine-man) at Awelo, named Okelo, gave me the following account. It is a solitary piece of evidence and is doubtless false in details, but it illustrates vividly the principle that I had deduced from my other observations. He gave me a list of *jok* manifestations, each of which, he said, was a disease and each of which must be treated with a special magical technique. The symptoms of the patient would give the clue to the manifestation of *jok* from which he was suffering. He would then go to an *ajwaka* who knew the technicalities of that manifestation of *jok*. Some of these diseases, together with their treatment, had been known in Lango from the beginning of time and therefore came under the generic term of '*Jok Lango*', but a number of the diseases with their treatments had come from the 'Peoples of the Lakes' (*Jo Nam*: the Banyoro, Bakenyi, Baruli, etc.). These diseases were termed '*Jok Nam*'. I had previously deduced this principle myself. My informant then gave me the following list of diseases, with their symptoms as far as he knew them.

A. *Jok Lango:*

1. *Jok Orongo.* Shiverings all over the body, due to killing a roan antelope (*ochwil*).
2. *Jok Omarari.* Plague.
3. *Jok Mama.* A type of madness.
4. *Jok Orogo.* A type of madness.

B. *Jok Nam:*

1. *Jok Abani.* Aches in head and chest.
2. *Jok Obanga.* Permanently bent back or other bones crippled.
3. *Jok Olila.* A disease like dysentery.
4. *Jok Kabejo.* Stomach-ache.
5. *Jok Odudi.* Aches in head and chest.
6. *Jok Nyarakoe.* Aches all over the body.

As I have said, this list of names and symptoms may not be

accurate—I had no time to verify it sufficiently—but I believe the principle to be true.

Sickness and disease are of the greatest concern to the Lango and much thought must have been expended on their causes and cures. This accumulation of experience has resulted in a threefold classification of sickness:

(a) *Sicknesses usually undergone by children.* These are termed *two*. They are considered as inevitable and their treatment is stereotyped, consisting of the inter-Clan ceremonies described below (pp. 83–97). In this category must be included common forms of sickness occurring to adults, which are not serious and are treated with well-known herbs, etc.

(b) *Incurable sicknesses.* These are also known as *two*. There is no explanation of them, but they are recognised as sicknesses (*two*) and not as due to *jok* power.

(c) *Jok sicknesses.* These are thought to be caused by the particular manifestation of *jok* power entering the sufferer's body. Of such a person it may be said, '*Jok Orongo* seizes him' (*Jok Orongo omake*).

A medical training is essential for the study of native diseases and their methods of treatment, if pronouncements as to the accuracy of diagnosis or the efficacy of native drugs and methods are to be of any value. I was given many roots and herbs by prominent *ajwaka* (medicine-men) and was shown how to prepare the drugs from them. The symptoms for which they were used were also explained to me. But this would have been of value only if an analysis could have been made on the spot. The combination of Anthropologist and Doctor might lead to the discovery of drugs at present unknown to science.

With this reminder of the worthlessness of a layman's views on medical matters, I may say that I was very struck by the definiteness of the distinction between the different types of sickness. Most of the *jok* afflictions comprised psychic disturbances or virulent diseases, such as plague. Rigid distinctions were made between the different types of psychic disease. Epilepsy, contrary to expectation, was not considered to be a *jok* disease. It ranked as incurable sickness (*two*) and was called *ekwinkwin*. It is realised that it is an affliction which cannot be treated. Okelo of Awelo also told me of an interesting affliction that is becoming more frequent. It takes the form of a fear of crowds. The sufferer falls to the ground shrieking if he sees a crowd of people near him, 'Because he fears the people'. He mentioned the case of an Aloro policeman. Okelo said that the name of this disease was *ongech*. Cold water would be poured on the sufferer to bring him to his senses. In the case of *ekwinkwin* and *ongech* Okelo insisted that *jok* power had nothing to do with them. Yet, when referring to them, he said, 'This is a bad *jok*' (*man jok marach*), meaning 'This is a bad disease', for he again expressly denied the presence of *jok* power in either of the diseases.

The following are a few disjointed yet significant pieces of evidence regarding these *jok* diseases. During a meal at Ngai with the local chief, the Aboki Dispensary dresser and my informant Philipo Lawottim, I was told that epilepsy (*ekwinkwin*) had nothing to do with *jok*, being a disease that made a man fall to the ground and froth at the mouth for which there was no cure. They said that other diseases, which caused the patient to behave as if mad, were due to *jok* power seizing the man's body; of such were: *Jok Orongo, Jok Abong, Jok Adongo, Jok Orogo, Jok Lango*. As soon as a person becomes ill he is taken to the *ajwaka* (medicine-man), who specifies what *jok* has seized him and what ceremony should be carried out in order to effect a cure. For instance, if it is *Jok Adongo* a sheep is killed and dragged into the bush. The chief (*jago*), a school boy of Awelo and a devout Christian, also said that *jok* is bad in that it causes diseases, but through the *ajwaka* it does good by telling you what to do to be cured. He added that the *jok* which seizes a man is Satan, while the *jok* which helps one, like Oming (p. 163), is *Obanga* (the Christian God). Oming, he said, is like a doctor. The Lango know, he continued, that if they go to the English doctor sometimes they are healed and sometimes not. The same is true of their own *ajwaka*, he said, but they are more frequently healed by the *ajwaka* than by the English doctor.

All types of madness are not immediately assigned to some aspect of *jok* seizure. A young man of twenty near Aduku lived in the open near his mother's house, sleeping in the ashes of his fire, naked and unable to talk coherently or do any work. His

mother denied that he was suffering from any type of *jok*
seizure and told me that she had come to the conclusion that
it must have been caused by a cow, which had knocked him
over and injured his head when he was a small boy. There was
a mad woman at Chiawanti, who abused me foully when I
greeted her. I asked what *jok* had seized her, but they assured
me that she suffered from no *jok*. They said that she merely
talked nonsense when the moon was full. The full moon marked
the highest points of her attacks of madness. This was not a
jok disease, they insisted.

On the other hand my informant Philipo Lawottim of Ngai
took me to see his sister, who was suffering from a form of
madness. She was living with her parents in a small hovel of
a hut. They had moved here from a large house as they thought
that the largeness of their old house might have something to do
with her condition. She was naked, could not talk but grinned
all the time, and she had to be moved about by her parents.
They said that it had started two years previously. Her husband
had gone like this first but had now recovered. They said that
Jok Orogo had seized her body (*jok orogo omako kome*). They had
been to the *ajwaka* Oming, who told them to kill a goat and
carry out a certain ceremony at her husband's village. The
mother told me that she considered this sickness to be the work
of an *ading* (sorcerer: p. 29). She explained that if someone
steals from a man, the injured person will go to an *ajwaka*,
who will divine (*tyeto*) and lay a spell on the offender, who will
become ill in some way. She considered that the husband had
been afflicted as a result of some theft and that he had com-
municated the disease to his wife. [They had heard of a man
at Aboki who had a cure for this disease and they had sent for
his medicine. It arrived on the following day, cost ten shillings
and consisted of a powdery fibrous substance wrapped up in
banana leaves. The girl was given this to eat. I do not know
if she recovered.]

The rigid distinction between curable and incurable psychic
diseases suggested to me the possibility that the *jok* diseases were
neuroses produced by social causes, that they fell into certain
categories designated by different *jok* terms, and that a specialist
in a particular *jok* disease was capable of curing the psychic

disturbance by means of his technique. The whole process would then be comparable to psycho-analytical methods. I have no proof of this and merely want to suggest it as a possible subject for inquiry. I had no time nor the necessary medical qualifications to carry out such an inquiry myself. But apart from this somewhat fantastic suggestion, the evidence is sufficient for me to say that diseases of a more or less unusual nature are considered to be due to the influence of *jok* power, which can be controlled by a magical technique known only to a specialist *ajwaka*. It will be seen later (p. 24) how, once the *jok* power is controlled in this manner, the patient is given a certain power over this manifestation of *jok*, so that he may become an *ajwaka* specialising in this line himself.

3. *Misfortunes.* The occurrence of misfortunes of an inexplicable kind denotes the presence of *jok* power. The best example of this occurred when my car turned over into the marsh on the Lira side of Akalu. There is a bend in the road which is narrow and steeply cambered with sandy margins. Careless driving can easily lead to an accident here, and two other cars had come to grief before me. A woman who passed at the time told me this and added that a lorry had run over her foot at this spot. She said that it was quite clear that there was *jok* power in the tree at the bend (*jok obedo i yat cha*).

D. **Jok power is present when human beings are in a highly excited emotional state.**

Under this premise come:

1. *Sexual intercourse.* It is not surprising that the excitement and ecstasy of the sexual act should mark it as an occasion fraught with *jok* power. Copulation might almost be considered as an act that generates *jok* power. As is explained below, the spiritual part of a man, his *tipo*, may be likened to a spark of *jok* power which enters the body of the woman at coition and is the source of life. When questioned as to the mystery of life, the Lango said that 'the *jok* power within a woman caused her to bear' (*jok ma tye iye omiyo dako nywal*). The Christians say that *Obanga* (the Christian God) causes the child to grow in the womb. This constitutes the chief reason for their belief in

Obanga. 'If *Obanga* does not exist,' I used to be asked, 'then who created you in your mother's womb?'

[I would go so far as to suggest that the very conception of *jok* power arises from, or at least finds its vindication in, the sexual orgasm. During the orgasm the individual feels himself to be under the control of an irresistible, mysterious force, which is seen to have the power of creating life. This force, which has created the man, accompanies him throughout life as his *tipo* (spirit) and at death returns to the source from which it came, to the land of spirits, to the world of the unseen, the realm of the superphysical power which must be the cause of all those inexplicable, unknown or uncontrollable happenings which occur in the land of the living.]

If the sexual act generates *jok* power, we may expect it to be ritually controlled. I cannot say whether any ritual is practised between man and wife, but the following prohibitions are sufficient evidence of the magically dangerous nature of the sexual act.

Adultery was rare and prostitution unknown before the coming of the British and with them the Indian traders. A woman committing adultery was said to 'spoil her Clan'. The danger came from this careless and forbidden generation of *jok* power. The children and spouse of the adulterer would become very ill and probably die. Adultery used to be a capital offence.

When the British first came to Lango, the bachelor's hut (*otogo*) was still in use. This was a small round mud hut built on a raised platform and used by boys on reaching puberty. Until the birth of his first child, a man could have intercourse only inside his *otogo*, otherwise his wife would become barren. Should he have had intercourse in the open, he would have been called an *ajok* (sorcerer). Even now the Lango will very rarely have intercourse in the open. They will arrange trysts with lovers in vacant houses.

The guardian of the hunting ground (*won arum*) has magical control over the hunt. He must perform various rites to ensure success, and on the night before the hunt his *Etogo* group come to invoke good luck (*gato winyo*, p. 149). The *won arum* must on no account have intercourse with his wife on this night.

Intercourse would liberate *jok* power that might interfere with the ceremonies that had been performed in order to direct *jok* power for effecting a successful hunt. Sexual intercourse was forbidden during the *ewor* ceremony (p. 69).

As soon as a woman has conceived her husband ceases to have intercourse with her until the child is weaned in about its third year. The Lango say that intercourse after conception would probably kill the child. For the object of sexual intercourse is to generate *jok* power in order to create another human being. When this object has been achieved, a further generation of *jok* power is merely dangerous, since it is undirected. [This long period of abstinence has been cut down now largely as a result of the example of those Christians who are perforce monogamists.]

The horror of sexual perversions and incest can be explained by the fact that *jok* power is thereby generated without procreation as an objective. A child born from an incestuous union would upset the whole pattern of relationship between individuals and groups. Those committing incest would never desire a child. In the old days death to the man was the invariable punishment for intercourse between clansmen or blood relations. Driberg (*The Lango*, p. 209) describes how a man who had committed incest had to pour water over the girl before he was killed in order to nullify the evil *jok* power he had brought upon her, for by his action 'he brings *jok* power upon the girl' (*okelo jok i kom nyako*). Anyone who commits incest is considered to be an *ajok* (sorcerer). I was once in the Aloro chief's court when a boy was brought in by his uncle. The uncle was demanding compensation from him for causing the death of his daughter by incestuous intercourse. The girl had died in childbirth and the boy admitted that he was responsible for her death on account of the incestuous intercourse he had had with her.

Driberg told me that he had ample evidence that an *ajok* (sorcerer), as part of his black magic, will have incestuous intercourse. By this means he generates a charge of *jok* power, the potency of which is enhanced by the fact that it is a heinous tribal crime. He directs this *jok* power to the required end by means of his nefarious rites. I have no evidence of this. But Ogwangatolomoi of Anep told me how a certain *ajok* called

Ogwalachu had 'tied up the rain' and caused a drought by hiding the urine of his wife and himself just after they had had intercourse.

2. *Dancing.* Dancing plays a large part in magical ritual. They dance for rain, they dance at the birth of twins, they dance at the Age Grade initiations before a raiding expedition. Caught up in the rhythm and excitement of the dance the individual feels himself endued with a power outside himself. *Jok* power is generated by the dance and is harnessed to the requirements of the Tribe by the accompanying ceremonial. This does not apply to the social dance to the same degree, though it may have applied to the old type of Lango social dance, now obsolete. The unfailing mark of an *ajok* (sorcerer) is that he dances at night and alone.

3. *States of dissociation.* In all exorcising ceremonies the patient is reduced to a dissociated state. This is effected by the *ajwaka* (medicine-man) with the aid of his women helpers, usually about five in number. These women sing monotonous and endless songs to the accompaniment of rattles (*aja*) made by placing seeds in long-necked calabashes. I have shaken these rattles to the accompaniment of the songs until my head has become quite dizzy, and can understand how easily a partial hypnosis is induced in the patient by these means. At the ceremony at Awei near Aduku the patient jerked her body convulsively, emitting great groans and dancing about the village in a demented manner (p. 153). As soon as she fell into this state the spectators said, '*Jok* has come upon her'. While in this state she announced the name of the *jok* that had taken possession of her. This *jok* was really a *tipo* (spirit), for the *tipo* then spoke through her lips and gave the names of its wife and children (p. 155).

The ceremony for catching a *tipo* in a pot (p. 156) is commenced by inducing a dissociated state in the patient. Under the influence of this the patient shouts out the name of the *tipo* which is 'seizing' his body. Later a similar state is induced in him by the rattle and chant technique, and at the climax of his excitement he expectorates the offending *tipo* into the little pot that has been prepared for its reception. On every occasion at which I saw a person in one of these dissociated states, I was told that *jok* power had come upon her (a woman was more susceptible than a man).

E. **Jok power is present in situations and objects dangerous to man.**

Under this premise come:

1. *The hunt and fierce animals.* The hunt with its dangers to the individual is an occasion pregnant with *jok* power. Those animals which are known to be particularly dangerous— elephant, leopard, lion, buffalo, rhinoceros—are also associated with *jok* power. If killed they will afflict a member of the slayer's family with *jok orongo* unless a purifying ceremony is performed (p. 141). Some witnesses denied that these animals possessed *tipo*s (spirits). They said it was the heads of the animals that came and afflicted the village. Others said that the animals did possess *tipo*. No one was clear on this point (see *The Lango,* p. 229). The special case of the roan antelope (*ochwil*) is described below (p. 141). I could find no better reason for the fear of this animal than that given by Driberg (*The Lango,* p. 121). Besides these animals, honey eaten from a tree will bring *jok orongo*. This may be due to the danger from bees, or to the fact that honey is most frequently found during a hunt, when it is usually seen simultaneously by a number of men. Should it be touched a quarrel might easily start and break up the hunt. For this reason honey may not be gathered during a hunt.

2. *Fighting.* The dangers associated with fighting need no emphasis. The whole occasion, from preparation for battle to the celebrations on returning, is pregnant with *jok* power. Naturally I never saw the ceremonies that used to be enacted before a fight, but Driberg describes some of them (see *The Lango,* p. 107).

3. *Journeys.* A person going on a journey, especially in the old days of internecine hostility, would be subjected to danger on all sides. This was a situation in which *jok* power was felt to be imminent, and the traveller was specially guarded by magical ritual before starting out, his father giving him *winyo* (p. 5).

4. *Breaking of tribal laws.* The integrity of a primitive society depends upon the rigid observance of the rules and customs of

that society. The more important the rule the greater the
generation of *jok* power if it is broken. This is well illustrated by
Driberg, who, as already mentioned, pointed out to me that
an *ajok* (sorcerer) would have incestuous intercourse before
carrying out a piece of black magic. Incest is the most heinous
crime as it is likely to cause quarrels inside the Clan. The *ajok*
is thus able to generate a strong charge of *jok* power for his
nefarious aims by secretly committing incest.

F. *Jok* **power is associated with every human being as
that part of him to which we usually apply the term spirit
or soul.**

The Lango term for this human spirit is *tipo*, and sometimes *chyen*.

1. *The nature of the* tipo *and* chyen. I would first refer to
Driberg's article on 'The Secular Aspect of Ancestor Worship
in Africa' (Supplement to the *Journal of the Royal African Society*,
January 1936, Vol. xxxv, No. cxxxviii). There Driberg deals
with the problem of the spirit world and the power principle.
I will here state the specific facts as they apply to the Lango.

The *tipo* can be considered as a spark of *jok* power which
enters the woman's body at coition and is the source of life.
The association of the sexual act with the generation of *jok*
power has been explained above. The Lango say that it is the
jok power within a woman which fashions the child in the womb.
As Driberg points out, *jok* power appears to be universal, form-
less and limitless, and though the *tipo* may be considered to be
a spark of *jok* power it is at the same time part of the totality
of *jok* power. This was well brought out at the ceremony when
jok nam was exorcised from Atim (p. 154). The spirit of a dead
person took possession of Atim's body and was never referred
to as a *tipo* but as a *jok*. Yet *jok* power in spite of its unity is
divided into a number of spheres of influence. The Tribe is
associated with a special sphere of *jok* power. Each Clan has its
own sphere of *jok* power within the Tribe. Each Family has its
sphere within the Clan. So that the individuals of each Family,
Clan and Tribe draw their spiritual components, their *tipo*s,
from demarcated spheres of *jok* power. Just as the individual
considers himself primarily as a member of the group, so his
spiritual beliefs show him the group character of his soul.

The ceremony for ritualising a child (*atin akwer*) illustrates this principle. At the *atin akwer* ceremony (p. 136) a name is given to the child by an old woman of another Clan. The name given will be one not commonly used in the child's Clan but appropriate for the old woman's Clan and hence associated with another sphere of *jok* power, which it is hoped will not be ill-disposed towards the child, whose older brothers and sisters have all died as a result of the malignancy of the *jok* power of their own Clan.

The word *tipo* is also used of a shadow. If asked whether a man possesses a *tipo* when alive, my witnesses pointed to his shadow and said that he did, but that it was of little importance to him when alive, save that it was often the cause of dreams. The *tipo* became important on death, for then it was released from the body and could affect members of its own Family and Clan. The ways in which the *tipo* of a dead man can affect the living are discussed below. The *tipo*'s visitations are always malignant, and prove that the funeral ceremonial has failed to translate it to the next status of ancestor. For death marks a change in status in the same way as do puberty and marriage, and the funeral ceremonial is a *rite de passage* that covers the period of transition. The funeral ceremonial is the concern of the *Etogo* group, as will be explained later. Dealings with the *tipo* when in this hypersensitive state can be very dangerous for members of the *tipo*'s Clan, and members of other Clans—the *Etogo*—can alone control it with impunity. Again this illustrates the principle that each Clan has a particular sphere of *jok* power peculiar to itself.

While the *tipo* is most noticeable when it is causing trouble, it is also used as a medium through which *jok* power may be approached and harnessed to the requirements of the living. This is the essence of ancestor-worship. A man when translated to the status of ancestor is in a position to utilise *jok* power for the good of living men. The individual will appeal to his own ancestors, that is to his Family's sphere of *jok* power, by building an *abila* (shrine), and in general will keep on good terms with this Family sphere by due observance of ritual and custom. In Chapter III I shall show how the whole company of the tribal ancestors was supplicated by the massed action of the *Etogo* groups in the two vital tribal interests of warfare and rain-making.

All peoples on earth appear to have believed in some form of immortality. Perhaps this is a mental necessity for an animal with a physiological system that urges self-preservation as a primary instinct, and possesses at the same time a cerebral cortex which provides him with the certain knowledge that whatever he does he is bound eventually to die. As Malinowski has put it: 'The substance of which spirits are made is the full-blooded passion and desire for life.' But the Lango seem to have no idea of a spirit world comparable to the Christian heaven or hell. At death the *tipo* leaves the body. It then leads a very vague existence. It is likened to air and is sometimes detected in eddies of air. The best example of this was at the ceremony of *gato two* at Akot near Aduku (p. 116), when the sick man told the assembled *Etogo* members that he had buried his wife near a certain rain pool. Once when he was washing himself in this pool he saw an eddy of air coming from the grave to the pool. This, he said, must have been the 'wind' (*yamo*) of his dead wife, for it gave him a bad headache. All those present agreed with him. As in the case just described the *tipo* is often found in the vicinity of the grave, but may move about freely. After it has been in this state for some time it is referred to as the *chyen* rather than the *tipo* of the dead man. I could not discover the exact point at which this occurred and each witness insisted that the *tipo* and the *chyen* were exactly the same thing. But one man, when pressed, said that if it became necessary to dig up a dead man's bones and burn them (*golo chogo*, p. 122), you would see the hair still adhering to the skull. 'This is the *chyen*', he said. This statement did not make the distinction much clearer to me. But it suggested that the *chyen* may be the spiritual counterpart of the *ajok* (sorcerer). The burning of the dead man's bones is the last extremity to which the *Etogo* will go in the case of a *tipo* that refuses to be pacified by the funeral ceremonial. My informants said that it would be impossible for the *tipo* of a man whose bones had been burnt to afflict the living. Perhaps the ceremony of exhumation and burning (*golo chogo*, p. 122) deprives the *tipo* of its status as ancestor, of which it has proved itself to be unworthy as a result of its malignant behaviour. The *tipo* has proved itself to be a *chyen* and is excluded from the line of re-incarnation just as the *ajok* (sorcerer) is excluded by omission of the funeral ceremonial. In support of this interpretation see *The Lango*, p. 241, where Driberg describes the killing of an *ajok* and says that all the people flee from the burning *ajok* in order to escape the vengeance of his '*chyen*'.

This brings me to the question of re-incarnation. I found very little evidence of this belief. Family names recur in alternate generations and one informant said that this enabled an orphan to be recognised, as he would have the same name as his grandfather. I pressed this witness on this point and suggested re-incarnation. But he emphatically denied the suggestion. Other informants when pressed said that some people believed that they would be reborn. It may be that Missionary teaching has made them unwilling to admit that such beliefs have ever been held by them. I am ready to believe that the assumption of re-incarnation is there even if the belief is not expressly formulated. A Missionary told me that an old man working down a well wanted some wood. The Missionary stopped the worker above from throwing down the wood, pointing out that it would kill the man below, but the latter replied, 'That does not matter, I have plenty of children'. This may imply a belief in re-incarnation. Professor Radcliffe-Brown pointed out to me that whether the belief in re-incarnation is there or not, it is clear that the son takes the place of his grandfather in the social scheme, and this is felt so intensely as to be almost the equivalent of re-incarnation. The Chinese author Lin Yutang expresses this view well when he says: 'The Chinese family ideal is backed by the view of life which I may call the "stream-of-life" theory, which makes immortality almost visible and touchable. Every grandfather seeing his grandchild going to school feels that truly he is living over again in the life of the child. His own life is nothing but a section of the great family stream of life flowing on forever.'

2. *How the* tipo *afflicts living people.* The funeral ceremonial (*achuban me gonyo tol*, p. 111, and *apuny*, p. 63) is sufficient in the ordinary course of events to pacify a *tipo*, which is considered to have feelings of jealousy towards the living. But

some *tipo*s will not rest content. Of such a *tipo* it is said, 'His head is bad' (*wiye rach*). The *tipo* may only afflict a member of his own Clan and usually it is one of his own Family. This is further evidence in support of the theory that there is a sphere of *jok power* peculiar to each Clan and Family. The wife is in a peculiar position, since she is of the same Family as her husband and yet of a different Clan. In the ceremony recorded below (p. 115) it was the sick man's wife's *tipo* that was troubling him. The anomaly is discussed further during the description of the ceremony (p. 121). A malevolent *tipo* of this type 'seizes the body' of the person (*omako kome*) and so causes him to be ill. The sufferer knows that a *tipo* has seized his body because he dreams of a dead relation. They say that a *tipo* brings dreams (*tipo okelo lek*), and it is this *tipo* that causes the dreamer to be ill. When examining a witness on this subject I was asked why I questioned him, since I must know that if a person dreamed of a dead relation he would certainly begin to die himself. I said that I often dreamed of dead relations without beginning to feel ill. Those who heard this remark disbelieved me. If a man quarrels with a relation during his life, at death the relation's *tipo* will bring him sickness.

Since the *tipo* can only afflict clansmen, the ceremonies by which it is encouraged to leave the body of the sick person must be carried out by members of the *Etogo* group. For the *Etogo* members, being of different Clans, are safe from the jealousy of the *tipo*. The ceremony by which a spell is laid on the sickness (*gato two*, p. 115) is the first in the series of ceremonies that are performed by the *Etogo* in order to pacify a malignant *tipo*. I suggest below (p. 121) that the ceremony of *gato two* is a form of mystic participation, by which the offending *tipo* is attracted into the body of an animal and then absorbed into the bodies of the *Etogo* members by their ritual eating of the meat of the animal. The *tipo* cannot harm the *Etogo* members since, being of other clans, their *jok* power is derived from spheres different from that of the *tipo*. But members of the *tipo*'s own Clan must not eat the meat ritually or the *tipo* will afflict them. Should *gato two* prove ineffective, the ceremony of killing a bull for sickness (*neko dyang me two*, p. 121) is performed.

At any period during a *tipo* visitation the sufferer may go to an *ajwaka* (medicine-man) who specialises in 'catching' or 'covering the *tipo*' (*mako tipo*, or, *umo tipo*, p. 155). Such an *ajwaka* entices the *tipo* into a pot, in which he imprisons it.

The final extremity to which the *Etogo* will go is the exhuming and burning of the dead man's bones (*golo chogo*, p. 123). It is usual to consult an *ajwaka* whenever a *tipo* is causing sickness, and he advises what ceremony is to be performed. According to several informants, if the *ajwaka* says that it is not necessary to dig up the bones, it is clear that the *tipo* is causing the trouble. But if the *ajwaka* orders an exhumation, and if the corpse has not completely decomposed and there is still hair on the skull, then it becomes clear that the *chyen* is troubling the sick man, and the burning of the dead man's bones will destroy the *chyen* for ever.

The *tipo* of a dead man may also afflict its descendants, usually its own or classificatory son, by causing impotency. This is attributed to jealousy of the son on the part of the father, whose *tipo* castrates the son (p. 141).

The *tipo*'s jealousy is always aroused by the sowing of the dead person's fields in the season following his or her death. The ceremony of mixing the seed (*rubo koti*, p. 123) is therefore performed by the *Etogo* to ensure that the crops grown in these fields will not be blighted by the *tipo*'s malevolence.

After the completion of the funeral ceremonial, if the *tipo* has shown itself to be well disposed, it takes its place among the ancestors, 'The people of the dead' (*jo ma to*). By virtue of the close association, if not actual identification, between the people of the dead and *jok* power, the people of the dead can help the living. They do this only on the supplication of the old men of the Tribe, the elders of the Clans. Their co-operation is sought especially against those two threats to the integrity of the Tribe—an enemy invader and drought. The massed *Etogo* groups supplicated the people of the dead at the ceremonies of *apuny*, *ewor* and rain-making (see Chapter III).

3. *Dreams*. Dreams are not considered to be very significant by the Lango, but certain dreams are important. I have already shown that the visitation of a *tipo* is recognised by the sufferer dreaming of the dead person. It is probable that dreams of dead relatives cause the mental disturbance known as a *tipo*

visitation, which is cured by the appropriate ceremony. In support of this view I may mention that an *ajwaka*, who was 'catching' the *tipo* in a sick woman, told his patient that she must not mourn for her dead mother unduly. The *ajwaka* told me that the woman's mother's *tipo* was bringing her dreams and causing her to be ill merely because the woman could not be consoled. My boy Okuja once said to me, 'If you dream every day that you are mad, you will become mad. Similarly, if you dream of a dead man, you will certainly die.' I show below (p. 30) how the traditional activity of the *ajok* (sorcerer) may be accounted for by dreams.

Ogwangatolomoi of Anep said that dreams just come into your head; you dream of a person or place because you have just been there or seen the person. A woman informant said that people dreamed chiefly of death (*to*); the people of the dead (*jo ma to*) made them dream and then the dreamer would die also. Philipo Oruro, *Jago* of Nabieso, who used to record his dreams (p. 169), said that when a man sleeps his *tipo* goes to *Obanga* (the Christian God). *Obanga* tells the *tipo* things and this is the man's dream. Philipo Oruro is a Christian and this is probably his own theory. But there is a tendency to account for dreams by the nocturnal wanderings of the *tipo* of the living man.

Driberg describes the cult of trees (*The Lango*, p. 218). I found no cases of this, except in regard to Oming (p. 164). But my informants admitted that they had heard of it. When questioned as to how the *tipo* announced its presence in the particular tree, my informants said that the *tipo* made its presence and desires known in a dream, whereupon the *abila* (shrine) was built and the offerings made as described by Driberg.

II. The Practice of Lango Religion: White Magic

White magic is the term used to designate all those activities which aim at harnessing *jok* power to the requirements of man, where such requirements are not of an anti-social nature. Magical processes constitute the practice of religion. This harnessing of *jok* power is effected by rites and spells which are interwoven into the ceremonies, descriptions of which I have recorded in the later chapters of this book.

The ends which the Lango strive to achieve by means of white magic are those which their empirical knowledge or technique is unable to grasp. All these occasions have been described in the section on the premises of Lango religion. They are the occasions where *jok* power is thought to be responsible and where human beings feel themselves to be impotent to control the powers at work by any means other than magic. Magical control over *jok* power is a dangerous operation only possible for those who have a proper knowledge of the methods. The greater the immanence of *jok* power, the greater the danger involved in the controlling processes. The old men, through knowledge and experience gained during their lives, are able to exercise this control. The *Etogo* have control over the dead, and in the particularly dangerous operation of digging up the dead man's bones (*golo chogo*, p. 122) only the chief old man of the *Etogo* group dares to do the actual exhuming. The old men and women always direct proceedings during the stereotyped tribal and clan ceremonies described later. All these ceremonies are white magic, and, by means of the principles of the scapegoat, sympathetic magic and *pars pro toto*, achieve control over *jok* power. While the rite and the spell are being enacted, those present are taught or reaffirmed in the religious dogmas that underlie all these practices.

There are certain occasions for which there is no stereotyped tribal or clan technique. Only a specialist is capable of dealing with such manifestations of *jok* power. These specialists are the medicine-men and medicine-women known as *ajwaka*. They combine the functions of doctor and priest in their ministrations. The majority of the *ajwaka* are general practitioners to whom the surrounding people go for advice and treatment for the ailments which cannot be cured at home. Others, besides their general ability, have learnt the technique of curing some special disease, and have acquired a notoriety in effecting cures. In order to understand the nature of the *ajwaka* it is necessary to see how a person becomes an *ajwaka*, what his methods are and what functions he performs in the culture of the Lango.

The *ajwaka*'s calling is not necessarily hereditary, except in the case of rain guardians (*won kot*). But an *ajwaka* wants to hand on his or her knowledge, and if his own or his classificatory

son or daughter show an aptitude, he will probably teach him
or her his technique. Rain guardians, such as those of Aduku
(p. 74), hand on their office to a direct descendant. Lingo
of Aduku had quarrelled with his eldest son, Oduralingo, and
so had handed on his esoteric knowledge to Ogwangalingo.
But there was much hesitation before the old men of the Clan
eventually agreed that Ogwangalingo was fit to become rain
guardian, as Oduralingo appears to have been the more capable
of the two brothers.

Most *ajwaka* augment their earnings by having one or more
apprentices, who help them at ceremonies and to whom they
hand on their knowledge and methods, receiving payment in
return. These apprentices have usually been cured of some
disease by the *ajwaka*. In the case of an *ajwaka* who specialises
in one of the *jok* diseases (pp. 7 and 10), his apprentices would
certainly have been cured of that disease, as in the case of Atim
(p. 155). In such cases it is the sensational nature of the disease
that marks out the person as being possessed by that type of
jok power and as being endowed with the ability of controlling
it, since it has been overcome in his own body.

The majority of *ajwaka* are women and in the village of every
ajwaka that I visited I noticed a twin house (*ot rudi*). I was
expressly told that it was not necessary for a woman to have
borne twins before she could be an *ajwaka*. But in every case
that I saw the *ajwaka* was either a twin, the mother of twins
or closely connected with someone who was associated with
twins, and there was a twin house in a conspicuous place in
the village. This is not surprising, since it is believed that *jok*
power is particularly immanent in both the mother and the twins.

One *ajwaka* I saw (p. 161) had only one breast, another
(p. 161) had one eye and peculiar teeth. These disfigurements
appear to have marked them out as sufficiently abnormal to
justify their practising as *ajwaka*. For the principle governing
the acceptance of an *ajwaka* by the people is that he should be
associated with some abnormality which can be recognised as
a manifestation of *jok* power. Philipo Oruro, *Jago* of Nabieso,
used to record and interpret his dreams (p. 169). *Rwot* Ogwalajungu told me that one day Oruro would be a great *ajwaka*
as a result of this ability, which obviously came from *jok* power.

The methods of all *ajwaka* are very similar in principle. The ceremonies, which I witnessed and which I record in Chapter VIII, are sufficient to show the more detailed nature of their practice. These methods may be generalised under the four headings of Cause, Diagnosis, Psychological Cure and Medical Remedy.

When an individual suffers calamities, whether sickness or otherwise, in the face of which he feels impotent, he will go to the local *ajwaka* and lay the facts before him. The *ajwaka* questions the sufferer to discover the cause of his misfortunes. If he has been dreaming of a dead relation it is obviously a *tipo* visitation due to the omission of some funeral rite, etc. If the sufferer has quarrelled with a clansman, this is the cause and he must make it up. If he has stolen anything, this is the cause and he must confess and return the stolen article. The *ajwaka* probably knows all the sufferer's personal affairs already. But in any case he soon discovers some omission in ceremonial, or some offence against custom or morality which is the cause of the trouble.

Having decided in his own mind what irregularity has been committed, he resorts to his magical divining technique. This is usually done by the *ajwaka* shaking his rattle (*aja*) and speaking in an assumed voice with his back to the patient. The assumed voice is supposed to be the voice of the particular manifestation of *jok* power which is controlled by that *ajwaka*. This voice tells the patient what is wrong with him, the cause of the trouble and what he must do to be cured (p. 167). Other methods are used, as with Akelo (p. 167), who threw sandals into the air and read *jok*'s orders from the positions the sandals assumed on the ground. Odur (p. 154) obtained his information from the positions assumed by cowries thrown from his hand. In one or other of these ways the diagnosis is made known to the patient, who is impressed by the fact that it comes by means of *jok* power.

The divining is accompanied by a conjuring trick of some sort, which is the invariable stock-in-trade of the *ajwaka*. This conjuring trick (for examples consult the Index-Glossary) has two functions. It is the psychological component of the cure and it serves as the *ajwaka*'s name-plate or advertisement, as I shall now show.

The most important part of Lango cures is that conveyed

by suggestion, to which the Lango seem particularly susceptible, as are all Africans. By means of this conjuring trick the *ajwaka* demonstrates vividly before his client's eyes the control that he has over *jok* power. His clients are interested only in the conjuring trick and the accompanying ritual. That the *ajwaka* also gives them a root to chew or medicine to drink is a minor consideration. Yet the *ajwaka* knows a great number of drugs. These he obtains from roots and herbs. This knowledge is the accumulation of centuries of experience passed on down the line of *ajwaka*s, and known only to the initiated. In every case that I witnessed the *ajwaka* gave his patient some root or herb concoction after the conjuring trick and ritual had been performed. I was given a number of these drugs in their vegetable form, but it was impossible to have them analysed. I placed a drop of one drug, which was used for applying to cuts and sores, on an ant and the ant was immediately killed. I have every reason to believe that the more important *ajwaka*s possess a detailed knowledge of drugs of great medicinal value, and that they effect cures by means of them. As the *Jago* of Ngai said, the people had discovered that they were more often healed by their own *ajwaka* than by the English doctor. But the value of native drugs is greatly diminished by the inaccuracy of diagnosis.

I have shown that the people are impressed by the *ajwaka*'s display of magic by means of his conjuring trick, and that the actual medicine, which they take, does not interest them much. The conjuring trick also acts as the *ajwaka*'s advertisement. The case of Oming (p. 164) illustrates this point well. Oming is the oldest manifestation of *jok* power controlled by an *ajwaka* that I was able to find in Lango. All over Lango I heard of him and his wonderful powers of healing. On each occasion my informants said that no one had ever seen Oming, for he was invisible and talked out of the ground. I expected to see a display of ventriloquism, yet the actual performance should not have deceived a child. Gira, who was the interpreter of Oming, undoubtedly possessed a very wide knowledge of drugs, and the crowds that visited him from all over Lango testified to their efficacy. But the crowds did not come to Gira because of his drugs; they came because *there* was the abode of Oming 'who spoke from the ground'. Without this tale of magic Gira's drugs would have been valueless to the Lango.

Every *ajwaka* is aware that he is deceiving his patient by means of his conjuring trick, but it is not a deceit practised for gain, at least it used not to be. He has been taught by the *ajwaka* to whom he was apprenticed that the conjuring trick is an essential part of the cure, which it undoubtedly is. In our civilisation scientific knowledge has pushed back the realms of the unknown farther and farther. Magic and religion deal with the unknown. With the Lango medicine and magic are barely distinguishable, for the cause of disease is unknown. The *ajwaka* is therefore both spiritual and medical adviser. So it appears to have been with the Christian church before the days of science. Following the discoveries in the scientific fields, religion was divorced from the technique of the physician. Comparatively recently the medical world appears to have recognised the value of the psychological accompaniment to the physical remedy. At the other extreme are the Faith Healers and the Christian Scientists, who can only recognise the psychological aspect of healing and refuse what science has to offer. In seeking to give the Lango the benefits of medical science, his mental requirements should be recognised as of paramount importance. 'It is no use going to the dispensary, they merely give you water to drink', said an old man to me. Confidence and faith are as essential as good drugs to an African community.

Although this section is entitled 'The Practice of Lango Religion: White Magic', I have dwelt more on the nature of the *ajwaka* than on the ceremonies which really constitute Lango magic. The reason for this is that in Chapters III to VIII I have carefully described the ceremonies which I saw performed in Lango, and a knowledge of Lango magic is best obtained from reading these descriptions. The relation of the *ajwaka* to this mass of ritual material is best explained by the following observation.

From the many ceremonies recorded in Chapters III to VIII it is possible to pick out actions and objects which occur again and again and which constitute what may be termed the 'ritual elements' of Lango religion. The different ceremonies are constructed by combining these ritual elements. In the stereotyped ceremonies of the Tribe, Clan, *Etogo*, Family and Territorial groups (see Chapters III to VII) these ritual elements are combined in a recognised order known to all. The difference between the stereotyped ceremonies and the more individual ceremonies performed by the *ajwaka* (see Chapter VIII) is that the *ajwaka* combines the same ritual elements in an order determined by himself. The *ajwaka*'s ceremony is therefore novel and original, but the ritual elements composing it are well known and therefore the ceremony is logical, acceptable and convincing to the people.

[I had not read Bateson's *Naven* before writing this chapter on Lango religion, and it now appears to me that Lango religion could be analysed according to Bateson's categories. Bateson would first generalise all details of behaviour into premises. These premises he would show as being parts of a 'logical' system which he terms 'cultural structure'. He would then try to elucidate the nature of this 'logic' which governs the manner in which the premises are combined to form the cultural structure. The nature of this 'logic' Bateson terms the 'eidos' of the culture.

When the Lango *ajwaka* fashions a novel ceremony out of the ritual elements of Lango religion in such a way that the ceremony is logical, acceptable and convincing to the people, it could be said of his ceremony that it conforms to the eidos of Lango religion. Let me explain this further. Each of the ritual elements of Lango religion is the nucleus of a premise. For example, the convolvulus, *bomo*, is used in twin ceremonies. It is associated with fertility and is therefore used at the sowing of the crops. The premise is that *bomo* promotes fertility and therefore it is 'logical' for an *ajwaka* to tie *bomo* round the loins of a barren woman in order to make her fruitful. The ritual elements in association with the premises, which govern them, form a 'logical' system which is the 'cultural structure' of Lango religion according to Bateson's definitions. When these ritual elements are combined into a ceremony by the *ajwaka*, they must be combined in a manner consistent with the logic of the cultural structure. Only such a combination will afford satisfaction to the mental requirements of the Lango spectators, will satisfy the eidos of Lango religion. Let me give another example in which the premises are that *bomo* promotes fertility while the leaves of the *epobo* tree cause sterility. According to the eidos of Lango religion it would be absurd for an *ajwaka* to give a barren woman an effusion of *epobo* leaves to drink in order to make her fruitful. But it is conceivable that in another culture, where the same premises hold good for *epobo* and *bomo*, the eidos of the culture might make it eminently logical to give an effusion of *epobo* leaves to cure sterility. The difference between the Lango culture and this hypothetical culture would be a difference in eidos.]

III. The Practice of Lango Religion: Black Magic

Black magic is the term used to designate all those activities which aim at harnessing *jok* power to effect ends of an anti-social nature. These activities may also be termed witchcraft or sorcery. This harnessing of *jok* power is done in secret by means of rites and spells, whereby one individual brings misfortune on another individual or on the whole community.

A person who uses magic against an enemy or for other anti-social purposes is called an *ajok* (sorcerer) and the punishment used to be death. The *ajok* is activated by jealousy (*nyeko*) according to all my informants. This jealousy may be of a general kind directed against society as a whole. Such an *ajok* might 'tie up the rain' so as to bring misfortune on the Tribe. Ogwangatolomoi of Anep gave me a good example of this. He said that long ago a man named Ogwalachu stopped the rain by hiding the urine of his wife and himself just after they had had intercourse. The people looked for this urine, they found it and the rain fell. Another method is to catch some rain water in a pot and hide it with appropriate ritual.

More often the malignance of the *ajok* is directed against a personal enemy who has excited his jealousy. Such an *ajok* may have heard of specific black magic processes, which he sets in motion against his enemy. These usually work according to the principles of sympathetic magic or the *pars pro toto* principle, as when Ogwalajungu discovered one of his wives with the excreta of her co-wife's child of whom she was jealous. She was taking this to have it treated secretly so that the child would die. An *ajok* of this type is called an *ading* and is not so dreaded as a third type of *ajok* who is recognised by his nocturnal habits, which have been so well described by Driberg (*The Lango*, p. 241). This is the most dreaded type of *ajok*, termed *achudany*, for black magic resides in him constitutionally. He may even be unaware of the malignant forces that he exerts. This type of *ajok* is hereditary. The son of a known *ajok* is himself considered to be an *ajok*. He is often abused openly by being called an *ajok*. It is believed that he has something inside his stomach that makes him an *ajok*. The unfailing evidence of such an *ajok* is that he dances and whistles at night. He dances round a person's house at night and then lies down near the doorway. His stomach swells up to a huge size. Then he goes away and the owner of the house dies.

Driberg's account of black magic is more to be relied upon than any evidence that I was able to collect. But one of my informants, having explained how the body of the *ajok* swells up, said that the person in the house did not actually see all this but dreamt it. He remained on his bed unable to move and dreamt the whole thing, crying out in his sleep. For this reason should you hear anyone calling you at night from the door of your house, you must never reply, as it is an *ajok* calling, and if you reply you will die. Driberg, however, thinks it is probable that the stomach of a man can be made to swell up by means of native drugs, and that the story of the *ajok* may well be believed in its entirety. The headmaster of Aduku said that he had always heard of these activities of the *ajok*, but had never discovered anyone who had actually witnessed such a scene. He said that it might be possible for the *ajok* to eat something that made him swell up. Another informant said that the *ajok* was unconscious of his nocturnal activities, which were performed as if in his sleep. It is impossible to obtain direct and concrete evidence of this type of *ajok*. Until more explicit evidence is forthcoming, I would favour the dream theory, as I do for the tree manifestation of the *tipo* (p. 22). The swelling up of the *ajok* would then become a type nightmare. As is well known the primitive is apt to confuse vivid dreams with reality.

The last aspect of black magic is that which is approved by society. It is aimed against those who have transgressed against tribal morality. A man has something stolen from him, so he goes to an *ajwaka*, who sets in motion a spell against the un-known offender. Death or sickness will fall upon the thief. This forms a powerful sanction to tribal law, the removal of which has led to a breakdown of tribal morality among the educated and Christianised Lango. [I made an inquiry why thieving was so prevalent among the Christians while it was practically non-existent in the remote villages. I was told that the Missionaries had taught that a man must not desire to kill anyone else, that the *ajwaka*s were swindlers and that Christians must on no account go to them. For these reasons Christians stole from each other without fear of magical retribu-tion, for the spell of the *ajwaka* no longer held any terrors for them.] No *ajwaka* will openly admit that he practises black magic even for the ends just mentioned. The people do not wholly approve even of this social type of black magic, but they grudgingly admit that black magic set in motion against an offender is justified.

The effectiveness of both black and white magic must be ascribed to suggestion as far as our present knowledge goes. But this is aided in many cases by poisons. Until British Administration became effective the Lango were very free from the terrorising aspects of black magic and from poisons. They still do not have such a dread of them as do many African tribes. But the use of poisons has increased and with it the fear of black magic.

I have very little direct evidence of black magic processes. But I give here a few pieces of information that I gathered.

1. Should a man wish to kill an enemy, he can obtain a photograph of the enemy and seal it up in a pot in the same way as an *ajwaka* catches a *tipo* (p. 155). The enemy will then die, for his *tipo* is caught in the pot. The Lango translation of the word photograph is '*tipo*', and taking a photograph is called 'seizing a *tipo*' (*mako tipo*). This process is often resorted to in the case of theft. The victim of the theft goes to an *ajwaka*, who divines the name of the thief. A photograph of him is obtained and this is sealed up in a pot. When I took photographs of the Lango I was sometimes asked if I was going to take them home to England in order to kill the Lango. The great desire of the Lango to have their photographs taken, in spite of the

possible use to which they might be put, shows how little they are under the terrifying aspects of black magic. The Bagishu of Mount Elgon on the contrary would never allow me to take a photograph of them.

2. My boy Okuja told me that a man had given him the following recipe for killing an enemy. He was not sure what the actual substance of the medicine (*yat*) was, but first you procured this. The medicine is placed in a heap on the ground very early in the morning so that no one sees you doing it. You then flutter (*buko*) a chicken over it, muttering the names of the people you want to kill as you do it. You then cut off the chicken's head so that the blood flows on to the medicine. If you omit to do any of the prescribed rites, you will yourself be killed by the medicine. You drink some beer, eat some food and go to sleep till the evening. In the evening you set off for your victim's village. You must not go along a frequented path as anyone met on the way will die. On reaching the village you climb up a tree and watch to see whether your victims are there. You wait until they are all asleep and then you place the medicine in the middle of the courtyard of the village. You must return home by a different path from that by which you went to the village. All your victims will then die.

3. Okuja also gave me the following pieces of information. If you point your finger at a man and think hard that you want to kill him, he will fall down dead. You must point your finger at his back and, should he look round at that moment, he will be saved. If a man walks round you he will kill you, for this is a sure sign that he has medicine (*yat*). If a man calls you by name when you are asleep at night and you answer him, you will certainly die. But if you keep silent all will be well.

4. *Rwot* Ogwalajungu told me of a case that came before him. A young boy killed a small squirrel-like animal called an *awurunguru*. An old woman saw him do this and said to him, 'Ah, your luck is in. Come to-morrow and I will tell you why.' When the boy returned to her she said, 'Cut off the tail of this animal and if ever you have a case or a quarrel with anyone all you have to do is to dip the tail of this animal in the water that your enemy's cows or goats drink and they will all die.' Ogwalajungu gave this woman two months in prison. 'For',

he said, 'everyone knows that the *awurunguru* is deadly.' If its tail is dipped in the water that cows drink, they will all die. On killing such an animal a man goes to an ant-hill from which swarms have already been caught. In this ant-hill he digs a deep hole and buries the animal there, stamping down the earth tightly.

5. When I was in the Kumam country I heard of a new form of black magic that was causing terror in the District and which had spread to Awelo and other parts of Lango. The victim would see fire at night jumping from tree to tree. He knew then that he would die unless he did something. One of the teachers at the Catholic Mission at Lwala complained that this fire magic had been set in motion against him. He asked leave of the Missionaries to visit a local *ajwaka* to discover who had a grudge against him. That night his house was burnt to the ground, so that he seems to have had a legitimate ground for fear. This type of black magic was looked upon with horror by all whom I questioned in that part of the country. But I had no time to elucidate the mystery.

6. During a beer drink with Ogwalajungu and others the discussion turned to the methods of the *ajok*. They said that a favourite device was to obtain a piece of the enemy's faeces. The *ajok* would plaster this round a piece of iron and work it on an anvil in the manner that a smith would make a spear. The victim would become sexually impotent.

Summary

This chapter will be made clearer if I now summarise the eight assumptions or premises round which the religious beliefs and practices of the Lango are organised:

A. *Jok* is a neutral power permeating the universe, neither well nor badly disposed towards mankind, unless made use of by man. The conceptions of this *jok* power we may term Religion. The practices by which man tries to harness *jok* power for his own requirements we may term Magic—White Magic where the ends are for the good of society, and Black Magic where the ends are anti-social.

B. Anything of an unusual and apparently causeless nature

must be associated with some aspect of *jok* power. Of such are:
1. Abnormal births. 2. Abnormal natural objects. 3. Mystifying occurrences. 4. Good and bad luck.

C. Phenomena affecting society, the vicissitudes of which,
while familiar, cannot be predicted or controlled empirically,
are associated with *jok* power. Of such are: 1. Natural phenomena, such as rain, hail, locusts and lightning. 2. Sickness and
disease. 3. Misfortunes.

D. *Jok* power is present when human beings are in a highly
excited emotional state. Of such are: 1. Sexual intercourse.
2. Dancing. 3. States of dissociation.

E. *Jok* power is present in situations and objects dangerous
to man. Of such are: 1. The hunt and fierce animals.
2. Fighting. 3. Journeys. 4. Breaking of tribal laws.

F. *Jok* power is associated with every human being as
that part of him to which we usually apply the term spirit or
soul. 1. The nature of the *tipo* and *chyen*. 2. How the *tipo*
afflicts living people. 3. Dreams.

G. The *ajwaka* or medicine-men and the elders of the people
control these manifestations of *jok* power and harness them to
the needs of society by means of the rites and spells which form
the ceremonial life of the Tribe. The ceremonies are performed
publicly; they are white magic; they are for the good of society.

H. The *ajok* or sorcerer, by means of esoteric knowledge
and secretly performed rites and spells, can harness this *jok*
power to further his own purposes. He works in secret; it is
black magic; it is anti-social.

CHAPTER II

LANGO GROUPS AND CEREMONIES

Man, with his poor natural weapons, has dominated the animal world through his power of co-operation. In backward societies this co-operation is essential for the existence of the individual, who is absolutely dependent on his group. The preservation and reproduction of the individual depends upon the preservation of the group. If the society is to survive, the group must have a power of resistance to disintegrating forces. There is no need to postulate a group mind in this connection, for the power to resist disintegration arises from the system of thoughts and sentiments that is in the minds of the individuals of the group, causing them to act in opposition to external or internal attacks upon the integrity of the group.

Among the Lango the Tribe was the main group. I found the Lango Tribe split up into a number of local and social groupings each of which had some part to play in the integration of Lango society. The inter-relations of these groups with each other formed part of the social structure of Lango society (cf. Bateson's definition, *Naven*, p. 26). Within this social structure of interacting groups the individual Lango was born and brought up. He was a member of several groups and each group played a part in training him for life within Lango society. The importance of the groups to the individual lay in their training functions, while the whole of Lango culture had its being within the framework of this social structure.

A culture must provide first for the nourishment and protection of the individual and for the production and care of his children. In other words it must promote the preservation and reproduction of the individual. At the same time, if it is to have any survival value, it must promote the preservation of the social structure upon which it is itself dependent. In addition to these fundamental requirements of a culture, there are the biologically less essential accretions of religion, art, economic organisation, and so on; in fact, all that gives human society its colour, interest and variety.

The importance of the Lango groups, which I am about to describe, was that through them the system of thoughts and sentiments of the individual Lango were standardised to the pattern of Lango culture (cf. Ruth Benedict, *Patterns of culture*).

In the previous chapter I analysed the system of thoughts which lay behind Lango ritual practices, and so I isolated the premises (cf. Bateson's definition, *Naven*, p. 24) of Lango religion. In this chapter I wish to show the structural devices by means of which the individual's sentiments of loyalty to his group were trained.

The most important of these devices were the ceremonies which are described in the following chapters. I found that each ceremony was concerned with one or other of the Lango groups, and the individual Lango attended the ceremony by virtue of his membership of that group. I have deduced the premises of Lango religion, as formulated in the previous chapter, from the behaviour of individuals at the ceremonies. These ceremonies play a great part in standardising the mind of the individual to the pattern of Lango culture.

In analysing Lango social structure as represented by these groups, I have tried to bring out the ways in which each group worked upon the individual member so as to standardise his psychology to the required pattern. For this purpose I have considered each group from four points of view. 1. Basis of membership of the group. 2. Integrating forces that maintain the unity of the group. 3. Inter-relations with other groups. 4. Value of the group, both in respect of the major group of the Tribe and in respect of the individual member.

Driberg gives a history in his book on the Lango, but as this is out of print a summary of his conclusions may conveniently be placed here. For it is necessary to have some knowledge of Lango history in order to understand the requirements of the Tribe and hence of its constituent groups.

The Lango are a nilotic Tribe showing close affinity to the Shilluk, Luo, Anuak, Acholi, Alur and Jopaluo. The nilotic homeland seems to have been somewhere between the Nile and Lake Rudolph, where the Lango were in close touch with the nilo-hamitic Langodyang and Langolok, which accounts partly for certain hamitic traits in Lango culture. As a result of the hamitic invasions from Abyssinia, which passed round the north of Lake Rudolph and across to the north of Lake Albert, and also as a result of Bari and, at a later date, of Madi pressure from the west, the Nilotes split up and migrated north-west and south-west to form the nilotic Tribes as we know them to-day. This movement began round about A.D. 1500.

About A.D. 1700, probably driven on by the increasing desiccation of their land, the Lango migrated south-west towards the Nile. At this period the Lango and the Acholi, who had preceded them, used to fight in alliance against the Madi to their north. During this phase some Lango Clans migrated south, as they were unable to navigate the Nile, and reached the Tochi round about 1720. These Clans were cut off from the main Tribe as a result of a state of enmity arising between the Lango and the Acholi, who had made peace with the Madi through fear of the Madi bow-and-arrow war tactics.

The main Lango Tribe was compelled to swing eastwards, and, after a further period of migration, reached the country neighbouring the Karamojong. Here there was a pause of eighty years or so before they made the final push into their present territory, passing by Mount Otuke. This was in the beginning of the last century, and by 1890 they had spread across their present territory and made contact with the section which had formerly reached the Tochi. At the close of the last century they first came in touch with Europeans.

The latter half of this account is still confirmed by Lango traditions, and I have no grounds for not accepting Driberg's hypothesis of the earlier migrations. But the actual facts are not important. All that it is necessary to realise is that the Lango have been in a state of gradual migration for long periods of their recent history. Migration entails war with Tribes encountered on the way, and an organisation enabling groups of people to move onwards in safety and yet still keep in touch with the main Tribe. These two considerations, I believe, were chiefly responsible for the great importance of children and the highly organised Clan system of the Lango.

The account of Lango groups given below will be the clearer for a preliminary survey of their names and relations to each other. Diagrams A and B facing p. 38 may help towards an

understanding of the social structure of the Lango groups, though
only a model utilising many different planes could represent the
situation truly.   Diagram A looked at separately shows the
social and diagram B the territorial groups to which the individual belongs. When they are superimposed upon each other
an idea is obtained of the network of groups to which the
individual owes loyalty and by means of which his moulding
into the pattern of culture of the Tribe has been achieved.

1.   The Tribe.
2.   The Clan.
3.   The *Etogo* (a religious group which links Clans).
4.   The *Jo Doggola* (a lineage within the Clan in the male
line).
5.   The Family.
6.   The *Wat* (relations on the mother's and father's sides).
7.   The *Neo* (the mother's brothers and their families).
8.   The *Okeo* (the sister's family).
9.   The *Rwot*'s sphere of influence.
10.   The *Jago*'s sphere of influence.
11.   The Village community.
12.   The *Wang Tich* (group that works in the fields).
13.   The *Jo Awi Dyang* (people who keep cattle in one
kraal).
14.   Age and Status groups (they stratify all other groups).
15.   ·Age Grades (they cut across all the other groups).

The Tribe, Clan, *Jo Doggola* and Family form a hierarchy
of groups within groups. The *Etogo*, *Wat*, *Neo* and *Okeo* are
groups linking up the Clans and their constituent groups. These
two sets of groups are socially determined.

The *Rwot*'s sphere of influence, the *Jago*'s sphere of influence,
the Village, *Wang Tich* and *Jo Awi Dyang* also form a hierarchy
of groups within groups, but constituted on a territorial basis.
The Age Grades link up all the groups so that they form a
united body against the external threats to the Tribe—famine
and the attack of an enemy.

[The Tribe is split roughly into four geographical divisions:
Jo Moita, *Jo Kidi*, *Jo Aber*, *Jo Burutok*, embracing respectively
the areas south of Lake Kwania, the north-east, the north-west
and the south-west. They are distinguished by slight variations

A Diagram showing the inter-relations of Groups

A.   Socially Determined

B. Territorially Determined

LANGO GROUPS AND CEREMONIES

in customs and material culture and probably signify separate waves of migration; *Jo Aber* being the descendants of the Clans originally cut off from the main Tribe; *Jo Kidi* and *Jo Moita* being influenced by the hamitic Teso and Kumam; *Jo Burutok* being influenced by the Bantu Baganda and Banyoro. These divisions are not important functionally, for the nature of the Lango territory, bounded by the lakes and the Nile, held them in one Tribe. Had there been more room for expansion they might have split into four different Tribes. Therefore I ignore them in this account of Lango groups, as there would be no profit in showing such small differences in custom as exist between them.]

The devices, which induce in the individual that system of sentiments and loyalties which keeps these groups in being and maintains their union one with the other, are the ceremonies, symbolisms, customs, institutions and beliefs of the culture.

The Tribe

Membership. The people occupying the Lango District spoke what they regarded as one language. They called themselves the 'Lango' and considered themselves to be one people, in spite of continual internecine war. This expressed itself in the fact that they would unite to protect their territory against invaders.

Unity. The basis of unity was a sentiment of loyalty to the Tribe, expressed in actions designed to protect it when threatened by enemy invaders or the vicissitudes of nature. Disasters shared in common are great promoters of group co-operation. The tribal ceremonies of *apuny, ewor* and *myel akot*, which tended to build up this sentiment and foster it at the required degree of intensity, are described in Chapter III. At the *apuny* all the *Etogo* groups of Lango assembled at one time at traditional places to celebrate past deaths and to constrain the ancestors to give them abundant crops. By the *ewor* the Age Grades were formed and Lango youth was taught the mysteries of rain-making and was marshalled on a war footing. By *myel akot* the ancestors were supplicated for rain in due season. Other unifying elements were a common language,

endogamy, common traditions, the linking up of the Clans by
the Age Grades and *Etogo* groups, common customs and beliefs,
ceremonies and institutions, in other words a common pattern
of culture.

Inter-relations.   As the Tribe was the major group, the
question of inter-relations does not arise. But it will be convenient here to note its relations with other Tribes. The Lango
used to assist Kabarega, king of the Banyoro, in his wars against
the Baganda and the Madi. Certain Nyoro and Lango traditions point to a close connection between the two Tribes, but
this is unimportant functionally. Warfare with the Acholi was
of the border raid variety, similarly with the Kumam. There
were clashes with the Karamojong in the dry season when they
came to the Moroto to water their cattle. When, at the end of
the last century, Bantu settlers began to occupy the lake and
Nile shores, there was fighting against them. The newcomers
obtained a footing however. They are called '*Jo Nam*' (people
of the Lake) and consist of Baganda, Banyoro Banyara, Baruli
and the Bakenyi water gypsies of the Lakes.

Value.   The Tribe would combine to protect its members
against invaders. But tribal feeling was not highly developed
and the protective machinery of the Clans was more important
from the point of view of the preservation and reproduction
of the individual. There was a sense of spiritual unity within
the Tribe which found expression in the rain ceremonies, where
the ancestors of all tribesmen were asked not to withhold the
rain. The Tribe was therefore essentially a protective group
defending the lives and culture of its constituent Clans from
the two external threats—an enemy invader and famine as a
result of drought. The first function was actual protection, the
second was magical.

The Clan

Membership.   Following the definition of a Clan given in *Notes
and Queries on Anthropology* (p. 55, Fifth Edition), the Lango Clan
(*atekere*) was composed of those people whose mothers were
married with cattle belonging to the Clan. Their fathers may
not have been clansmen, but may have been war captives or the

okeo (sister's son) of a clansman, who were provided with wives through cattle belonging to the Clan. Or they may have been born illegitimately, their mothers later marrying into the Clan. So that the Clan must be reckoned as an exogamous, patrilineal group of persons all the members of which (*jo me atekere*) held themselves to be related to one another and bound together by a common tie of clanship. This tie was based on the fact that the individuals concerned were the products of unions sanctioned by the handing over of cattle belonging to the Clan. The tie of relationship therefore was not necessarily biological.

Clans tend to split up in the following manner: 1. A Clan living in a certain locality may increase so greatly that one half begins to feel that it is not closely related to the other. Some boy may have intercourse with a girl in the other half, whereupon it will be decided that the two halves are separate Clans and inter-marriage will be allowed. [This is about to happen in the Clan *Arak me tung Ogwal* at Awelo. They are waiting for a case of incest to declare the two divisions distinct Clans.] 2. Two brothers may quarrel so that one collects his cattle together and migrates to another district. His children may marry those of his brother, as he has declared that he has founded a new Clan, the important symbol of which is the division of the cattle. The tendency to identify the Clan with its cattle makes it a logical procedure for the Clan to be divided when half the cattle have been taken elsewhere under conditions of hostility. 3. A quarrel between a father and a son may lead to a similar division. 4. Should a section of a Clan migrate and a long separation ensue, the migrating section may no longer deem itself to be one with the parent Clan. 5. Should a section of a Clan have found inadequate protection from raids, it might migrate in order to ally itself with a stronger Clan, whereupon it would change its name and be considered a separate Clan.

When offshoots of a Clan split away as just described, the seceding section changes its form in regard to its name, its Clan cry, its ritual observances, the variations in its ceremonies, the exogamy rule. These changes are striking proofs of the suggestion that all these elements are symbolisms of Clan unity, and that they tend to maintain the integrity of the group.

Unity. Loyalty to the Clan was the strongest sentiment developed in the individual, who depended for his existence on Clan approval. It is natural, therefore, to find many devices at work in the Clan tending to create a strong sense of unity and to maintain this sentiment at a high level of intensity. These devices may be summed up as: 1. Name of Clan and of individuals in the Clan. 2. Clan cry. 3. Clan chief. 4. Ritual observances. 5. Ceremonies. 6. Variations in ceremonial. 7. Exogamy. 8. The *Etogo* group. 9. Communal ownership of property. 10. Communal responsibility and mutual help.

1. *Name.* Every individual knew the name of his Clan. It was the symbol of his interests. Driberg's list of a hundred and fourteen Clans (*The Lango*, pp. 192–204) is sufficient to show the types of names used, and there would be little value in adding the further forty-four names that I discovered. When a Clan divided, as described above, the seceding section changed its name by adding to the original Clan name: 1. The name of the founder of the new section. [*Arak* became *Arak me tung Owiny*; *Rwot* Owinyakulo, the founder of this section, is still alive.] 2. A nickname due to some event occurring to the new section. [*Arak* became *Arak me Opelo*. Opelo means that they speared their own legs, which apparently happened to some members of the section long ago in battle or the hunt.] 3. The name of the strong Clan to which the section migrated for protection. [*Oki* became *Oki me Otengoro*.]

There were also a number of personal names for individuals in the Clan. Only for exceptional reasons would a clansman be given a name that was not in use in his Clan, as when a child was given a name appropriate to another Clan in order to avert evil influences at the ceremony of *atin akwer* (p. 136).

2. *Clan cry.* Every Clan had what was known as the 'Bull of the Clan' (*twon me atekere*). This was the name or names of one or more famous ancestors, generally the founders of the Clan. The Clan cry (*twon me gigwongo*) consisted of allusions to these ancestors. Thus the *twon* of the Clan *Arak me Ongoda* was 'Agumakol, Obero, iloro atin Kidi ilapilop, Apyeli. ateri i ota. Adoo, Adoo adol otach.' The meaning of this was not clear to my informants, but the sense understood by them was that *Agumakol, Obero, Apyeli* and *Adoo* were famous ancestors and ancestresses;

Apyeli had a huge penis and his wife, *Adoo*, used a grass head pad (circular in shape with a hole through it) to protect herself from *Apyeli's* penis, which 'could kill a woman'. This Clan cry was known to the initiated men and women and to the wives of the clansmen (*mon me atekere*). It was shouted by the dancers at the twin ceremony while feinting with spear and shield. It was called out at rain-making, battle and on other public occasions. It was in essence a cry of victory. A woman would shout both her own and her husband's cry. When a Clan divided, the Clan cry of the seceding section was changed, a new one being concocted about the founders of the new section.

3. *Clan chief.* Each Clan had a leader (*adit me atekere*), who settled disputes between clansmen and led his people in war. He was installed by the ceremony of *chibo adit me atekere* (p. 103), when he was anointed with oil before his clansmen. His most popular and able son inherited his position. Driberg pointed out to me that the Clan chief incarnated the Clan *jok* power, which is crystallised in the founder of the Clan and handed down to his successors in office, as with the Didinga. So that the super-physical bond between clansmen was symbolised in the person of the chief.

4. *Ritual observances.* Each Clan had from one to five ritual observances (*kite me kwer*), which had to be kept by every woman married into the Clan. A new wife was taught them by her mother-in-law and observed them after the ceremony of *tweyo lau* (p. 84). In the case of a divorce, a woman kept her first husband's observances until *tweyo lau* had been performed by her new husband, whereupon she left off the observances of her first husband. These observances, which were met with every day of the week, were a strong bond between clansmen together with their wives.

The nature of the ritual observances may be summarised conveniently under four generalisations:

1. Variations on the question of not eating the meat of, or sitting on or touching the skins of: duiker, bushbuck, reedbuck, cob, waterbuck, goat, etc.

2. Prohibitions as to the eating of: wild cherry, honey, wild fig, vegetable marrow, the vegetable *gulu dek*.

3. Prohibitions against passing, going under the shade of, or

crossing: fig tree, clear space in the bush (*laro jok*), roots of trees showing across a path, trees struck by lightning, trees fallen on the ground, the plant *adyebepar*, a place where there has been a recent birth, a cattle kraal (if pregnant). Most of these observances were particularly urgent if the woman was pregnant.

4. Prohibitions against directing remarks or gestures at a pregnant woman: a reference to her state of pregnancy, a feint at her with a spear, and so on.

The Lango are extremely fond of children and the ritual observances were designed to curb the anxieties of wives, since miscarriage and infant deaths were very frequent, chiefly as a result of chronic malaria (according to the medical authorities). The penalties attached to non-observance of a ritual prohibition may be generalised as:

1. Where they applied to the wife (which was predominantly the case), she would become sterile; if pregnant, she would immediately miscarry; if she had a small child, it would die.

2. Where they applied to the child, it would die; or its head would go bald in patches and swell up; or its head would break out in sores.

3. Where they applied to the husband (which was rare), he would become impotent.

When a Clan divided, the ritual observances of the seceding section were changed slightly, as a result of incidents associated with the founders of the new section, or in imitation of the Clan whose name had been added to form the new name of the section.

5. *Ceremonies*. In Chapter IV I shall show how various Clan ceremonies bring clansmen together and stress their dependence upon one another. The following ceremonies serve this purpose: 1. Installing the Clan chief (p. 103). 2. Marriage (p. 82). 3. Tying on the marriage skin (p. 83). 4. Dance in celebration of twins (p. 97). 5. Sprinkling a mother of twins (p. 99). 6. Bringing ornaments for the children (p. 88). 7. Killing a bull for a sick child (p. 91). 8. Killing a goat for a sick child (p. 94). 9. Washing a child's sore eyes (p. 96). 10. Burial (p. 106). 11. Killing a bull at a dead man's grave (p. 108). 12. Feast marking the end of mourning (p. 111). 13. Mixing

the seed for sowing a dead man's fields (p. 123).   14. The *apuny* ceremony for a dead man (p. 63).

6. *Variations in ceremonial.* Although the ceremonies are the same for all Clans in the Tribe, yet in every ceremony each Clan has some small variation peculiar to itself. These variations are known to the clansmen and serve to mark them off from other Clans. The ceremonies at birth and during the bringing up of children are particularly subject to this Clan variation. When a Clan divided, the seceding section evolved new variations in its ceremonies based on the experiences of the founders of the new section, or in imitation of the stronger Clan whose protection had been sought.

7. *Exogamy.* The rule of exogamy tends to lessen quarrels. Quarrels arise most easily over food and women. By disallowing as incest intercourse between clansmen, such quarrels could not arise within the Clan. The importance of this institution is seen in the death penalty that used to be the punishment for incest within the Clan. Incest aimed a blow at the very structure of the Clan, on which the integrity of the whole Tribe depended. If a Clan divided, the exogamy rule did not hold between members of the seceding and the parent Clans.

8. *The* Etogo *group.* Through the *Etogo* institution meat was distributed among clansmen with a minimum of quarrelling. This was well illustrated at the ceremony at Abongamola (p. 122), when the *Etogo* man, who had killed the bull, gave instructions about the division of the meat. He took pains to warn them not to quarrel about this, saying that the disease would become worse if the clansmen quarrelled. He directed that the child's father was to have the breast, loin, ribs, neck and stomach, the girls of the Clan were to have a leg, and the rest was to be divided among the men of the Clan and their wives. It soon became evident how necessary his instructions were. The clansmen sat in three groups in the village dividing up the meat among themselves. The group near me seemed to be doing this very quietly. Only the calm suggestions of each individual that a little more meat should be added to his or her pile denoted the strain underlying their self-control. The tension suddenly broke when some one made a grab at a piece of meat. Immediately everyone was up, scrambling and shouting for

meat. The father of the sick child and the *ajwaka* (medicine-woman) were furious, as they had been told not to quarrel by the *Etogo* man, and now the child would probably get worse.

9. *Communal ownership of property.* Property of all sorts and wives (who represented cattle) had to be inherited by clansmen. Should the Clan be dying out, the sister's son (*okeo*) might inherit. But this *okeo* would have been given a wife by his mother's brother (*nero*). His children therefore belonged to the *nero*'s Clan, since they were the products of a union sanctioned by the handing over of the *nero*'s cattle (p. 55). They would eventually inherit the Clan property through their father, the *okeo*, and so the property would remain in the Clan. Cattle were the most important form of property communally owned by the Clan. Specific animals were assigned to individual clansmen by the ordinary form of father-son inheritance, and such an owner (*won dok* = guardian of the cattle) could dispose of the animals more or less as he wished, subject to Clan requisitions. But he would always inform at least his brother should he intend to kill or sell an animal. Most owners looked upon their cattle as a trust which must be preserved and multiplied so that their descendants might have sufficient with which to marry. The Lango was devoted to his cattle, the source of his milk supply, a food reserve in time of famine, a necessity for Clan ceremonial, but above all the means by which wives were obtained. Though individuals had control over certain animals, the totality of cattle belonged to the Clan. A poor clansman had merely to show his worthiness by doing hard work and he would be given a cow, which would form the basis of his herd. So great was this sentiment for cattle that the Clan was practically identified with its cattle and they formed a strong link between members.

10. *Communal responsibility and mutual help.* The important principle of communal responsibility was the foundation of the legal and political system of the Lango. For the Clan admitted responsibility for the actions of its members, paying any just compensation due from a clansman and demanding compensation for wrongs done to a clansman. A boy obtained cattle from his father, his father's brother or some other clansman when he wished to marry. He would only go outside the Clan,

to his *nero*, if his Clan was too poor to help him. It may be noted here that a wife who thought that she had been badly treated by her husband would voice her grievances loudly before the other clansmen at some ceremony, so that they would compel him to reform his ways, for a divorce would entail the surrender of the cattle distributed among them. This occurred during the *tweyo lau* ceremony I saw at Achaba. A man looked after his parents when they were old but not yet senile. When they were quite helpless, however, he left them behind when he migrated and they were eaten by hyaenas. Although members of the same Clan might live in widely separated localities, visiting each other on ceremonial occasions, yet most clansmen lived in one locality. They could then assemble easily for ceremonies, they dug the fields together, they were easily available for marriage questions concerning the cattle, above all there was a sense of security as being among their own people.

Inter-relations. Clans were linked together by means of: 1. The *Etogo* groups, which were composed of several Clans meeting together for ceremonies concerned with the *tipos* (spirits) of the dead. 2. Exogamy, which made it essential for each Clan to contract marriage alliances with other Clans. 3. The Age Grades, which cut across all other local and social groupings. 4. All those devices which bound families together (p. 53). The ceremonies which forged these links by bringing the Clans together and showing their interdependence were: 1. The *apuny* ceremony for a dead man (p. 63). 2. The *ewor* ceremony for the formation of Age Grades (p. 66). 3. Rain-making ceremonies (p. 73). 4. Feast marking the end of mourning (p. 111). 5. Dance in celebration of twins (p. 97). 6. Sprinkling a mother of twins (p. 99). 7. Marriage (p. 82). 8. Sprinkling a woman after marriage (p. 88). 9. Bringing ornaments for the children (p. 88). 10. Killing a bull for a sick child (p. 91). 11. Killing a goat for a sick child (p. 94). 12. Washing a child's sore eyes (p. 96). The last six ceremonies are performed in a reciprocal series, visits to the husband's Clan alternating with visits to the wife's Clan. This shows that the chief value of these ceremonies was to keep alive the alliance of two Clans united by marriage.

Value. The Lango did not migrate as a whole Tribe. Lango Clans were suitable units for migrating, as they could preserve tribal culture and they formed good fighting units. But the Clan, while largely able to protect itself, was yet retained within the tribal system by the institution of exogamy, which made it impossible for Clans to exist alone. The *Etogo* provided a mystical link. The Clan regulated marriage and hence the production of children, so essential for a fighting community, birth, on account of its uncertainties, being controlled magically by the system of ritual observances and ceremonies to ensure fecundity. Property was inherited by, and the fields dug by, clansmen. Communal responsibility for and redress of crimes against a clansman were the bases of tribal law, and provided that poor clansmen did not starve. When travelling far from home, a man could expect hospitality from a clansman as a right. A religious function lay in the fact that the *tipo*s of the dead could plague their own clansmen only. The services rendered by the Clan therefore from the individual's point of view were: 1. Protection. 2. Economic. 3. Social (marriage). 4. Legal. 5. Religious. 6. Security in adversity. From the point of view of the Tribe, the Clan was the group wherein the preservation and reproduction of the individual was carried out. The Tribe was too large a group for the individual to grasp effectively, and so all his energies and emotions were directed towards the Clan and its advancement. The Clan was essentially a protective group defending the rights and lives of its constituent Families.

The *Etogo*

Membership. The *Etogo* was a grouping of certain Clans, all of whom were conscious of the other Clans as belonging to their *Etogo*, and who met together primarily to eat a ritually killed animal. In general the *Etogo*, sitting according to the three meat groups into which it was divided, had to eat a bull, goat, sheep or chicken ritually, in circumstances which made it very dangerous for a non-member to join the eaters. The important members of the *Etogo* were the old men of the associated Clans. The initiated men of the younger generations were also full

Etogo members, and when the older generation died off, they took their place. Women and children also attended the *Etogo* meal but sat apart from the ritual eaters.

The members of the *Etogo* were divided into three meat groups according to the parts of the animal eaten:

1. *Jo Ekori:* ate ribs and shoulders.
2. *Jo Aboi:* ate all the viscera.
3. *Jo Oguru:* ate the back, loins and legs.

The head went to the owner of the animal. Only small pieces of the meat were eaten ritually, most of it being taken home or eaten on the spot later. Three pots of beer were also brewed, one for each group. The animal was always killed by the leader of the group of the dead man whose *tipo* was the cause of the ceremony.

The initiation of boys into the *Etogo* is described later (p. 64). Inquiries as to the formation of the *Etogo* groups resulted generally in the assertion that from the time of their ancestors they have always been constituted as they are now, a man belonging to the same *Etogo* as his father. But many informants from different parts of the country were agreed that Clans or Families might become affiliated to an *Etogo* group in one or other of the following ways:

1. If a Clan split up (as described on p. 41), the parent Clan and its offshoots would remain members of the same *Etogo*. Some witnesses asserted that this process was the origin of the *Etogo*, and had Clans not split up there would have been no *Etogo* groups.

2. On migrating to a place out of reach of his own *Etogo*, a man would attend the celebrations of a local *Etogo*, sitting apart and being given pieces of meat. He himself could not become an *Etogo* member, but his sons would be initiated into this *Etogo* in the ordinary way and their descendants would call this their *Etogo*.

3. If a certain *Etogo* continually quarrelled over the division of the meat, a member might decide to go over to another *Etogo*. He himself could not change membership, but his sons could be initiated into the new *Etogo* in the manner described later (p. 64).

These methods of changing from one *Etogo* to another were responsible for the fact that the Clans associated in an *Etogo*

in one part of the country might be different from those in an
Etogo of the same name in another part of the country. It is
very difficult to obtain accurate information on this subject,
because the younger men often do not know much about their
*Etogo*s, while not every old man knows (perhaps this is concealment) the name of his *Etogo* or the names of the Clans in it.
He knows the individuals with whom he eats in the *Etogo*, and
to what meat group he belongs. It is, however, clear that, if a
man goes to another part of the country, he will eat ritually
only at an *Etogo* of the same name as his own, though he will
sit apart and will be given meat at any *Etogo* feast.

The *Etogo* may be considered as an indigenous Lango institution, though it became associated with the Age Grade system,
which was an importation from the Hamites.

Unity.   Each *Etogo* had a name. A sentiment of awe was
the chief binding link of the *Etogo*. It was a religious group, and
the magical control of the old *Etogo* men over the *tipo*s of the
dead was necessary for the members in order to allay their
anxieties over malevolent spirits. This dependence upon the
old men of the *Etogo* was inculcated by the ceremonies at which
they performed and at which the *Etogo* members met each other.
These were: 1. Feast marking the end of mourning (p. 111).
2. The *apuny* ceremony for a dead man (p. 63).   3. Drawing out
the evil *tipo* from a sick man (p. 115).   4. Killing a bull for
sickness caused by a *tipo* (p. 121).   5. Digging up a dead man's
bones (p. 122).   6. Mixing the seed before sowing a dead
man's fields (p. 123).   7. Rain ceremonies (p. 73).   8. *Abila*
for impotency caused by a *tipo* (p. 141).

As a working institution the *Etogo* was based largely on locality
and united the people of that locality. When a *tipo* 'seized the
body' of a man, it was impossible for him or his clansmen to do
anything about it. The *Etogo* alone could deal with the situation.
By eating the animal in which the offending *tipo* was immanent
as a result of the preliminary ceremonial, the *Etogo* drew the
tipo out of the sick man (pp. 20, 121).   The *tipo* could not hurt
the *Etogo* eaters, since they were not of its Clan. This curative
function of the *Etogo* was a very strong link between the Clans
of a locality.

Inter-relations. At the tribal ceremonies of *apuny* and rain-making the various *Etogo* groups of the locality performed together. The Age Grades also linked up the *Etogo* groups.

Value. From the individual's point of view his *Etogo* was the only means by which suitable relations could be maintained with the dead, so that they should not afflict him with adversity. Certain types of illness were caused by the *tipo*s of the dead and only the *Etogo* could effect a remedy. The *Etogo* with its superphysical control over the dead relieved all anxieties on account of the spirit world. This was its primary function and it controlled all funeral ceremonial, the object of which was to translate the *tipo* of the dead man to the status of ancestor. It may be that the word *Etogo* is derived from the word *tego* (to ripen), as being the agency through which the *tipo* matured or ripened into the status of ancestor (see Glossary under '*otogo*', last paragraph). It also linked up Clans on a territorial basis. Its ceremonies provided a suitable opportunity for handing on tribal traditions.

One of the most striking functions of the *Etogo* to an outside observer was that of killing and distributing meat with the minimum of quarrel. A man's emotions were so centred in his cattle that he found it very difficult to bring himself to kill one of his animals at all, let alone having to do the deed himself. The meat supply was ensured, however, by the ceremonies, most of which required the killing of some animal. The distasteful task of slaughter was assigned to a man outside the owner's Clan. The *Etogo* leader of the meat group of the dead man did the actual slaying. The division of the *Etogo* into the three meat groups—*Jo Ekori*, *Jo Aboi* and *Jo Oguru*—ensured that the meat was divided up into the ritually apportioned parts. No one was limited to eating his part alone, but that part was his legally, and on that point there could be no disagreement. He might give some of it to others in exchange for their portions. This limited quarrels over the distribution. The tendency to quarrel whenever meat was being distributed was very great, and on these occasions everyone was warned that any quarrelling would spoil the magico-religious effectiveness of the proceedings. This was brought out very clearly at the Abon-

gamola ceremony (p. 122), when the *Etogo* man, who had been
summoned to kill the bull, explained exactly how the meat was
to be divided up among the clansmen, and warned them that,
if they quarrelled, the child would die.

THE *Jo Doggola*

Membership. The *Jo Doggola* (people of the doorway) were
a group based on lineage. It was a group of agnates, which
comprised all those descended through the male line from a
given individual. A man's *Jo Doggola* were all those persons
of either sex who could trace their descent through males to a
common ancestor. The term *Jo Doggola* was relative, since the
group of individuals contained in it depended upon the particular person who was selected as the point of departure. The
Jo Doggola group was similar to the lineage group (*thok diviet*)
of the Nuer Tribe (cf. 'The Nuer, Tribe and Clan', Evans-
Pritchard, *Sudan Notes and Records*, 1933, Part I, p. 28). It
differed from the Nuer group by being less crystallised, since
the Clan was the more important group among the Lango.
A man's *Jo Doggola* meant his father's kinsmen, and the number
of people included in the expression would vary according to
how far back memory reached. But the relationship between
members of the *Jo Doggola* could be traced more specifically
than the relationship between clansmen.

Unity. All that has been said about the Clan applies to the
Jo Doggola, save that the sentiment of loyalty to the *Jo Doggola*
was more intense than Clan sentiment. In the ceremonies as
given for the Clan it was actually the *Jo Doggola* who performed,
though theoretically the whole Clan took part.

Inter-relations. The bonds linking *Jo Doggola* together were
identical with those which maintained Clan unity.

Value. As far as the individual was concerned the *Jo
Doggola* were those members of the Clan from whom help was
sought when difficulties arose. All that has been said of the
Clan applied equally to the *Jo Doggola*, who may be considered
as the practical unit whereby Clan interests were maintained.

The Family

Membership. The Family was a group composed of husband, wife or wives, and children.

Unity. Propinquity was the chief bond of the Family. The functions of the Family, by their direct and immediate nature, formed the deepest emotional ties between the members. The dependence of the individual on his Family was emphasised in the following ceremonies: 1. Marriage (p. 82). 2. Birth (p. 130). 3. Sprinkling a man at his mother-in-law's village (p. 127). 4. Killing a bull for his mother-in-law (p. 129). 5. Safeguarding a child by ritualising it (p. 135). 6. Twin ceremonial (p. 97). 7. Purifying a man by sprinkling him (p. 137). 8. Killing a bull in honour of one's father (p. 138). 9. Migrating to a new house (p. 139). 10. First fruits (p. 139). 11. Ceremonies to cure sterility and impotency (p. 140). 12. Drawing out the spirit of a dangerous animal killed in the hunt (p. 141). 13. Blessing a spear to cure sickness (p. 144). 14. Burial (p. 106).

Inter-relations. Families belonging to one Clan were linked together by reason of this Clan membership, and all that has been said of Clan and *Jo Doggola* applied to them. They were linked to other Families within the Tribe by common membership of a village, the *Wang Tich* group, the *Awi Dyang* group, and by marriage. The ceremonies concerned with this linking, besides those concerned with linking Clans, were: 1. Sprinkling a man at his mother-in-law's village (p. 127). 2. Carrying flour to one's son-in-law's village (p. 128). 3. Killing a bull for one's mother-in-law (p. 129). These ceremonies formed a reciprocal series, visits to the mother-in-law's village alternating with her visits to her son-in-law. This shows that the chief purpose of these ceremonies was to keep alive friendship between the two Families.

Value. The family was the primary and essential unit by which the biological law of the preservation and reproduction of the individual was carried out. Its functions may be cited as: 1. Producing and educating offspring. 2. Producing and consuming food. 3. Organising marriage.

THE *WAT*

Membership. The term *Wat* was used in a very wide sense to cover all those people connected with the speaker through his mother, father, brother, sister or wife.

Unity. The totality of tribal ceremonial served to keep members of the *Wat* group aware of each other, while the exogamy bar between members of a common *Wat* group emphasised their affinity.

Inter-relations. The *Wat* was not strictly speaking a group, but the term served to cover all cognates and relatives by marriage. The *Wat* therefore formed a pattern of intersecting groups.

Value. There was general friendliness between members of the *Wat* group, which by its nature was large. It was an exogamous group, for once a marriage had been contracted with another Family no further marriages could take place between the *Wat* group and that Family. The strictness of this rule was modified by the distance of the connection. The feasibility of marriage between distantly related members was decided by public opinion rather than by any precise rule. The usual test was that, if anyone knew of a connection by Clan, however remote, of the ascendants in the direct father's or mother's line, the marriage was forbidden. A man's wives had to be from different Clans, unless a sister was given in place of a dead or unsatisfactory wife.

THE *NEO*

Membership. The mother's brothers (*nero*) and their children belonged to this group, the members of which were known collectively as *Neo*.

Unity. The same ceremonies as those linking Families served to link the *Neo* groups. There was a privileged relationship between a person (the *okeo*) and his mother's brother (the *nero*). Theoretically the *nero* had to grant all requests for small gifts made by the *okeo*. The *okeo* might seize a chicken in his *nero*'s house and take it off. There was also a joking relationship with the wives of the *neo* of his own generation. This consisted of: 1. Abuse or jokes of a sexual nature. [The *okeo* might say, 'You don't pluck your pubic hairs'. The woman replies, 'You have an enormous penis'.] 2. Lewd gestures. [When anointing each other at the twin dance, they would make a thrust at each other's private parts with the *tanga* paste.] 3. In the ceremonies of *donyo oko* (p. 135), *tweyo lau* (p. 86) and *kayo chogo* (p. 93) the *okeo* strikes his *nero*'s wife with an *epobo* stick and is struck back. All these actions reflected the fact that the *okeo* was likely to inherit his *nero*'s wife one day. He called her *chege* (wife). The *nero* had to be given a heifer on the marriage of his *okeo*'s sister. On the other hand the *nero*'s wife was usually unfriendly to her husband's *okeo* if he was dependent upon his *nero* through family misfortune, and she would treat him badly.

Inter-relations. The *Neo* group provided the bonds which linked Families together by marriage, and the question of inter-relations was merged in that of the wider groups.

Value. Should a man be so poor that he could not obtain a wife and none of his Clan could help him, he would go to his *nero*. He would build his house there and would work for his *nero* as one of the Family. In due course the *nero* would provide him with a wife (often the widow of a clansman) and would also give him some cattle. His wife kept his *nero*'s ritual observances and the *nero* was said to have married her, though he had no sexual rights over her. The *okeo* could never leave his *nero*. Should he have done so, he had to leave his children and wife behind, for they belonged to the *nero*'s Clan. The value of the *Neo* group to the individual was that it provided a refuge in time of poverty. A man might send his daughters or sons to live temporarily or permanently with their *nero*. In any case they had to visit him for a week or so. A father, who knew that his son would not have sufficient cattle with which to marry, would send him to a rich *nero*. If a girl married while with her *nero*, he sent the cattle home to her father, keeping a bull and a heifer for himself. In the ordinary course of events he would have claimed a heifer only. The *Neo* was a group performing for the individual similar services as 'the dole' in our culture. From the point of view of tribal integration it served to link Families and Clans.

THE *OKEO*

Membership. The *Okeo* group was the reverse of the *Neo* group. It referred to the speaker's sister's Family (*okeo* = sister's son; *akeo* = sister's daughter).

Unity. The bonds of union between the *okeo* and his *nero* were the same as those between the *nero* and his *okeo*. The *okeo*'s mother (*wayo*) demanded a bull on the marriage of the *nero*'s daughter, just as the *nero* demanded a heifer on the marriage of his *akeo*.

Inter-relations. These were the same as for the *Neo* group.

Value. The *Okeo* institution enabled a weak Clan, or one that was dying out, to strengthen itself. For the *okeo* added his work and strength to the village of the *nero*, and his children were members of the *nero*'s Clan. It was not possible, therefore, for property such as the *arum* (hunting ground) to leave the Clan, since, if all else failed, it would be inherited by the *okeo*, who in due course handed it on to his children, who were members of his *nero*'s Clan (p. 55).

THE SPHERES OF INFLUENCE OF THE *RWOT* AND THE *JAGO*

Membership. Before the establishment of British administration no Lango ventured far from his village alone or unarmed. The loose political system in Lango was based on local, ephemeral alliances between Clans which organised themselves on a military basis. A local leader would dominate the Clans in his neighbourhood. These Clans would ally themselves under him and style him their *Jago*. A *Jago* with outstanding military successes would exert an influence over a wider sphere, the neighbouring *Jagi* acknowledging their subservience to him and styling him their *Rwot*. The Tribe was therefore divided up into ever-changing territorial spheres under the influence of the *Jagi* and the *Rwodi*. These territorial leaders were at the same time the leaders of their respective Clans.

Unity. On the installation of the successor of a Clan chief who had been a *Jago*, the ceremony of *chibo adit me atekere*

(p. 103) was celebrated with especial elaboration and the Clans within the dead *Jago*'s sphere of influence would attend. It was the knowledge of the *Jago*'s prowess and success in battle that united his people under him for self-protection and for raiding purposes. There must have been other forms of symbolism of a unifying nature now difficult to discover. But some kind of political machinery to keep a balance between group interests was a necessity and the functions of that machinery were the chief means of unifying the group. By virtue of their positions as leaders the *Jago* and the *Rwot* settled inter-Clan quarrels within their spheres of influence. The Clan chief, as we have seen above (p. 43), was an incarnation of the Clan *jok* power. An alliance between Clans may well have been an alliance between *jok* power as well. I have no evidence on this, since it did not occur to me until after I had left Lango. Nor have I any evidence that the *Etogo* was really formed out of these allied Clans. But a non-member of the *Etogo* might attend the celebrations of a local *Etogo* group. He would sit apart and be given pieces of meat. He could not become an *Etogo* member himself, but his sons would be initiated in the ordinary way and their descendants would call this their *Etogo* (p. 49). If a *Jago*'s sphere of influence remained stable for many years, there would be a tendency for the *Etogo* groups to be composed of the allied Clans. This would have made the allied Clans spiritually as well as temporally dependent upon each other within the *Jago*'s sphere of influence. I have no evidence on this and merely suggest it as being logical of Lango culture.

Inter-relations. The *Jago* groups were held together by virtue of their association within the *Rwot*'s sphere of influence. The *Rwodi* were rivals and were the cause of the intermittent civil strife in Lango. But their rivalries were expressly suppressed at the tribal ceremonies of *ewor* (p. 69), *apuny* (p. 66) and rain-making (p. 73). During *ewor* a strict truce was observed throughout Lango (cf. *The Lango*, p. 246) and after it the various *Rwodi* would unite under a *Twon lwak* (Bull of the crowd) to raid a neighbouring Tribe.

Value. The *Jago* or the *Rwot*, by his control over the man-power of the associated Clans, protected his people from the hostile actions of other *Jagi* and *Rwodi*, and organised his people in raids for plunder. He settled disputes within his sphere of influence and his verdicts were backed ultimately by a sanction of force, for he could call out the man-power of the other Clans against a recalcitrant Clan within his sphere. In this way he maintained the balance between group interests within his sphere of influence, thus preserving it from disintegration from within.

THE VILLAGE

Membership. The Village consisted of from ten to a hundred and fifty huts and was not built to any special plan nor was it fortified. Each Family built together, roughly in the form of a segment of a circle (see Plate I at p. 58). The villagers were not necessarily of one Clan, though one Clan would usually predominate. The members of the Village built together primarily for protection.

Unity. Mutual aid and entertainment (beer drinking and dancing) were the chief unifying factors, though the actual fact of growing up together formed bonds of sentiment between villagers. Unsociable individuals were driven away. Ownership of water and grazing rights were vested in the Village community. Villagers attended all ceremonies which took place within their Village.

Inter-relations. At dances, hunts and on raiding expeditions the various Villages within a *Jago*'s sphere of influence united with each other. The tribal ceremonies also brought members of the different villages together.

Value. The Village was an economic group, the members of which co-operated to produce food from the earth and to herd cattle. At the same time it formed a strong protective group at a time when internecine raids were frequent.

THE *WANG TICH*

Membership. *Wang Tich* means literally 'Work line'. The members of this group were permanent and numbered from twenty to forty, often embracing a whole Village. They ap-

PLATE I

The village of Alai

Rwot Ogwalajungu with some of his family in Lango Dress

pointed their strongest member to be *won Wang Tich* (guardian of the *Wang Tich*). He was responsible for order at the beer party after work in the fields, for each member of the group would help to dig the fields of every other member in turn. As an incentive to work (not as a reward, for repayment consisted in working each helper's fields in return) the owner of the field brewed beer, or killed chickens (one chicken to two men), or provided some other form of meat. According to the amount of refreshment provided the man obtained the number of workers that he required. Should a member, having refused to work, come to drink the beer in the evening, the owner of the field would treat him similarly when his turn came. The *Wang Tich* used to consist exclusively of men. Women may now be members, which shows how the division of labour has broken down as a result of the introduction of the new economic crops.

Unity. The actual organisation of the *Wang Tich* was a sufficient bond, but the influences that united the Village applied to the *Wang Tich* as well. Anyone who quarrelled continually or did no work was expelled. Men would only work with people with whom they were on the best of terms.

Inter-relations. Two or more *Wang Tich* might have combined to do a particular piece of work by arrangement between their respective leaders, who had mandates from their people to refuse or accept work according to their own discretion.

Value. The *Wang Tich* provided a co-operative form of labour, which enabled more work to be done than would have been possible were each man to have dug his fields separately. Any member could call the *Wang Tich* merely by brewing beer. Digging and weeding were the chief occasions, but the *Wang Tich* might have been called to plaster a house. It was exclusively an economic group.

The Jo Awi Dyang

Membership. The *Jo Awi Dyang* were the people who kept their cattle in one kraal (*awi dyang*). Anyone might have done this by applying to the *won awi dyang*, who was the person who first made the kraal, or his heir. All those who kept their cattle in the kraal had to help build a new one when this became necessary. The *won awi dyang* was an important person and disputes concerned with cattle were often brought to him.

Unity. There was a ceremony on the opening of each new kraal (p. 148). If a member sold an animal to be eaten, the duodenum (*echau jok*), testicles and meat from the neck and flank had to be given to the *Jo Awi Dyang* to eat. They were linked by the Village tie also.

Inter-relations. Owners of cattle liked to distribute their animals in different kraals as an insurance against raids and epidemics. It also prevented inbreeding to some extent. This tended to unite the *Jo Awi Dyang* of different localities.

Value. The *Jo Awi Dyang* were a stock-raising group. Economy in herding was achieved, as one herdsman looked after the cattle of the whole kraal. A member would leave his cattle in the kraal for some time and, when they had multiplied, would give the *won awi dyang* a heifer. This was also done if someone from a foreign kraal left his cattle there for safety. The *Jo Awi Dyang* had the milk of all cattle left in the kraal.

STATUS GROUPS

The whole Tribe was stratified by groups based on status. These may be tabulated as:

1. Children. From birth to puberty.
2. (a) Boys. From puberty to parenthood.
   (b) Girls. From puberty to parenthood.
3. (a) Men. From parenthood to grandparenthood.
   (b) Women. From parenthood to grandparenthood.
4. (a) Old men. From grandparenthood to ancestorhood.
   (b) Old women. From grandparenthood to ancestorhood.

These Status Groups were not formally organised, except in the Age Grade system described below. But the status of everyone was obvious to all, and he was treated according to the pattern of behaviour due to a person of his status. The two important stages were those of youth and parenthood. At puberty the boy built himself an *otogo* (small hut raised on piles), in which he slept until the birth of his first child, whereupon he built himself an ordinary house, the symbol of his new status as a father. The biological landmarks of puberty and procreation were denoted by initiation into the *Etogo* group (p. 64) and the building of a proper house, social landmarks which served to mark the progress of the individual from one behaviour pattern to the next.

AGE GRADES

Membership. Boys who had been initiated into the *Etogo* at the *apuny* ceremony (p. 64) were initiated into the tribal Age Sets at the following *ewor* ceremony. The succession of *ewor* ceremonies produced four Age Grades, a new Age Set within one Grade being formed at each celebration of the ceremony. The names of these Age Grades and the intervals between the formation of each Age Set were:

1. *Amorung* (rhinoceros).   Interval of four years.
2. *Lyech* (elephant).   Interval of four years.
3. *Kwach* (leopard).   Interval of four years.
4. *Jobi* (buffalo).   Interval of nine years.

Then the cycle recommenced with *Amorung*. The whole cycle covered a period of twenty-five years. A boy initiated at the *Amorung* year remained an *Amorung* all his life, and similarly with the other Grades.

Unity. The intensive instruction at the *ewor* ceremony in tribal lore, hunting, fighting, rain-making, and so on, bound the members of an Age Set together, as did their special animal songs and common name, which also united them with the other Age Sets within the same Age Grade.

Inter-relations. Although theoretically the last Age Set to be initiated was responsible for the rain until the new Set was formed, actually all the Sets took part in the rain-making ceremonies. Control of the ceremonies was reserved for the Age Grade in office and certain other privileged persons. Different Grades were linked by the *achapon* institution (p. 64) and the reciprocal obligations between the initiated and his adopted father.

Value. The Age Grades cut across Clan loyalties and linked the Clans together within the Tribe. Their main functions were to educate the individual in tribal lore and teach him hunting, fighting and rain-making. The whole Tribe had to co-operate with a common will to obviate the two external threats to tribal integrity—enemy invaders and drought. The Tribe-wide organisation of the Age Grades was entrusted with these two tasks.

CHAPTER III

CEREMONIES CONCERNING THE TRIBE

Though the Clan was the most important group for the individual, the safety of the Lango Clans depended upon their alliance within the Tribe. There were two major threats to the integrity of the Lango—the aggression of neighbouring Tribes and famine as a result of drought. By the three tribal ceremonies of *apuny*, *ewor* and *myel akot* the ancestors were supplicated for victory and rain, while the new generation was organised into Age Grades, given a military training and taught the mysteries of rain-making.

(*a*) **Apuny.** The *apuny* was a final burial rite for the dead. It ensured a good rainfall, which the dead might withhold if not propitiated by this ceremony. It took place at the end of November or the beginning of December at intervals of two or three years. Lingo, the late rain-maker of Aduku, used to give the order for the celebration of *apuny*. News spread from Aduku throughout Lango, and every village then celebrated its own *apuny*. The ceremony was performed as a final burial rite only for a grown man and not for a woman or immature boy. The Lango believed that, if it were not held, the rain would not fall and the crops would not grow.

The *Etogo* group, owing to its special powers of control over the ancestors, was the working unit of *apuny*. The various *Etogo* groups of a locality assembled in the traditional pasturage. Each *Etogo* group killed a bull in memory of a dead *Etogo* member. The meat was then eaten ritually by the three meat groups into which the *Etogo* is divided (p. 49). During the eating the new generation was initiated into the *Etogo*. This in brief was the ceremony of *apuny*.

If many *Etogo* members had died at about the same time, it might be twenty years before *apuny* was performed for one of them, because only one bull was killed by each *Etogo* group. The bull was demanded from the widow of the dead man. If she refused to provide a bull, the *Etogo* would beat her and her new husband with *epobo* sticks. They would hold her in a black ants' nest until the pain of the ant-bites forced her to agree. But if she persisted in her refusal she would be shut up in her house with her husband, and the *epobo* sticks would be broken and placed in front of the door. Should they open the door and step over the *epobo* sticks, it was believed that they would die. [Ebibi, a man who lived near the C.M.S. station at Boroboro and supplied one of the Missionaries with milk, told me that the *Etogo* had once done this to him. He opened the door and stepped over the *epobo* sticks, but nothing happened to him or his wife. In these days a man will go to the Courts if beaten, and such coercive measures are therefore no longer used.]

Having obtained their bulls, the *Etogo* groups collected in the pasturage. The bull was killed by three spear-stabs given in turn by the leaders of each meat division of the *Etogo*—*Ekori, Aboi* and *Oguru*—commencing with the meat division to which the dead man belonged. There were certain local variations of this practice.

The bull was not skinned, the meat being cut away with the skin, which was burnt off in the subsequent roasting. Each meat division of the *Etogo* cut away its due portion and took this to the place where the members of the division sat apart. Some of the meat was then roasted and eaten ceremonially.

The women (who were considered to belong to the same *Etogo* as their husbands) sat behind their husbands and were given pieces of meat to eat. Children sat informally near their mothers. But a boy on reaching puberty was formally initiated into his father's *Etogo*. Such boys decided among themselves, at the suggestions of their fathers, which of the *Etogo* members each would choose to be his adopted 'father' (*papo*). This 'father' could not belong to the same Clan as the boy but had to belong to the same meat division as was intended for the boy. The first son ate at a different meat division to that of his father, the second son at the remaining division, the third son at the same division as his father, and so on in rotation. As soon as the *Etogo* members began to eat, the initiates sat near their adopted 'fathers' and the 'fathers' handed them pieces of meat to eat, thus initiating them into the *Etogo* group (*achapon bang loni* = I have been initiated through that man). They ate this meat with the old men. But the men of the generation below these old men ate in a group apart. At the following *apuny* the initiates would join this younger group of *Etogo* members.

Some time later the initiated boy would go with his friends to dig the fields of his adopted father, who would present him (should he give satisfaction) with brass wire for his neck, leg and arm ornaments, spears, hoes and a he-goat. The boy was not allowed to marry his adopted father's daughter, but this prohibition was not extended to his brother. The initiated boy would act as the 'son' of his adopted father at the next *ewor* ceremony, thus linking the *Etogo* with the Age Grade system. [A Christian after being baptised will go with his friends to do some work for his Godparents. This is clearly borrowed from the *Etogo* exemplar.]

Strangers at an *apuny* ceremony sat silently some distance away. Should they come near the *Etogo* eaters or should they ask for meat, it was thought they would die. But the eaters might hand them some meat, which they could eat with impunity. The ritual eating of meat by the *Etogo* was always a very solemn affair and was fraught with great danger if all the rules were not carefully followed.

Not all the meat was eaten at that time, but it was all divided up on the spot. The head, certain intestines and a shoulder were given to the owner of the bull. The *Ekori* meat division took the ribs and shoulder, the *Aboi* took the viscera, the *Oguru* took the back, loins and legs. It was very inauspicious to quarrel. Such of the meat as was not eaten ritually was taken home, but it had to be eaten before the new year's crop was sown. Certain individuals might 'tie up the rain' if not given some meat. Lingo would do this. At Amaich an old man of the Leopard Age Grade had a similar reputation. According to Chief Ogwalajungu, the leader of the *Etogo* (*adit me Etogo*) had to be given a leg of all animals killed by the *Etogo*.

Lingo, as rain-maker of Aduku, once sent his son Ogwanga-lingo round the country appointing certain old men to be his agents for rain. These men were called buffaloes, 'because the buffaloes ripen the millet' (*pien jobi ocheko kal*). Lingo probably chose members of the Buffalo Age Grade for this purpose. These buffaloes went to the local rain tree on the occasion of *apuny* and butted it with their heads to ensure a good rainfall.

The leader of the meat division of the dead man sprinkled the widow and her new husband with water, saying, 'May you have good health' (*komwu obed ayot*).

It was believed that the dead would be pleased at this mass action of the *Etogo* groups and would send rain in due season to water the crops. Drought was one of the two main threats to the integrity of the Tribe. At *apuny* Clan rivalries were forgotten and internal peace was maintained. The ceremony was therefore important as promoting the unity of the Tribe.

An *apuny* was performed in 1935 and I was told that it would be performed in 1937 for Lingo himself, who died in July 1936. Unfortunately I had to leave Africa in the middle of 1937 and do not know whether the ceremony was performed. I have not witnessed an *apuny* ceremony, and the above account is derived from verbal evidence. In my description I have used the past tense because I believe that the *apuny* ceremony is dying. The fear of famine as a result of drought is no longer so pressing on account of the grain reserves (see Plate II at p. 66) maintained by the government and the introduction of cassava, which withstands the severest drought. With ordered government the Tribe need no longer fear internal disruption as a result of Clan rivalries. The younger generation are not anxious to take part in the ritual of their fathers, and therefore the organisation of the *Etogo* is slowly decaying.

(*b*) **Ewor.** The ceremony of *ewor* and the Age Grade system that it created have disappeared from Lango culture. I collected evidence from the old men and prominent individuals from all over Lango. The results showed that even memory of *ewor* and the Age Grades was fading. Let me first quote Driberg's account of the ceremony.

'An account must be given of a quinquennial festival known as the *ewor* or *aworon*, the festival of honouring the aged and the men of old, as, though it is concerned with all aspects of native life, its main motive is the instruction of the young men in the mysteries of rain-making. This festival is universal among the Lango, with the exception of the *Jo Aber*.

'The *ewor* is essentially a quinquennial festival, but at the end of every sixteen years there is a gap of nine years instead of four, after which the cycle recommences. This is explained

PLATE II

A Dance near the Famine Reserve Granaries at Orumo

Day School at Aduku

by the fact that for rain-making purposes the initiates are divided into four groups, named after certain animals:

A. LYECH (elephant), with which are associated *ekori* (giraffe), *aputiro* (*kul*, wart-hog), and *ektu* (zebra).

B. KWAICH (leopard), with which are associated *ekwaro* (serval) and *ogwang* (merekat).

C. AMORUNG (rhinoceros), with which is associated *alop* (hartebeest).

D. JOBI (buffalo), with which are associated *engato* (lion) and *apoli* (waterbuck).

'Each individual *ewor* is named after one of these animal groups, and the rain festivals for the next four years are said to belong to that group (though actually the initiates in the group have few special privileges and no duties). The cycle of *ewor* is as follows, starting with the *amorung* group:

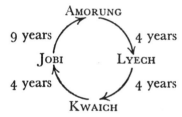

'The last festival took place in 1915 and was a *jobi* year, and the next should thus be due in 1925. The reason for the interregnum after the *jobi* is that the *jobi* are said to ripen the grain (*jobi ocheko kal*), and accordingly their influence persists longer than that of the other groups. No connection is evident, however, between this belief and the current local view which assigns heavy rains and floods to cycles of twenty-one years. There is a second and possibly more plausible reason given for this interval, viz. to allow initiates to die off and to make room for their successors. Already representatives of the *amorung* and *lyech* groups are scarce.

'The *jobi* call the *lyech* their fathers (*papogi*), and the *kwaich* call the *amorung* theirs, for reasons which will subsequently become apparent; and the few discrepancies in practice in the four *ewor* groups will be found to be between the *lyech* and *jobi* on the one hand and the *kwaich* and *amorung* on the other.

Further, though each group has its own specific songs, it is significant that the *jobi* and *lyech* share *awele* (pigeon) and *aweno* (guinea-fowl) songs, while *amorung* and *kwaich* share *awalu* (crested crane) and *okokom* (vulture) songs.

'The festival takes place in November at three different localities. The *Jo Burutok*, embracing Chakwara, Awelo, Ekwera, Aputi, Ngai and West Dokolo, hold it at Ekwera; the *Jo Kidi*, embracing Bata, Bar, Aloi, Orumo, Ariego, Omoro and East Dokolo, at Abako; and the *Jo Moita*, embracing Chiawanti, Aduku, Abyeche, Inomo, Agwata, Amaich and Akalu, at Alipa. It should be added that though the *Jo Aber* do not hold the *Ewor* festival, a few representatives from the west, near Kibuji, usually attend the *moita ewor*.

'When the festival is due, the *awobi*, or young men who have reached the age of puberty and have not yet been initiated, gather from all the places detailed above at their respective points of assembly. With them come the old men, versed in the mysteries, especially all the old men whose group year it may be; these have no option, but must attend. Thus in 1915 all the surviving *jobi* initiates of 1891 were bound to attend. When they have all gathered, the *awobi* are led by the old men to a traditional sycamore tree, and under this the *awobi* have to sleep for the next three nights. The old men return at nights to sleep in villages, but spend the days in teaching the *awobi* the duties of citizenship, the lore of hunting, the art of fighting and the traditions of their race; lastly they are taught the mysteries of rain-making, together with the rain dances and the songs appertaining to their group.

'Just before dawn each day is sung the bird song peculiar to the group whose *ewor* it is. These songs are only sung at the *ewor* and have no bearing on rain-making.

'All the day is spent by the *awobi* in undergoing tuition, and in the evening they go to fetch food. They may not enter a village during these three days, but the food (in the cooking of which no salt may be used, while the beer must be served cold) is placed ready for them by unmarried girls in the *bar* or goat pasturage, and there each struggles to get as much as he is able. *Awobi*, who come from a long distance, bring uncooked food with them, and it is cooked by women in villages near at hand. During this period there is an absolute truce, even in pre-administration days when it was unsafe for an unarmed man, much less a woman, to walk from one village to another during the day. All spears except the sacred spears of the old men are left in the houses, and may not be brought out under pain of death; a man's worst enemy is saluted by him, even though a recent blood feud is between them. Any transgressor of the peace truce is killed and his village is burnt. The *awobi* are armed only with hide lashes and withies of the tree *epobo* and ropes of plaited grass, and with these they severely trounce any passer-by and anyone who remains in a village, without fear of subsequent retaliation. No sexual intercourse is permitted during these three days, and only old men and children and *awobi* who have already been initiated may enter villages. The *awobi* bring the old men, their teachers, food every evening under the tree, after which the latter go to sleep in the neighbouring villages. Thus for three days and three nights the *awobi* are taught and sleep under the sycamore tree, and on the fourth day they return to the village.

'Before returning to the village, however, the *awobi* first kill a ram of the colour of a small grey bird called *alibor*, and hence named after it. It is cut up ceremonially and is put on spits over the fire under the sycamore tree. While it is cooking the *awobi* and the old men proceed together to a *nam* (a lake, river or marsh) to the traditional spot, and there the former are washed and have water poured over their heads by the old men. On their return the old men sit and eat the meat of the ram under the tree, while the *awobi* go and wait outside the village; they may not partake of the meat. Having finished their meal, the old men gather up the ram's *we* (chyme) with the grass on which fell the blood of the slaughtered animal (called for this occasion only *kodi*) and eat it. They also collect all the refuse of the meal and all the ashes of the watchfire and carefully deposit them in the river at the spot where the *awobi* were washed.

'Having done this, they proceed to where the *awobi* are waiting outside the village (about 2 p.m.), and the women of the village perform the ceremony of aspersion (*kiro*—to sprinkle ceremonially). The *awobi* stand in a circle round them and are sprinkled with water in which has been mixed the root of a tree called *kwong*, which has been first masticated by the old men; the leaves of a lilac called *olwedo* are used for aspersing. Were the ceremony not observed all the *awobi* would die.

'Warm beer and food cooked with salt are ready in the village for the *awobi*, but before they may enter there is still one ceremony to be undergone. They are each anointed with the beer and the food by the old men on the forehead, each cheek and each breast. They are now free to return to the village, but may not drink the beer till sundown, when the *awobi* who have been initiated drink it in little pots apart.

'Meanwhile the women have been busy brewing beer for the teachers, the flour having been collected by voluntary contributions, and now the *awobi* have to plaster the floor of a large house with cow dung and to strew leaves on it, that the teachers may drink there in the evening. Each teacher has now a disciple or servant, who addresses him as father, though he may be no relation. The servants of *lyech* teachers are chosen from boys whose age denotes that they will some day be initiated as *jobi*; and the servants of *amorung* are similarly chosen from prospective *kwaich*—explaining why the *jobi* and *kwaich* call *lyech* and *amorung* their fathers, as noted above.

'Purposely the old men leave their chairs at a distance from the village at which the beer is to be drunk, and at sundown send their temporary servants to fetch them. They must run as fast as they can there and back in order to get the best place for their father in the beer-house, and while the old men are drinking, each stands behind his master's chair to wave away the flies and to prevent them falling into the beer. Some of the beer is left to be drunk next day. An old man who is pleased with his servitor, with his attentions and zeal, will in future make him presents from time to time, and will even pay the indemnity due for the latter's sexual indiscretions.

'The *ewor* festival or initiation ceremony is now complete, and if it is a *jobi* year all the initiates become *jobi*, *kwaich* of a *kwaich* year, and so on, irrespective of the group to which their fathers belonged. They are taught by all the teachers, whether the latter belonged to that year's group or not.'

I quote Driberg because I could obtain no detailed account such as he gives, though the gist of his description was confirmed. The ram killed and eaten by the old men was clearly an *Etogo* meal as described in the *apuny* ceremony. Driberg was not aware of the *Etogo* group, the presence of which is a clear indication of the solemn spiritual nature of the *ewor*, by means of which the ancestors were supplicated for rain and victory. I was told that the 'father' whom a boy acquired at the *apuny* ceremony would also be his 'father' at *ewor*. In view of Driberg's statement the 'father' acquired at *apuny* would therefore have to be of the alternate Age Grade to that into which the boy would be initiated at *ewor*.

I was given the following information. The initiates, in addition to learning all the customs of the Lango, such as *tweyo lau, gonyo tol, gato kom, myel akot*, the arts of fighting and hunting, were also given certain esoteric knowledge which could never be divulged. After learning all this, a raid was made against the Kumam. [As Driberg points out, complete internal peace ruled during *ewor*. It was therefore an occasion for the usually hostile *Rwodi* (chiefs) to unite under a commander-in-chief (*twon lwak* = bull of the crowd) for a raid against some neighbouring tribe.] During the raid a Kumam and his dog were killed and their genital organs were cut off. The scrotum of the man and that of his dog were stuffed with the millet seed brought by the old men from their respective villages, a little bit from each man's contribution being used. The rain dance was performed and then the millet was redistributed. On returning home the old men mixed this specially treated millet with their own seed before sowing, and the result was an excellent crop.

After the *ewor* ceremony the *apuny* was celebrated before the next *ewor*. The last *ewor* took place in 1915, which was a *Jobi* year, so that the next celebration was due in 1925 according to Driberg. It did not take place, owing to the discouragement of the administration, so the Lango maintain. The Baganda, who were given positions as Agents in Lango at the commencement of British administration, used to suppress Lango ceremonial. The more prominent tribal ceremonies were naturally most affected by this policy. But this cannot entirely account for the complete disappearance of *ewor* and the Age Grades.

I agree with Driberg that the Age Grade system and the rain dance were importations from the Hamites. They came from the more Hamiticised Tribes, such as the Teso and Kumam. When I asked anyone about *ewor* or *apuny*, he always pointed to the south-east, the direction of the Kumam country, and said that when the ceremonies were due to be performed news reached the Lango from that direction. I believe that the Age Grade system was not very deeply engrained in Lango culture. The *Etogo* group with its *apuny* ceremony was a genuine element of Lango culture, to which the Age Grade system became attached by borrowing from the Hamitic Tribes.

At a time when old beliefs were being discredited, recently acquired customs might well be the first to go. The Age Grades and *ewor*, together with *apuny* and *myel akot*, were designed to guard against the attack of enemy Tribes and famine as a result of drought, by uniting the Tribe on a war and religious basis. British administration has abolished these two threats to the integrity of the Tribe. There is no more inter-tribal fighting. The famine reserve system and the introduction of cassava have made the terror of famine a thing of the past. Ceremonies that helped to sustain the integrity of the Tribe are no longer required when that integrity is no longer threatened. Moreover, the trials and exertions of *ewor* were not popular. Should anyone be beaten in the manner customary at *ewor* he would now bring a case in the Courts. Should elephant or rhino be killed, as required during *ewor*, the killers would now be prosecuted by government for violating the game laws.

One point that arose out of my investigations into *ewor* is worth noting. Not one of my witnesses substantiated Driberg's statement as to the cyclical nature of the Age Grades. Ogole, Clan brother of Lingo the rain-maker of Aduku, who played the leading part in the *ewor* ceremony, said that the initiates at the *ewor* were not given a single animal name, but were divided up into *Jobi*, *Kwaich*, *Lyech* and *Amorung* just as the leading old man present chose. The old men of Kibuji said that all the initiates at the *ewor* were termed *Jobi*. When they became old they were turned into *Lyech* by the leading old man. When very old they were turned into *Kwaich* and kept away from the ceremonies, because *Kwaich* were very bad, making the sun shine and withholding the rain. The old men of Amaich said that animal names were not bestowed until a man was old, when he became a *Jobi*. Later, if the leading old man (who used to be Lingo) thought that certain people were too old for the rain ritual, he turned them into *Kwaich* and they could no longer take part in the rain ceremonies. *Kwaich* were very bad, as they caused the sun to shine, while the *Jobi* ripened the millet by bringing rain. Men, too old even to dig their fields, were turned into *Lyech*. My informants, who were themselves *Jobi*, had never heard of *Amorung*.

These accounts, which are typical of others from all parts of the country, are sufficient to show how memory of *ewor* and the Age Grades has become confused. My informants were very emphatic that it was only the older men who were given animal names, not the boys, and that the names were not permanent, their bearers being changed successively from *Jobi* into *Kwaich*, *Lyech* and *Amorung* according as they grew older and older. I think that the explanation for this lies in a lapse of memory as to the principles involved. The last *ewor* was performed in 1915; since then the system has been at a standstill. An individual reflecting on the situation would be justified in thinking that when he grew older he would become another animal. For he sees the older men above him being termed successively *Kwaich*, *Lyech*, *Amorung*, and he has not seen the younger Grades being formed as in the old days.

Had it not been for Driberg's account, I should have given a very different picture of this *ewor* and the Age Grade system. This shows how easy it is for an investigator to make serious mistakes in reconstructing a culture when relying on the memories of the old men.

Driberg had some unpublished material on the *ewor* ceremony. He withheld this at the instance of the Lango, who initiated him into their secrets on condition that he should tell no one. Since the whole system seems to have broken down, he told me that he would publish this secret information. It will be of great value as demonstrating the forgetfulness or deliberate concealment of the Lango.

(*c*) **Myel akot.** This is the rain dance, which has been described so well and fully by Driberg (*The Lango*, pp. 248–63). His account should be read to obtain an accurate view of the annual rain-making activities of the Lango in the past, for they no longer exist in the form that he knew.

Anxiety about the rainfall loomed large in Lango psychology and the rain ceremonies were necessary to soothe and give confidence as being the only method known at that time by which control over the food supply might be exercised. These anxieties have been largely dispelled, for the government granaries (see Plate II at p. 66) maintained at the head-quarters of every chief are a continual reminder that drought no longer means death. Every Lango now grows a patch of drought-resisting cassava. Empirical control has usurped the magical.

However, unlike warfare, which no longer exists, drought is still an evil to be dreaded. Rain magic therefore continues, whereas the Age Grades have entirely disappeared. But the nature of rain magic has changed. In Driberg's day *myel akot* was performed annually and it was a democratic ceremony based on the Age Grades. Now, if performed at all, it is only when the rains are particularly late in falling and danger of drought is imminent. Moreover, the control and organisation of the proceedings have been concentrated in the hands of powerful *won kot*s (rain guardians), to whom deputations come from all over Lango with requests for rain.

The supreme example of this was Lingo, the *won kot* of Aduku. His history is an interesting example of culture borrowing. Lingo's father Okelo was a Madi, captured during a Lango-Nyoro raid into Madi. He was told to bring his possessions with him and he brought:

1. Two large quartz rain stones (*kide kot*) which are buried next to each other at the edge of the village of Amiayta outside Aduku. One was two feet long with seven inches showing above the ground, and was called the 'husband' (*chwor*). The other, one foot long with five inches showing above ground, was called the 'wife' (*dako*).

2. A spear-head, which is stuck point down by the side of the rain stones.

3. A large two-mouthed pot (*dogaryo*), kept at Lingo's village of Akoreloke about a mile from Amiayta.

4. An iron spear, kept at Akoreloke.

5. A solid ovoid of pottery nine inches long, kept at Akoreloke.

Okelo was given a wife by the Ogora Clan and so his descendants are Ogora. Madi rain-makers are very powerful individuals, and Lingo, who was taught the secrets of rain-making by his father, undoubtedly learnt from him that the rain-maker's power should be the dominant factor.

Lingo became famous all over Lango. According to my informants, if he said that rain would fall it certainly would. At the sowing of millet in February and March the old men from all over the country used to come with goats, grain and beer to beg for rain. He used to give the word for the *apuny* and *ewor* ceremonies to be held. He sent his son, Ogwangalingo, round the country appointing two or three old men of the *jobi* Age Grade in each Gombolola (British administrative area) to be his agents for rain. These old men would dance for rain in the traditional place in their localities. They collected grain and other offerings from their districts to take to Lingo.

Lingo must have been a very capable man. He combined Madi principles with Lango practice by appointing the *jobi*, who 'ripen the grain', to be his agents. He died a very wealthy man in July 1936 just before my arrival. His son, Ogwangalingo, inherited his esoteric knowledge.

Ogwangalingo told me that in an exceptional drought, when even the rain dance, as described below, fails to bring relief, the following procedure is prescribed by Lingo. The rain stones and spear-head are dug up and taken to the village of the *won kot*'s oldest brother (the man who will succeed to the office of *won kot*). Beer is made in the two-mouthed pot. It is drunk from calabashes by the old men, who assemble from all over the country. A little beer is left in the pot, the mouths of which are wreathed with *bomo* (a convolvulus). The pot is placed on the ground and the rain stones, spear-head and two iron spears (one manufactured by Lingo) are stuck in the ground around it. The old men wash the *won kot*'s brother over the pot, so that the water trickles off him on to the pot, stones and spears. He provides a black goat which is in like manner washed over the pot. The old men spit the beer left in the pot over the stones. They then do the rain dance under the traditional tree.

To prevent hail the *won kot* places the two-mouthed pot in

front of his house and puts the pottery ovoid (see item 5 on p. 75) in one of the mouths. The hail will then turn to rain.

To ward off locusts the *won kot* goes secretly far from the village with two old men. They spend two days digging a deep hole. A small new pot is taken and a male and female locust put inside. A piece of new winnowing-mat is placed over the mouth and plastered down with marsh mud. It is then placed in the hole. The legs of a black sheep are cut off at the knees and thrown in the direction of the advancing locusts. The sheep is then buried alive in the hole.

I will now describe the rain dance that I saw at Aduku on 26 February 1937 exactly as it occurred, so that it may be compared with Driberg's description. The following are the main differences: only forty old men took part; not a single young man and not a single woman was present even as a spectator; the ceremony was finished in one day, whereas in Driberg's time it lasted for four; the whole ceremony was truncated; no goat was killed; there was no procession to neighbouring villages.

The old men, who had been summoned by Ogwangalingo and Ogole, Lingo's Clan brother, arrived on the previous night. There were representatives of sixteen Clans comprised in four *Etogo* groups. Out of the forty performers twenty-four were of the *Etogo* Obar, which is the *won kot*'s *Etogo* and is particularly associated with rain-making, being called the 'Etogo of the tree' (*Etogo me yat*) or the 'Etogo of the sycamore' (*Etogo me olam*). The importance of the *Etogo* on this occasion again shows how the major perils of the Tribe can be avoided only by the massed action of the *Etogo* groups, who, with their special powers of control over the spirits of the dead, can effectively supplicate the ancestors.

The millet had been sown and had started to germinate as a result of some showers. But it was now being scorched by the sun, and rain was necessary to save the crops.

All the performers went to the traditional sycamore tree (*olam*) by the side of the main Aduku-Nabieso road near Lingo's village, Akoreloke. Most of the old men had *bomo* round their heads. They waited under the tree.

A certain old man was told to fetch water from the marsh; this had always been his duty. He had a large calabash (*wal*), into which he first put some marsh mud, being careful to pick pieces of mud containing grass, which he and Ogwangalingo termed 'vegetables' (*dek*). Then he filled the calabash with water and we went back to the *olam* tree.

All the old men carried spears. Most of them were ordinary hunting spears, but Ogwangalingo carried the two iron rain spears, the heads of which had fallen off and were carried separately. Some spears were wreathed with *bomo*. Apparently there should have been another rain spear, but it had been stolen from Lingo's grave. They suspected a certain Philipo Ebi of the Ogora Clan, an ex-policeman, who was posing as an *ajwaka* (medicine-man). He was very jealous of Ogwangalingo, as he wanted to be *won kot* himself. He refused to come to the rain dance. The old men asked Chief Ogwalajungu, who was with me, to allow them to beat Philipo Ebi as they would have done in the old days when anyone refused to dance. But the chief said that that was no business of his and he must not be associated with it.

They all lined up under the *olam* tree. It was about 11 a.m. Ogole stood in front and everyone held his spear point downwards. Should they point them to the sky, they said, there would be a terrible drought, as the rains would be scared away. Ogole, and occasionally another old man, chanted sentences in the manner known as *gato*, the company repeating the last word with a lunge of spears. The gist of the chorus was, 'If the rain falls, good. If the millet grows, good', etc.

They then danced and sang, trotting once round the tree. Having encircled it, they caught hold of the twigs and branches of the tree and sang and danced, pulling the leaves of the tree to the rhythm. The old man then climbed up the tree with the calabash of water he had fetched, another man helping him, and sprinkled the water over the dancers with a spray of *olwedo* leaves. He also threw water over the tree, saying, 'We want rain' (*wamito kot*). He himself was then sprinkled 'for good health' (*pi yot kom*).

They trotted in single file to Lingo's village, about a quarter of a mile away. Circling the village, they approached Lingo's grave warily. They circled it carefully and then closed in singing and dancing. This continued for about three-quarters of an hour. The old man sprinkled them by means of the *olwedo* branch with water from his calabash.

After this they went to the *abata* tree on the main road, where they continued to dance. Meanwhile Ogwangalingo's brother and another man plaited a grass rope about fifteen feet long. It was placed across the road and the performers stood in a line behind it facing towards Nabieso. They then did a *gato* chant-chorus to the effect that the man who had stolen the rain spear should die.

They proceeded to an *etek* tree on the other side of the road. On the way they picked up light, toffee-coloured pebbles, with which they weighted each end of the grass rope, which was placed in a semicircle round the foot of the *etek* tree. Ogole also placed a pebble at the base of the tree with a smaller one balanced on top of it. This rope would tie up the wind, they said. The *gato* chant-chorus was repeated under the leadership of an old man, while they walked slowly round the tree with spear lunges at each chorus. The substance of the invocation was, 'If the rain falls, good. If the millet ripens, good. If the sorghum ripens, good. If it thunders, good. If it rains without wind, we do not want the wind, good. May the rhinoceros, which charged the *Rwot*, die. May its head be confounded.' (This was with reference to the hunt at Chiawanti which I attended when a rhino nearly killed Chief Ogwalajungu.)

They returned to the *abata* tree and the proceedings were over. It was about 2 p.m. Each man enveloped his spear-head with *olwedo* leaves. They said that, on arriving at their villages, they would take water and throw it up to the sky with the *olwedo* leaves. They would lay their spears near the water pots in their houses. When sufficient rain had fallen, they would put the spears on the wall, but would replace them if more rain was required. That evening there was a heavy shower of rain, which the C.M.S. teacher of the Aduku Day School assured me was due to the rain dance. 'For the rain dance is a prayer to God in the old style.'

I was told that as soon as the old men of other parts of the country heard that *myel akot* had been performed at Aduku, they would come in batches and dance with Ogwangalingo, so that the rain might fall in their part of the country. This did not occur, and I was told in other parts of the country that Ogwangalingo was still young and untried. He must prove his ability before being generally accepted. They assured me, however, that he would be a great *won kot*, since Lingo had told him all the secrets.

I have said above that, while the Age Grades had disappeared and the rain ceremony had been concentrated in the hands of a powerful individual, anxiety over the rainfall necessitated local rain magic, often of a purely private nature. I will conclude this account with a few illustrations of this point.

The people of Atura go to the great *ajwaka* (medicine-man), Oming, who lives near Ngai, if they want rain. Or they go to Atworo, who lives six miles from Oming. When I was at one of Atworo's séances a man asked why rain did not fall on his fields, while his neighbour was always lucky. Atworo asked the man if he had brought any presents, as he would not give him rain unless he brought something. The man said that he would come again with some sesame.

At Aloro there was a tall tree, at which the *jobi* appointed by Lingo used to dance for rain. If it did not fall, they went to Oming.

On the west side of Alito rock there is a small cave. A few days before my arrival there, three *jobi* had washed a black goat at their village and then gone to this cave to dance, placing leaves of *olwedo* and *olutokwon* in it. They called the cave the house of *jok* (*ot jok*).

A few days before my arrival at Amaich the old men had danced round an outcrop of rock near the rest camp, about ten yards from the house. They showed me two pieces of stone which they called *kide jok* (stones of *jok*). They showed me how these fitted together, and the stone thus formed was a Bushman digging-stick weight. They said that this had always been in the crevice at the top of the rock. Formerly there had been two of them, but one had a habit of flying to other parts of the country. They had heard that it was now at Abako hill, for rain was required there.

At Dokolo I was taken to an outcrop of rock near the village of Angwechibunge. Here I was shown a tunnel-like cave formed by two leaning rocks, which they called house of *jok* (*ot jok*). The old men had danced round the rock recently and crawled through the cave. In the cave had been placed a little beer in small calabashes (*agwata kech*) and the *bomo* wreaths which the dancers had worn.

Some days before I arrived at Awelo the old men had danced round and swum across a rain-water pool (*atapara*) in the bush. This was the usual custom if the rains failed.

Conclusion. These three ceremonies, which concern the Lango Tribe as a whole—*apuny, ewor* and *myel akot*—have broken down under the new conditions. The *apuny* ceremony still survives, as does the *Etogo* system. But *ewor*, being concerned chiefly with fighting, is dead, and I believe that the rain dance I saw at Aduku is likely to be the last of its kind in Lango. These ceremonies no longer have a vital part to play in the life of the Tribe, which is guarded by the *pax Britannica* and by an organisation for famine relief.

Another factor is responsible for the decay of these and other ceremonies. There is a marked antagonism between the old men and the younger generations. The boys who have been through the Day Schools (see Plate II at p. 66) want to have nothing to do with the old men. They want new customs, the customs of Christianity by which the White man has obtained 'wisdom'. They want to be 'wise' too and to forget their old Lango customs, which were doubtless of use in the days before the White man came. But so rapid an abandonment of age-old traditions would not have been possible had not the Baganda Agents in Lango suppressed performance of these ceremonies by violent means. It is the foreign Tribes, Baganda, Alur and Banyoro, who have been chiefly antagonistic to Lango traditions. The individuals of these Tribes were able to affect Lango culture by virtue of their positions in Lango as Agents to 'advise' the *Jagi* (lesser chiefs) and as *Rwodi* (higher chiefs), as Pastors and as Schoolmasters.

CHAPTER IV

CEREMONIES CONCERNING THE CLAN

The interests, sentiments and hopes of the individual Lango have always been centred in his Clan: Loyalty to the Tribe, on the rare occasions when it existed, was a secondary consideration dictated by necessity, for the ultimate safety of the Clan depended upon its alliance-with other Clans within the Tribe. This alliance was achieved by the important religious group of the *Etogo* and by the inter-marriage which Clan exogamy necessitated.

The preservation of the individual depended on his Clan, the preservation of the Clan depended on its alliance with other Clans. It was therefore natural to find a prolific crop of ceremonies which served to inculcate in the individual sentiments of intense loyalty towards the Clan, and to invest the marriage alliance of two Clans with a religious sanctity. That this was the main purpose of the inter-Clan ceremonies is proved by their serial and reciprocal nature. The series commenced with the marriage negotiations, when the two families concerned visited each other on alternate occasions until the marriage goods were finally handed over. Then followed the *tweyo lau* ceremony, when the husband's Clan attached the leather strip to the young wife's waist as a sign that her pregnancy had consolidated the marriage pact. After this the husband's Clan visited that of the wife to perform the *kiro dako* ceremony. The wife's Clan next visited the husband's for the ceremony of *yeyo lyeto*, which was followed by a visit of the husband's Clan to the wife's Clan for the ceremony of *kayo chogo*. The ceremony of *ngolo ki dyel* was next performed during a visit of the wife's Clan to that of the husband. The series was concluded by another *ngolo ki dyel* ceremony, when the husband's Clan visited the wife's. The specific occasion for most of these ceremonies was sickness arising among the offspring of the union. On the first sickness of any of the children *yeyo lyeto* was performed; on the second illness arising among the progeny *kayo chogo* was performed, and so on. The significance of these inter-Clan ceremonies to the individual Lango was that they caused the wife to be fruitful, and protected her and her children from the perils and diseases of birth and childhood. There must be no inversion of the customary sequence. Even in these days of neglect two ceremonies may be telescoped into one, so that the sequence is not violated. This occurred at the ceremony I saw at Achaba. The *ajwaka* (medicine-man) had prescribed *yeyo lyeto* as a remedy for the sick child, but *tweyo lau* had not yet been performed, so *tweyo lau* and *yeyo lyeto* were telescoped into one.

(*a*) **Marriage.** *Tweyo lau*, as next described, is the real marriage ceremony. I merely record here the negotiations that take place between the two families, since they are the beginning of that alliance between the Clans which the subsequent ceremonies keep alive. I have published a full description of the marriage institution elsewhere (*Uganda Journal*, April 1940, Vol. vii, No. 4).

Contrary to the former rule of pre-nuptial chastity, the Lango now have trial marriages. The couple then decide that they are mutually compatible and the girl's mother consents to the match by accepting the four shillings proffered to the girl by the boy's friends. The boy's father then goes to the girl's father and discusses the details of the marriage goods to be handed over for the girl. He is entertained hospitably. A day is appointed and he goes again, accompanied by his son's friends and taking ten shillings for the girl's mother. The guests are given beer and food. Another day is appointed and the father with his son's friends takes the money portion of the marriage goods, which may be anything up to four hundred shillings, to the girl's father. Beer and food are again produced for the visitors. On a subsequent day the girl's father and clansmen go to the boy's village to see the cattle, the essential element in all marriages. Beer will have been brewed for the guests, but will only be drunk as a sign that the cattle have been accepted. Food will be prepared and the boy kills a bull for his girl's clansmen.

From the beginning of his courtship the boy will have avoided his future mother-in-law. A day is now appointed when he stands at the edge of her village and they look at each other well for the last time, so that they will be sure to know each other for future avoidance. It remains for the marriage to be formally registered in the *Jago*'s *lukiko* (chief's court).

(*b*) *Tweyo lau.* Marriage, in the eyes of the Lango, is consolidated by the arrival of a child. When this is assured, the real marriage ceremony, *tweyo lau*, is performed. *Tweyo lau* means 'to tie on the skin', and refers to the tying on of the leather 'tail' which extends from the small of the back of a married woman to the ground. Lango have likened this action to the putting on of the wedding ring in Christian marriages. To the Lango, marriage (*nyom*) is the handing over of marriage goods, primarily cattle, to the girl's Clan. Christian marriages are termed *ribere* (mixing together), and *tweyo lau* is equated with *ribere*.

Formerly *tweyo lau* was performed as soon as the girl was pregnant. In these days of neglect it may not be performed until she has borne children, and then only if she does not conceive again quickly or if any other misfortunes occur to wife or children.

I saw *tweyo lau* performed at Achaba, and the women of a village near Aboki gave me a demonstration. It was described to me in every part of Lango.

When it is decided to *tweyo lau*, the husband's clansmen are informed and assemble at the village. The director of proceedings is the wife's mother-in-law, though one of her husband's other wives or an important old woman of the Clan may deputise for her.

A cowhide is spread in front of the doorway of the mother-in-law's house and the new wife, who is completely naked, sits on this with legs straight outstretched. A small girl and boy sit on each side of her to encourage her to bear children, I was told.

The mother-in-law brings a *chip* (small cotton pubic fringe) and a *lau*. This *lau* is always an ancient one handed down from mother-in-law to daughter-in-law. It is made of oribi (*amyem*) skin. [If a wife, who has already undergone *tweyo lau*, bears a succession of children of one sex, they perform *tweyo lau* again with the *lau* of another old woman of the Clan.] The *lau* and *chip* used to be the only articles of clothing worn by a Lango woman. Since all but the very old people now wear clothes, the wife wears her newly invested *lau* and *chip* for the three or four days' duration of the ceremony only. She then hides them away carefully and puts on her clothes again. The *lau* and *chip* have magical properties. A husband suspecting that his wife is about to leave him conceals them, for by treating them in a special manner he can prevent her from bearing children. He will only hand back the *lau* and *chip* when the marriage goods have been returned and the divorce completed.

Most Clans possess a piece of *echach* stick which is used on ceremonial occasions. This *echach* stick is produced and smeared with clarified butter (*mo dyang*). It is then leant against the wife's shoulder.

The wives of the Clan (*mon me atekere*) begin to abuse the naked wife sitting on the cowhide, saying, 'Why do you come here to bring misfortune upon us? When visitors come, you do not give them any food. You do not know how to cook properly. You are a worthless creature.' They pinch her and generally make her feel her lowly position in the Clan. The mother-in-law then tries to tie the *lau* and *chip* round her waist. The wife fights to prevent this in a ceremonial manner, for, I was told, it is difficult to divorce her husband once she has been ritualised by *tweyo lau*. If she does leave him, she will very likely become sterile. Throughout the proceedings the assembled women abuse and insult the young wife.

The new wife and the boy and girl are then smeared (*wiro*) with clarified butter by the mother-in-law, who says, 'We want you to have good health'. *Modo* grass is tied round her waist and neck and, taking her hand, the mother-in-law leads her away from the cowhide with the shrill cry of victory (*jira*).

The second phase of the ceremony commences with the action of washing the pot (*lwoko gulu*). Everyone crowds into the mother-in-law's house. The cowhide is spread out and the new wife sits on it. A large pot of beer (*kongo*) is placed in the centre of the house. The exterior of this pot is washed by the *mon me atekere* (wives of the clansmen) with water and smeared with clarified butter, while they shout out at the new wife all the ritual observances of her husband's Clan, warning her to keep them strictly in future: 'Remember not to sit on the skin of a bushbuck; mind you never eat wild figs. . . ', and so on. The ceremony of *tweyo lau* is often called *nyuto dako kwer* (showing the wife the ritual observances). Every Clan has a number of observances (pp. 43–44), which the women married into the Clan (*mon me atekere*) must keep if they want to remain fertile. Until a girl is a fully fledged *mon me atekere* she need not observe these taboos. But after *tweyo lau* she will keep them strictly. If she is divorced, she observes her late husband's ritual observances until *tweyo lau* has been performed by her new husband's people. But she may revert to her old husband's observances in addition to the new if she suffers any misfortunes in the child-bearing processes. A woman who is past the age of bearing does not trouble to keep the observances.

Having heard the ritual observances, the new wife takes some beer into her mouth from the pot and spits it back again twice. The beer is then decanted into calabashes (*agwata*) and tasted by all. The *mon me atekere* are smeared (*juko*) with it. Straws (*cheke*) are inserted and all drink. Having had a drink from this pot, most of those present retire outside, where other pots of beer are waiting, and they spend the afternoon drinking.

The new wife may not leave the house for three days. If compelled to do so, she must place a winnowing mat (*oderu*) on her head. No one could tell me the reason for this. Perhaps the sun is dangerous to a person in a ritual state. But on the evening of the first day she comes out with the winnowing mat on her head to be shown how to cook. Together with the little boy and girl she grasps the handle of a hoe, which the mother-in-law also holds, in order to dig a small hole in front of the doorway of the mother-in-law's house. The mother-in-law shows the new wife how to place three stones round the hole and to lay a fire. This instruction in making a fireplace is called *tongo keno*. Fire sticks are brought. The wife, assisted by the little boy and girl, does a few preliminary twirls and then some man drills fire and sets it in the fireplace. A new pot is washed by the *mon me atekere* and *modo* grass is tied round its neck. Various vegetable sauces (*dek*) are now cooked in the pot. If anything has to be pounded in the mortar, the mother-in-law will do this while the new wife with the little boy and girl hold the pestle. This phase, as with the other parts of *tweyo lau*, is all concerned with showing the woman in a formal manner her duties as a wife, though actually of course she knows it all before. Meanwhile *kwon* (the staple millet porridge) has been cooked. The first lot will have a piece of grass stuck in it, for it must be used in the subsequent smearing ritual.

The cowhide is now spread near the fireplace and the new wife sits on it with the boy and girl. The *kwon* and *dek* (sauces) are placed nearby. The mother-in-law then smears (*gwelo*) the wife and children with the *kwon* and with small pieces of the various forms of *dek*. Finally she takes a lump of *kwon*, dips it in *dek* and feeds it into the mouths of the wife and the two children. The other women and children then gather round and finish off the food. But only those who have already been ritualised by *tweyo lau* may partake. Should a child, whose mother has not been ritualised, touch the food, 'his mother's body will be spoilt' (*kom totere ebibale*), meaning that she will become sterile.

The mother-in-law now leads the new wife up from the cowhide by the hand with the shrill victory cry (*jira*), and takes her to the doorway of her house. The wife stands there holding an *epobo* switch, as does a young boy, her husband's *okeo* (sister's son). She hits the *okeo* on the shoulder. He hits her in return and runs behind the house in confusion, while all the spectators laugh.

Food is then eaten by the remainder of the Clan, who dance and drink beer late into the night.

After her three days' seclusion in the house, the new wife goes to the marsh carrying a small calabash (*apoko*). She is accompanied by her husband's brother, who has a stout *epobo* stick. Having filled her calabash at the marsh, she returns to the village, but suddenly the husband's brother chases her with the stick. She drops the calabash, breaking it to pieces, and is chased into her mother-in-law's house. This is all done with much laughter, but the wife is scolded by her mother-in-law in the house for being reckless, and when she comes out all the *mon me atekere* pinch her well and abuse her, asking why she is so careless as to break her mother-in-law's pots.

After this the new wife is taken to collect fire-wood, which she ties with a new grass rope. On returning to the village, her husband or his brother breaks off the *modo* grass which had been tied round her neck and waist. The day is ended with beer drinking and dancing, and the new wife is at last one of the *mon me atekere*. She may not visit her mother's village nor may she shave her head until the ceremony of *kiro dako*, as next described, is performed, which will take place any time up to about three months after *tweyo lau*.

The ceremony of *tweyo lau* is the true marriage ceremony. It initiates the new wife into the Clan to take her place with the *mon me atekere*. From henceforth she keeps the ritual observances of her husband's Clan and will be able to leave her husband only with grave danger to her reproductive functions, which alone enable her to be someone's wife. She is shown her position among the *mon me atekere*. Being the latest arrival, she must be humble and obedient; therefore she is treated as a worthless woman, who has no idea of performing her domestic duties efficiently. The ceremony serves to reaffirm all the *mon me atekere* in their allegiance to the Clan, and it strengthens Clan sentiments by providing an occasion upon which all the clansmen meet to eat and drink together.

Tweyo lau is performed throughout Lango. It is a ceremony which will die with difficulty, though there is a movement among Christians to abolish it together with all Lango ceremonies. But if anything goes wrong with the birth and child-rearing processes of a woman who has not undergone *tweyo lau*, the husband will be blamed by his Clan and the ceremony will be performed. A schoolmaster would lose his post for taking part in such a ceremony. But if his children are dying or his wife not bearing, he will allow his father to take her away secretly to perform the ceremony. When a Christian refuses to let his wife be ritualised by the ceremony, the *mon me atekere* come to her and say, 'Your husband will not allow us to perform *tweyo lau*? Very well then, these are the ritual observances of our Clan, see that you keep them.' She will be instructed accordingly and will certainly keep the observances. The general neglect in performing the traditional ceremonies in these days was well brought out at Achaba, where *tweyo lau* and *yeyo lyeto* were telescoped into one. The three days' seclusion in the house was omitted and the whole ceremony was performed in a great hurry.

(c) **Kiro dako.** After *tweyo lau* the newly initiated wife may not enter her mother's house, eat her food or shave her own head, until she has undergone the ceremony of *kiro dako* (sprinkling the wife), also known as *tongo keno* (making the fireplace). Formerly it took place after the birth of the first child, at the conception of which *tweyo lau* had been performed. Now it is done about three months after *tweyo lau*, since this ceremony itself may not be performed until after birth.

I have not witnessed a *kiro dako* ceremony. But it was explained to me by many informants and the various ritual elements described could be recognised as similar to those witnessed in other ceremonies.

The older women of the *mon me atekere* of the husband's Clan take the wife to visit her own family. The wife digs a hole in front of her mother's doorway with a hoe, makes a fireplace and lays the fire. Fire-sticks are brought and she gives them a preliminary twirl, after which her brother or father drills fire and places it in her fireplace. A small new pot is produced by her mother and food is cooked in it. This pot is called *gulu lau* (pot of the *lau*). It is kept by the wife's mother and is used again when the ceremony of *kayo chogo*, as described later, is performed. The wife is smeared (*gwelo*) with the food. She then sits in the doorway of her mother's house and her mother sprinkles her with water from a calabash by means of a head of *modo* grass. After this she may eat her mother's food and enter her house. She is also sprinkled at the doorways of her other relations in the village, especially her brother. The wife and *mon me atekere* then go back to their village.

The ceremony is a demonstration to the wife's mother that the wife has been fully accepted as one of the *mon me atekere* of her husband's Clan. The visit of the *mon me atekere* helps to maintain friendly contact between the two Clans, which have been united by this marriage.

(d) **Yeyo lyeto.** After *kiro dako* and when the first illness occurs among the progeny of the wife, the ceremony of *yeyo lyeto* (bringing the ornaments), also known as *bolo lyeto* (throwing the ornaments), is performed, the wife's Clan visiting that of the husband on this occasion.

The *lyeto* are strips of metal about three inches long and half an inch broad, which are worn, five or six in number, by young children at the back suspended by a loin string. But the term *lyeto* is extended to all the gifts brought by the wife's Clan to the husband's Clan on the occasion of *yeyo lyeto*. At the ceremony that I witnessed the following articles were presented by the Anyeke Clan to the Achaba Clan: three ostrich egg-shell necklaces, three ankle bells, a new *lau*, a new *chip*, ostrich egg-shell wristlets and anklets, a new knife, a new awl, a new hoe blade and a piece of cloth. These gifts vary according to the number and ages of the wife's children, each of whom has to receive something. The ornaments which are to be seen on most Lango children are the result of *yeyo lyeto* ceremonies, and are not put on haphazardly by proud mothers, as might be thought.

Though I only saw one *yeyo lyeto* ceremony at Achaba, I was given accounts of such all over Lango.

Three days before the ceremony the *mon me atekere* of the wife's Clan bring *moko kongo* (flour for preparing beer) to the husband's village. Since three days are required for brewing beer from beer flour, it must be prepared in advance to be ready for the appointed day. The wife's Clan also bring with them the *lyeto* articles and much food, such as fried termites (*aripa*), sesame oil (*mo nino*), etc.

For convenience in description I will reproduce the ceremony I actually saw, at which there were three children, the baby being the sick individual on whose behalf the ceremony was being performed.

In the morning the wife's mother and mother-in-law stitched a new carrying skin (*abeno*) for the sick baby. A member of the husband's Clan had to sew on the right strap of the skin and a member of the wife's Clan the left. A cowhide was spread in front of the wife's mother-in-law's doorway and the wife, with legs outstretched, sat on it, as did her children. Her brother had brought the Clan *echach* stick and this was leant against her shoulder. She and the children were then smeared (*gwelo*) with *kwon* (millet porridge) and the various kinds of *dek* (sauce), which her Clan had brought. Beer was spat at their chests. Food was then put into their mouths, the woman who did it making two passes at the wife's mouth and putting it in at the third go.

The baby's calabash sun-shade (*wal wich*) was put on the wife's legs. In it was placed the newly made carrying skin. Some red-ochre powder was placed in the skin and sesame oil was poured over it to form a red paint. All the articles of *lyeto* were then rubbed in this so that they became red. The carrying skin was now picked up with all these things in it and gently thrown (*bolo lyeto*) from the *mon me atekere* of the wife's Clan to the *mon me atekere* of the husband's Clan and back again. This was repeated several times. The women of the husband's Clan then touched the chests of the wife and her children with the articles and proceeded to put them on the children. The bells went on to the left ankle of each child. Each child had a necklace, while the wife donned the *lau* and *chip*.

The wife and her children were well smeared with the red-ochre paint on backs, shoulders and chests. The wife's brother (the *nero* of the children) then caught up each child in turn and danced it up and down to make the bells tinkle. He then threw the piece of new coloured cloth to his sister after the fashion of *bolo lyeto*—it would have been spoilt by the red ochre had it been placed with the other things—saying, 'I want you to have a healthy body, and may any embryo in your body be peaceful'.

The wife and children were then lifted away from the cow-hide with the shrill victory cry (*jira*). The baby was placed on the wife's back in the new carrying skin. Then the wife, remaining in a squatting position, jumped over two wooden millet porridge spurtles (*lot kwon*) which were placed in front of her. They were again placed in front of her and she repeated the performance four times, because her first child had been a girl. Had it been a boy, they said, she would have jumped only three times.

Everyone crowded into the mother-in-law's house and a large pot of beer was placed in the centre. The wife and her children drank a mouthful straight out of the pot. All put their hands on the pot and washed it on the outside with water and sesame oil, saying, 'We want good health'. Then they settled down to drink the beer. This was the end of the ceremony.

This ceremony of *yeyo lyeto* provides an occasion for general conviviality between the two Clans, serving to strengthen the internal loyalties of the Clans and their bonds of alliance with each other. The gifts brought by the wife's Clan are symbolic of the good will that the wife's Clan bears towards her husband's Clan. For, according to Lango belief, the wife's Clan can bring misfortune upon the children of the union or sterility upon the wife, if it should be displeased with the husband's Clan. Should a child, who has not undergone *yeyo lyeto*, lay hold of the *lyeto* of another child, it would become ill and die, and could only be saved by the prompt performance of *yeyo lyeto* on its behalf. Should a woman not bear a child for some time after marriage, her parents bring a carrying skin and beer. The *yeyo lyeto* ceremony is then performed and the wife wears this skin on her back, as if she had a child there, until she does bear, when she will use that skin for her child. This is an obvious piece of sympathetic magic very typical of Lango psychology. The social value of cloth in modern times is brought out by its introduction into the ceremony that I have just narrated.

(*e*) **Kayo chogo.** When the next serious illness, usually dysentery, occurs to any of the wife's progeny, the ceremony of *kayo chogo* (biting the bone) is performed. As with the other ceremonies of this series, *kayo chogo* is performed once only for any one wife with her children. Should another child become ill at a later date, *ngolo ki dyel*, the next ceremony in the series, and not *kayo chogo*, would be performed. The children of one wife are considered as being one individual.

I saw *kayo chogo* performed at Akwon near Aduku and at Adyeda near Aloro. It is a very common ceremony and is described by Driberg (*The Lango*, p. 145).

The husband informs his wife's father that his grandchild is ill and inquires whether he will consent to kill a bull for *kayo chogo*. The father will agree, if satisfied that the illness is sufficiently serious, and a day will be fixed.

Some Clans perform *kayo chogo* with a goat, others with a bull. On the appointed day the husband, accompanied by his wife, children and clansmen, and taking a heifer or unmated ewe, according to whether a bull or goat is to be killed, goes to his father-in-law's village. The animal taken is given to the father-in-law to replace the animal which is killed.

The wife and children wait outside the village until a bull is selected from her father's herd. There is usually a quarrel over this as the father tries to palm off a small specimen, while the husband's Clan demand a large animal. The legs of the bull are tied and it is dragged to the wife's mother's doorway. This is done by the husband's Clan, who then proceed to kill the bull. A rope is tied tightly round its neck and the carrying skin (*abeno*) of the sick child is pressed over its mouth and nose (see Plate III at p. 92). Another carrying skin is pressed over its anus and its ears are covered by hand. The wife, her brother, her co-wives with their children, her husband and her children sit on top of the bull. The children shriek with fear. The bull usually struggles, and so they come off it again until it is finally killed, which is done by beating it on the head with a wooden pestle.

As soon as all movement ceases the same individuals climb on to the bull again. The *echach* stick of the husband's Clan is leant against the wife's shoulder and some scrapings from it are mixed with clarified butter in a calabash. The wife, her children and the dead bull are smeared (*wiro*) with this by the co-wife, who also washes them and the bull with water. She then leads the wife away from the bull with the *jira* cry of victory.

A new fire must now be made. The wife and children together do a preliminary twirl of the fire-sticks, and fire is then drilled by a man. Meanwhile the bull is skinned and the entrails examined for omens. White spots on the liver are bad, while a red spot on the tip of the heart is a very good sign.

A fireplace is made (*tongo keno*), the wife and her children assisting in the ceremonial way as described in *kiro dako* (p. 88). The *gulu lau* pot, which was first used at *kiro dako*, is placed on the fire with *dek* in it, having first had *modo* grass tied round it and clarified butter smeared on it. If necessary another fireplace is similarly made and another new pot with food is placed on it, after treatment similar to the *gulu lau*.

The meat of the bull is divided up with much quarrelling. It all belongs to the husband's Clan, but the head and right shoulder are left with the father-in-law, the owner of the bull. Slices are cut off the neck, flank and duodenum (*echau jok*) for the people

PLATE III

Killing the bull at the *kayo chogo* ceremony at Adyeda

Killing the goat at the ceremony of *ngolo ki dyel* at Anep

who keep cattle in the dead bull's kraal (*jo awi dyang*: people of the cattle kraal). The skin belongs to the *mon me atekere*. The chyme (*we*) is thrown away secretly by the wife's parents, for the sick child will die if anyone steals it. A little of the meat is roasted on the fire and eaten by the husband's Clan.

A cowhide is spread in front of the wife's mother's doorway. The wife and her children sit on it. Round their necks are placed necklets (*tumo*) of the dead bull's skin, and they are smeared (*juko*) with chyme, blood and certain intestines by the husband's clansmen. The intestines, with which the wife is smeared, are those commonly forbidden to a woman who is still capable of bearing a child. A small rib bone with meat on it is held near the wife's mouth and she bites off some of the meat (*kayo chogo*). She is then led away from the cowhide with the *jira* cry of victory.

There follow beer drinking and feasting. The beer drinking is preceded by a ritual washing of the pot (*lwoko gulu*) as described in the *tweyo lau* ceremony (p. 84). Whenever food is prepared, the wife and children help in the symbolic manner as already described. They are also smeared with the various foods and are ritually fed, as described in *yeyo lyeto* (p. 89).

The wife stands in front of her mother's doorway holding an *epobo* stick and a porridge spurtle (*lot kwon*), on the end of which is placed a lump of *kwon* and *dek*. Her husband's *okeo* (sister's son) stands opposite her carrying the bone she has bitten in addition to an *epobo* stick and a porridge spurtle similarly laden with *kwon* and *dek*. They then beat each other on the shoulders with the *epobo* sticks, the *okeo* running in confusion behind the house, while the onlookers laugh.

The bull's breast-bone with all the meat adhering is hung round the wife's neck; the man doing this says, 'May your body be well. *Jok* help you always. If you have another child, may it be well' (*Komi bed ayot. Jok okonyi nakanaka. Ka ibinywal atin onene, kome yot*). She is led away from the doorway with the *jira* cry and goes home to her husband's village with the breast-bone round her neck and accompanied by her husband's Clan.

On the way home, some of the meat, which has already been cooked, is eaten, but they are careful to sit with their backs towards the village they have just left. On the following

morning they cook the meat of the breast-bone on a fire made
by drilling. They smear (*gwelo*) each other with the meat and
the members of the husband's immediate family eat it. This
is the end of *kayo chogo*.

Like the other ceremonies, *kayo chogo* furnishes an opportunity
for strengthening Clan loyalties and the bonds linking the two
Clans, this time by the husband's Clan visiting that of the wife.
The necessity of having the good will of the wife's family, if the
children are to prosper, is again brought out. The special relationship between the *okeo* and his *nero*'s wife is emphasised in
the ritual familiarity between them in the beating episode.

Kayo chogo is popular, as it is an excuse for a feast of meat.
But the performance of ritual details has become very slack.
The ceremony I saw near Aduku was performed by a Christian
as a last resort for the illness of his wife and three children.
The ceremony was therefore hurried. Instead of suffocating
and beating the bull to death, the carrying skin was held for
a few seconds over its nose and then its throat was cut. Instead
of making the new fire by means of drilling, they asked me for
matches. Instead of carrying the breast-bone round her neck
till she reached home, the wife put it in a basket as soon as she
left the village. Instead of a convivial feast between the husband's and wife's Clans, the former were in a hurry to go home.
They drank no beer and ate no meal, and merely disgraced
themselves by quarrelling over the division of the meat. So
that my boy Okuja said to me: 'I shall never do this if I have
a sick child. These people are glad that the children are ill,
for they have obtained meat as a result. One man says that
he hopes someone else will soon be ill in the Clan, for then those
who are not satisfied now will have as much meat as they want.
See also how they quarrelled with the wife's father for not
giving them his largest bull. This is very bad behaviour.'

(*f*) **Ngolo ki dyel.** There are two ceremonies of *ngolo ki
dyel* (judging by means of a goat), which are identical in form
but take place at different villages. The first is performed after
kayo chogo, when sickness again falls upon any of the wife's
children. *Kayo chogo* is performed at the wife's father's village,
so the first *ngolo ki dyel* takes place at the husband's village and

PLATE IV

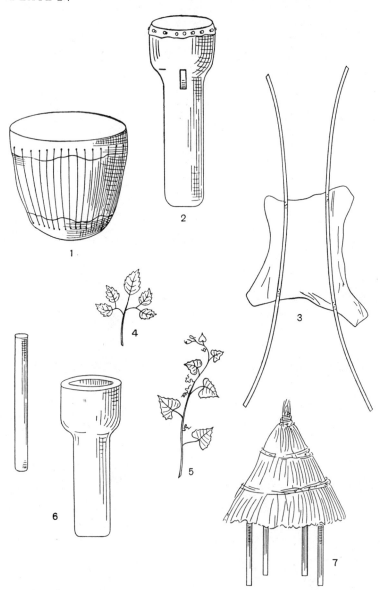

Drawings of various articles

1. Drum (*bul*).
2. Drum (*atimu*).
3. Baby's carrying skin (*abeno*).
4. *Anono*.
5. *Bomo*.
6. Pestle and mortar (*alekpany*).
7. *Abila*.

he provides the goat. Should sickness arise among the wife's children after this *ngolo ki dyel*, the ceremony is repeated at the wife's father's village and he provides the goat. This ends the series of ritual observance ceremonies (*kite me kwer*) and any further misfortunes will be treated as individual matters to be taken to the *ajwaka* (medicine-man) for his advice.

I saw *ngolo ki dyel* performed at Anep near Ngotokwe and obtained accounts of the ceremony in many parts of Lango.

An invitation is sent to the wife's parents informing them that *ngolo ki dyel* is to be performed for the sick child. On the appointed day the wife's Clan assemble at the husband's village, as do his own clansmen.

A goat is held in front of the husband's mother's doorway. The wife and sick child sit close to it while its throat is cut (see Plate III at p. 92). It is skinned and its entrails are laid out on leaves, being carefully washed with water. A skilled individual then reads the omens (*ngolo chine*: to judge the entrails). [In the ceremony that I saw the verdict was that they were inauspicious, because they had white patches on them. The man went on to say that many of the husband's Clan would be ill and the child would become worse. The wife, he said, must have a new house built and must not use the broom of any other woman. He demanded a speckled chicken. The wife and child held the shaft of a spear, the point of which was placed on the chicken's neck. The wife pressed it down and killed the chicken. The omen reader then slit open the chicken's back and pulled out the entrails. These proved auspicious and he said that after all the child and clansmen would recover. I interpolate this episode, which is not a regular part of *ngolo ki dyel*, because it shows the influence of an *ajwaka* (medicine-man). The ritual ceremonies are usually divorced from the *ajwaka*, who, however, becomes the adviser as soon as the series of ritual ceremonies is terminated by the second *ngolo ki dyel*.]

Fire is drilled, the wife and child sitting close to the drillers, or perhaps giving the preliminary twirls. The necklets of skin placed round the necks of wife and child at *kayo chogo* are now taken off, and fresh necklets of the goat's skin are put round their necks (*tumo*). The wife and child are then smeared (*juko*) with the chyme (*we*) of the goat.

The head and a shoulder of the goat are retained by the owner to be eaten later, but the remainder of the meat is roasted at the newly-made fire. Some of it is eaten in a ritual manner by the men present (women may not eat goat flesh), the rest being reserved for the evening meal and beer drink.

In these two ceremonies of *ngolo ki dyel* the reciprocal nature of the ritual ceremonies is again evident. The misfortune of illness is again turned into an occasion for strengthening Clan loyalties and the inter-Clan alliance.

(*g*) *Lwoko wang atin.* There is one other ritual ceremony, which may take place at any time during the series of ceremonies recorded above. This is *lwoko wang atin* (washing the child's eyes), also known as *kiro wang atin* (sprinkling the child's eyes). It is not an essential ceremony, but since one of the children is certain to suffer from eye trouble the ceremony is almost always performed at some period of their upbringing. It may be combined with any of the ceremonies of the series, and I was told that it could act as a substitute for *kiro dako*, as recorded above, in freeing the wife from the taboo against visiting her mother.

Lwoko wang atin was combined with the *kayo chogo* ceremony I witnessed near Aduku, and Philipo Lawottim of Ngai gave me a good account of it.

If the wife sees that her child's eyes are troubling him, she goes to her mother's village and appoints a day. She brews a little beer and her mother prepares a great quantity of beer.

On the appointed day the wife goes to her mother's village with the *mon me atekere* of her husband's Clan, carrying a small calabash (*apoko*) full of beer. On arriving at the village she and her fellow-travellers are sprinkled with water by means of a sprig of *modo* grass. The pot in which the wife's mother has brewed beer is now washed on the outside (*lwoko gulu*).

The wife and child sit in the doorway of the mother's house and some beer taken from the calabash (*apoko*) is put in the child's eyes. The beer pot is again washed with water and smeared with clarified butter. The necks of the wife and child are also smeared with clarified butter. The wife's brother sits in the doorway with her. The wife's co-wife takes a calabash (*agwata*) containing water and a smooth round stone, which she has brought from her own village, and washes the child's eyes in this water. She sprinkles the people sitting in the doorway by means of a sprig of *modo* grass. She then rubs the stone (*kide atyeng*) round the faces of the wife, the child, the wife's brother and herself.

After this they settle down to drink the beer, returning home with a small pot (*taba*) for the people who remained at home to drink.

The stone and the calabash are left in the wife's mother's village. When the wife has another child of the same age as the sick child, she will go to her mother's village. Beer will have been brewed, the stone will be placed in the beer and this will be taken back to the wife's village.

(*h*) **Myel arut.** *Myel arut* (twin dance), with its various ramifications, is the most frequent and widespread of Lango ceremonies. The most important performance takes place soon after the birth of the twins. But it is also performed either in whole or in part on many other occasions, such as the death of a twin and the return of a twin from a long journey. In the two ceremonies that I saw, it was carried out in full on behalf of wives who had failed to bear children after some years of married life. On the sympathetic principle typical of Lango psychology it was believed that *myel arut* would cure their barrenness.

I saw *myel arut* at Oget near Orumo and at Alira near Aduku. I also saw many minor phases of it—at the birth of a single child by a mother who had previously borne twins, on the return of a twin from a visit to Kenya, before a father of twins went to the hunt and so on. Driberg gives an account of the ceremony in *The Lango*, pp. 142–4. The following description is based upon the ceremonies I saw, and a comparison with Driberg's account will show how the essentials of the ceremony have not changed since his day.

When twins are born the midwife places the placenta and umbilical cords in a single pot. [Driberg says that each cord was placed in a separate pot. I never found this and think it unlikely. If one of the twins died, which was very usual, it would be placed in a pot which would be put next to the pot containing the after-birth, so that two pots are often seen under the twin house.] The father builds a rectangular platform of *okango* wood, measuring one and a half by two feet and raised about two feet off the ground by means of four corner posts. This is called *ot rudi* (twin house) or *ot jok* (house of *jok* power). [I never heard this called *peru jok* as stated by Driberg. But *peru* is the technical term for any building having no walls, so that the *ot rudi* is also a *peru*.] The *ot rudi* is built at the edge of the courtyard. Grass is spread on top of it and underneath are placed three conical-shaped termites' nests (*tuk*) obtained from the marsh. On the *tuk* is placed the pot containing the after-birth and it is plastered all over by the midwife with clay from the marsh. Bundles of the convolvulus *bomo* and *anono* are laid on top of the *ot rudi*.

The clansmen of the wife and husband are informed of the birth so that they may assemble for *myel arut*, which usually takes place on the seventh day after the birth. Spears, shields and hunting nets are placed near the *ot rudi*. A paste called *tanga* is made from sorghum flour and water. It is put in two small new calabashes (*agwata kech*), which are laid on top of the *ot rudi*. Two sorghum stalks are placed in the *tanga*.

Since dawn two squat-shaped drums and the long *atimu* drum have been beaten. The women, wreathed with *bomo* and *anono* and carrying spears, axes or porridge spurtles, dance up and down raising the shrill *jira* cry of victory. This dancing continues off and on the whole day. The older men and women rush to the edge of the village brandishing their spears threateningly and shouting their Clan cries as in warfare (*gigwongo twon me atekere*).

A white chicken is fluttered (*buko*) round the *ot rudi* and then beaten to death against it. A white cockerel and pullet are then fluttered over the *ot rudi* and round the wife's head by the women while she stands near the *ot rudi*. These chickens are shut up in her house till the evening. They are never killed.

A brown sheep is then killed near the *ot rudi* so that its blood runs under the platform. The women are anointed (*juko*) with this blood. Necklets of the sheep's skin are placed round the necks (*tumo*) of the wife and her twins. The skin will be used

PLATE V

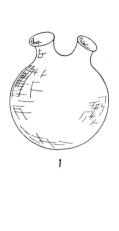

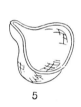

Drawings of various articles

1. Two-mouthed pot (*dogaryo*).
2. Spurtle (*lotkwon*).
3. Rattle (*aja*).
4. String made from *kworo* bark.
5. Half calabash (*agwata*).
6. Drinking tube (*cheke*).
7. Large calabash (*keno*).
8. Ceremonial calabash (*obuto*).

later as the carrying skin of one of the twins. The sheep is cooked near the *ot rudi* and ashes from this fire are smeared (*juko*) on the women.

The *tanga* paste in the two small calabashes is now dabbed by means of the two sorghum stalks on the chests of all present, especially on the wife and those women who are anxious to conceive soon. It is also dabbed on the *ot rudi*, the *tuk*, the pot, the *atimu* drum, the hunting nets, etc. This is called *goyo tanga* (striking with *tanga*).

A two-mouthed pot (*dogaryo*) full of beer is placed in front of the *ot rudi*. The mouths of the pot are wreathed with *bomo*. The beer is decanted into calabashes and the women drink it straight from the calabashes without the use of drinking tubes (*cheke*), which are used, however, as soon as this ritual drinking is over. The women, requesting the men to retire, dance by themselves and sing crude sexual songs, while the men settle down to drink beer. Every now and then a man picks up his spear and dashes among the women shouting out his Clan cry (*egwongo twon me atekere*). He has a mimic fight with one of the women, while she raises the shrill victory cry (*egoyo ijira*). They run threateningly to the edge of the village brandishing their spears at the bush. This is called *gato jok*, which is best rendered as 'laying a spell upon *jok* power.

The visitors have brought contributions of food with them and these are added to the meal which is prepared for the evening. The dancing, beer drinking and feasting extends late into the night.

I have translated *rut* throughout the above description as 'twin'. But a more accurate translation would be 'abnormal birth'. For the word *rut* is applied to triplets, leg and breech presentations and other abnormal occurrences of this sort. In any of such cases the *myel arut* ceremony will be performed. The significance of the twin ceremonies will be considered after the description of the burial of premature twins (p. 103).

(*i*) ***Kiro dako ma nywalo rudi.*** After bearing twins a woman may not enter the houses nor eat the food of any of her own family until the ceremony of *kiro dako ma nywalo rudi* (sprinkling a woman who has borne twins) has been performed. It usually takes place about a year after the birth. Should the wife break the prohibition, it is believed that she will become sterile and her twins will die.

Details of the ceremony described below are drawn from the only performance that I witnessed. This was at Apire near Aduku (see Plate VI at p. 102).

On the day appointed for the ceremony preparations are made in the villages of the husband and the wife's father. The wife's father builds a new *ot rudi* and her mother will have brewed beer in a two-mouthed pot (*dogaryo*). Some of this beer is put into a small lozenge-shaped calabash called *obuto*. A *tuk* is placed under the *ot rudi* and *tanga, bomo, anono* are placed on the *ot rudi* in readiness, as for *myel arut*, of which this ceremony is really a repetition.

In the husband's village two squat drums and the *atimu* drum have been beaten since dawn. From time to time the husband's clansmen and wives dance and brandish spears, as described for *myel arut*. This they do for 'We want *jok* to be pleased and not kill the twins'. Meanwhile the *mon me atekere* of the husband's Clan shave their heads and put on their best clothes.

When ready they assemble at the original *ot rudi*, which was put up at the birth of the twins, and there they anoint each other with *tanga*. The drums are anointed and are then carried towards the wife's father's village, while the husband's Clan follow, singing and trotting to the rhythm of the drums. The women wreathe themselves with *bomo* and *anono*.

Half-way to the village the husband's Clan are met by some of the wife's Clan, who are similarly wreathed with *bomo*. A sham fight ensues, the two Clans shouting threats at each other and brandishing their spears. Then they join forces and continue to the wife's father's village, where a similar though more involved sham fight takes place. The *jira* victory cry is raised continually and they dance the twin dance to the beat of the drums.

Anointing with *tanga* now takes place, the wife being liberally splashed by all the women. The drums are anointed and the new *ot rudi*, against which the spears and shields are leant. The two-mouthed pot and the lozenge-shaped *obuto* are brought to the *ot rudi*. Some beer dough is poured from the two-mouthed pot into a calabash (*agwata*) and to this is added some from the *obuto*, to the evident satisfaction of the women, who say, 'That's right, that's good'. One by one they take this beer dough in their mouths and spit it at each other's chests.

Now the essential *kiro* ceremony is performed. The wife, carrying her year-old twins, sits in the doorway of her mother's house and her mother sprinkles her with cold water from a calabash (*agwata*) by means of a head of *modo* grass. This is repeated at the doors of her brothers' houses. Everyone dances, shouts and brandishes spears after the fashion of *gato jok*. The doorway of the mother's house is the chief object of the threats and spear lunges.

During the next lull in the dancing the wife's father brings two brown sheep from his flock. In the ceremony that I witnessed one of the twins had died previously. The wife sat with her remaining twin in front of the *ot rudi*, her feet straight outstretched. One sheep was led round her anti-clockwise and its nose was bumped against the twin's chest. The twin was then placed astride the wife's back in the position usual for carrying a baby, and the sheep was held astride the twin's back. Several old men and women then washed the sheep with water, which trickled from the sheep over the wife and her twin. After this the sheep was put on the ground and water was poured into both its ears. It was let free and ran off.

The dancing and singing was recommenced. Bells were tied round the wife's left leg, and when she jumped up they raised the *jira* cry. The drums were sounding all the time.

The other sheep was brought. The wife's father cut its throat with a knife, which he had previously given to the wife and the twin to hold for a few moments. The blood flowed under the *ot rudi*. The old men and women smeared (*juko*) the wife and the twin with this blood. The sheep was skinned and placed on the *ot rudi*. It was to be eaten on the following morning, after being cooked on a fire made by drilling.

Beer drinking and feasting finished the activities of the day. But first the wife's mother prepared food of every description and with this the wife was smeared (*gwelo*), being fed with it in a ritual manner. After this she was free from the prohibition against eating food in her father's village. The dancing went on late into the night and whichever Clan lasted the longest was entitled to take the drums home as the prize.

(*j*) **Burial of premature twins.** I will now describe the various magical precautions which were taken at Ngotokwe, near Orumo, when the wife of the *Won amagoro* (petty chief) bore twins prematurely. The twins died about six hours later. I happened to arrive at Ngotokwe on the day following the mishap. Though this ceremony is nothing to do with the Clan as a social unit, I thought it best to place it here, as it illustrates well the real significance of the twin ceremonies.

The *Won amagoro* had not yet heard of his wife's miscarriage, but her parents were in the village and her father had built an *ot rudi*. Her co-wives had collected marsh mud and grass, which was placed near the *ot rudi*. The midwife wrapped the dead bodies in pieces of cloth and placed each in a separate pot. Pieces of potsherd were placed over the mouths of the pots. These pots, together with the smaller one containing the after-birth, were then propped up on stones under the *ot rudi*. The whole collection of pots and stones was then heavily plastered with the marsh mud by the midwife (see Plate VI at p. 102).

Tanga was made in two small new calabashes. This was anointed on the wife's chest by means of two sorghum stalks, which were wreathed with *bomo*. She sat near the *ot rudi*. The wife then anointed the midwife and her father, and splashed *tanga* on the ground in front of her co-wife. She did not anoint the co-wife. The wife's father then anointed the pots, the midwife and his daughter. Her co-wife took a length of *bomo* and stripped it of leaves. This she gave to the wife, who tied it round her waist.

Later in the day the midwife spat some beer dough, which had been made in a two-mouthed pot, at the pots containing the bodies. When asked why she did all these things, she said that were any of the ritual omitted the wife would not be able to bear again. The two-mouthed pot was now taken to the *ot rudi*. Hot water was poured into it and the beer was decanted into calabashes, from which those present drank. They said that on no account were they to drink this beer with drinking tubes (*cheke*) at this stage.

PLATE VI

Twin celebrations at Apire

Burial of premature twins at Ngotokwe

Later in the day an old woman chanced to come to the village. She was immediately taken to the *ot rudi* with the wife and the anointing with *tanga* was repeated all round.

The birth of twins signifies to the Lango the presence of *jok* power of great potency. This is so of all abnormal births. Where the abnormality is purposeless, such as breech or leg presentations, dentulous births, monsters and so on, the event is looked upon with horror and fear. When, however, this manifestation of *jok* power results in the unexpected arrival of two individuals to increase the strength of the Clan, the occasion is marked by rejoicing. But it is a joy tinged with fear and anxiety. The parents and their twins are marked individuals for the rest of their lives. The twin ceremonies must be observed scrupulously and on every subsequent ceremonial occasion or critical undertaking some part of the twin ceremony, usually the anointing with *tanga*, must be performed for the sake of safety. In this way the dangerous charge of *jok* power is brought under control and converted to man's benefit. The tragedy of the premature twins, just described, denoted an evil appearance of *jok* power, necessitating the most careful magical ritual to prevent the mother's reproductive powers being impaired. I was very struck by the solemnity of every action.

There may well have been other occasions on which the Clans visited each other as a result of the birth of twins. I only discovered the two occasions already described. These show how the twin ceremonies serve to bring the Clans together in festive manner and so strengthen the Clan and inter-Clan bonds.

(*k*) ***Chibo adit me atekere.*** I had heard from the old men that there used to be a ceremony of installation for a new Clan chief, called *chibo adit me atekere*. The account I give below is derived from the work of several educated Lango, who were asked by the District Commissioner to investigate the matter. In their account there was much detail obviously borrowed from the Acholi—leopard skins, stools, etc. I have cut all this out. But I cannot vouch for the accuracy of the remainder, which I reproduce for what it is worth. All that I can say definitely is that there was some ceremony of installation and the account given me seems likely enough.

In Lango every Clan had one leader who was known as *adit* (chief) and whose duty it was to lead his people in war. When such a chief died his most popular son took his place. The son's seniority was not important. He was elected by the people's judgment. He was bound to be a man who could lead the Clan's team of warriors against other chiefs. The heir had to be a man with a sense of responsibility and adept at using his spear and shield in the fight. Besides being a war leader he had to settle such matters as might arise in the village. These Clan chiefs were anointed before taking up chieftainship.

The day of the ceremony was made known to the people about three or four days beforehand, and the old people of the Clan prepared beer and food for the occasion. In the meantime the news was sent round to all the Clansmen and they were expected to be present on the day. The people assembled outside the house of the heir and his father's stool was put near his evening sitting-out place (*otem*) by the fire. A bowl of sesame oil (*mo nino*) was placed near by. The heir was then called from his house, and he came with his most popular wife, who was to be anointed with him.

When the heir and his wife were seated in the centre of his people, the oldest and most respected man of the Clan came forward and anointed (*wiro*) them with the oil. All the men and women present were then expected to anoint them in turn. The heir had the Clan *echach* stick leaning against his shoulder all this time.

The new chief was instructed in the art of ruling his people well. The old men admonished him as follows:

1. Now that you succeed to your father's stool, do not forget your people in future.

2. Now that you succeed in your father's footsteps, do not refuse the old men.

3. Now that you succeed in your father's footsteps, do not cast your eyes down upon your people.

4. Now that you succeed in your father's footsteps, never be a coward.

5. Now you are in your father's place, never speak harshly to your people.

6. Now you are in your father's footsteps, look after us well.

Each old man spoke a few of these sentences as he anointed the heir with the oil. The old women also admonished him as they smeared on the oil:

1. Now, boy, you are in your father's footsteps, remember old women.
2. Now, boy, you are in your father's footsteps, never hate old women and quarrel with them.
3. Now, boy, you are in your father's footsteps, never refuse the advice of old women.

Having given these admonishments, the clansmen left the new chief with four or five of the old men and he conversed with them. If his father was rich, he would prepare a feast for his clansmen. A week or two later the new chief would call the warriors together to practise warfare drill. He would have to show his powers as being the best of them all with his spear and shield. He would then kill a bull for his warriors. They would pick the meat from the fireplace with their teeth, not using their hands. [This was usually done as a method of swearing an oath before the chief. To prove that he was speaking the truth a man would take a red hot coal into his mouth.]

The ceremony of *chibo adit me atekere* is no longer performed, unless it is done in secret, for the chief (*jago* or *rwot*) appointed by the Government is no longer the legitimate Clan chief.

(*l*) **Blood-brotherhood.** Driberg found blood-brotherhood being practised in north-west Lango, and at Ngai in Atura I was given similar information, though I never witnessed a ceremony.

There are three methods: 1. A cut is made in each man's forearm. He puts his finger to his partner's cut and then licks the blood off. 2. They take an arm bracelet of brass wire and tug at it until it breaks. Each man then keeps his half of the bracelet. 3. They break a flying termite (*ngwen*) in half, and each man eats his half.

Should either of the partners become ill or die hereafter, a like fate will fall upon the other. The ceremony is an importation from the west and in these days, my informants told me, it is very unpopular. But should two men be so attached to each other that life without the other would be intolerable, they may even in these days perform the ceremony. Should their respective families hear of it, they will order a dissolution of the bond. This is done by building a grass hut of small dimensions in the nilotic style. The blood-brothers go inside and the entrance is blocked up. They then make two holes in the wall and creep out through these separate exits. Women may perform the ceremony. The Clan disapproves of the ceremony because it affects in like manner the classificatory Clan brothers of the two friends.

(m) **Yiko dano ma to.** I never witnessed the burial of a dead person (*yiko dano ma to*), and this description is drawn from verbal evidence. It applies only to adults.

When a death occurs, the women of the village immediately raise the funeral wail, so that the neighbourhood should be informed. This is a high-pitched wail that carries a long distance and sounds very eerie.

Men of the dead man's Clan or his relations by marriage dig the grave, which is very deep and just outside the edge of the village. The afflicted family do not take part in this for 'they are too sad'. A clansman or relation by marriage lays the dead man in the grave. He is laid just as he would sleep on his mat, the knees are bent but not drawn right up to the chin, nor do the heels touch the buttocks. He is placed on the cowhide that had served as his sleeping mat. In these days he is often wrapped in cloth. He is laid on his side with his hands drawn up and placed under his cheek. The side on which the dead person lies, whether man or woman, is immaterial, but he must be facing into the village. Should he face towards the bush, it is believed that his *tipo* (spirit) is certain to bring sickness upon the members of his family.

Before the dead man is placed in the grave, a patch of hair is shaved off his head at bregma, the meeting place of the coronal and sagittal sutures (*chwiny wich*). If this place is not shaved, it is believed that the man's widow will never be able to bear another child. The spot is always referred to as the place in a baby which still has no bone. At the same time this shaving of the *chwiny wich* furnishes evidence as to whether the dead man was a sorcerer (*ajok*). If an *ajok* is caught red-handed, a nail is driven through his head at bregma. This would be seen by his family when the shaving takes place. Another cowhide is laid on top of the dead man and his ears are stopped up with pieces of hide. Then the whole family take earth in their hands and throw it on the corpse, standing at the edge of the grave, which is then filled in by the diggers. A mound is left on top and the earth is trampled down tightly.

The grave-diggers are given a chicken, which they eat at their village. There follow three days during which the widows must remain in their houses, except for necessary purposes. Meanwhile the other females of the village go round to the dead man's relations to inform them of the death. They wail as they go.

On the day of the death, the widow or mother of the dead man prepares beer from beer flour (*moko kongo*) and the fermenting agent (*bilo kongo*). This is fit to drink in three days. It is therefore ready on the day of coming out (*donyo oko*), when the widow is allowed out of her house. On this day the clansmen, relations and friends of the dead man arrive early. They come silently till near the village, then there is an outburst of crying and wailing. All the women wail, while tears of genuine grief may be seen in the eyes of the men, though they remain silent.

An inquest is next held by the assembled clansmen to ascertain how their brother died. If he was an old man, they decide that it was old age. But the death of a younger man is thought to have been caused by an enemy. The widow and the dead man's brothers give their evidence. Should a nail have been found on shaving the head at bregma, they know that the dead man was an *ajok* (sorcerer) and no more is said about his death, for even his Clan are glad of the fact that he has been killed. [The dead man will, however, have been buried in the usual way, even though proved to be an *ajok*, unless he died away from home, in which case he would have been left to the vultures. A suicide is buried in the same way, but demonstrations of grief are not so excessive, as he sought death voluntarily. Suicide is most frequent with women who have lost their children. They hang themselves.] Perhaps the dead man stole something and his victim has killed him through the spells of an *ajwaka* (medicine-man). Perhaps some man has quarrelled with him and brought about his death. Anyway they decide definitely that someone has killed him, and if there is any explicit evidence the news is taken to the *Won pacho* (village chief) and so to the Courts (*lukiko*) (see Plate IX at p. 146).

The people then shave their heads. A sheep is killed and eaten. Its skin is worn by the widow or husband, as the case may be, either round the waist in the form of an apron, or in a strip round the head. It is worn for a month or so. Formal wailing is finished on this day. But the near relatives may continue to cry for several weeks with real grief, and suicide is not uncommon on the part of the mourners. The day is ended by drinking the beer that has been prepared.

Christians are buried differently in these days. A teacher buries them with the proper Christian service. They sing hymns and pray. They do not shave the head nor bend the knees of the dead. The body is wrapped up in new cloth. The man's bed is placed in the grave and the body laid on it. They kill the chickens for the diggers of the grave and also the sheep on the day of *donyo oko*, but the skin of the sheep is not worn.

The ceremonies of *yiko dano ma to* and *neko dyang me wi lyel*, as next described, together with the first four ceremonies associated with the *Etogo* group, form a consecutive series concerned with the disposal of the dead. By these ceremonies the *tipo* (spirit) of the dead person is laid to rest. It is the particular concern of the *Etogo* group to exert control over the *tipo*. But the *Etogo* takes no part in these first two ceremonies, which are the concern of the Clan.

(*n*) **Neko dyang me wi lyel.**   I never saw *neko dyang me wi lyel* (killing a bull for the grave). But accounts of it were numerous, especially in connection with sickness due to the visitation of a *tipo* (spirit). If the dead man's son does not provide a bull to be killed, the *tipo* will 'send dreams' to his family. The dreamer will become ill and die unless the ceremony of *neko dyang me wi lyel* is performed.

The ceremony is carried out any day after the *donyo oko* ceremony described above. Sometimes it is done on the same day as *donyo oko*, as they like to have it done as soon as possible through fear of the *tipo*. A bull is not killed for a woman.

The son of the dead man provides the bull, which is killed by the men who have dug the grave. The assembled clansmen divide up the meat. The grave-diggers take a leg for themselves and the son keeps the head and a shoulder, since he is the owner of the bull.

Conclusion. The ceremonies described in this chapter show the reciprocity which exists between Clans which have been united by marriage. Loyalty to the Clan and the maintenance of inter-Clan alliances were of prime importance in the days when the individual's interests could be protected only through his Clan. The network of Clan ceremonies built up these sentiments of loyalty and kept them at the requisite degree of intensity.

The Clan is still the focal point of the individual's interests, but he is not so dependent upon Clan support as he used to be. British administration, with its education, money economy and law courts, enables the individual to act independently of his Clan. The marriage alliance between Clans has become important more as a means of redistributing the newfound wealth through the institution of the marriage goods (see *Uganda Journal*, vol. VII, No. 4, April 1940, p. 159).

These changes have had their effect on the due performance of the Clan ceremonies. We have seen that the tribal ceremonies have died out almost completely as a result of the *pax Britannica* and the new famine organisation, which have made warfare and famines things of the past. The Clan ceremonies are still in existence, but are becoming more formal and less real. The modern tendency is to avoid the ceremonies wherever possible. This is the desire of the Christianised Lango. Schoolmasters may take no part in them on pain of dismissal. Consequently certain of the ceremonies may not be performed until misfortune comes upon the family. This is soon attributed to their neglect of the ceremony, which is hurriedly performed. A number of ceremonies may be telescoped into one as a result of this tendency. If a child becomes ill and *tweyo lau* has not been performed (it should have been done before birth), the difficulty would arise of doing *yeyo lyeto* out of its turn. A compromise is reached by doing more than one ceremony on the same occa-

sion, so that the due sequence is not upset. The marriage negotiations, formerly spread out into a number of reciprocal visits,
are often telescoped into one or two meetings between the parties
in these days.

Rodia, a devout Christian of Aloro, said that none of the
inter-Clan ceremonies would ever be given up by the Lango.
She said that these ceremonies were concerned with *Obanga* (the
Christian God) and not with *jok*, who was only concerned with
the practices of the *ajwaka* (medicine-men). This attitude pre-
vailed among all those who lived near the administrative centres
and were therefore in contact with modern developments.

But whatever rationalisations may be made to justify the
existence of ceremonies, which were dear to the Lango and on
which their social structure used to depend, the practice of the
modern Lango is to avoid or curtail these ceremonies. Where
Christians are concerned, the ceremonies are performed merely
as medicinal remedies. As such performances become more
and more formal, the social functions of the ceremonies, those
that promote group and inter-group loyalties, will disappear,
and the ceremonies are likely to reach the status of pure super-
stition or picturesque survival.

CHAPTER V

CEREMONIES CONCERNING THE *ETOGO*

Control over the *tipo* (spirit) of a dead man is exercised by his *Etogo* group. I have shown in Chapter III how the massed action of the *Etogo* groups constituted the practice of the tribal religion. For the *Etogo* groups control the *tipo*s of the tribal ancestors, which are in close association with *jok* power, and *jok* power is thereby harnessed to the prime tribal requirements of rain-making and victory in war.

The death of a man is followed by a consecutive series of funeral ceremonies by means of which his *tipo* is translated to the status of ancestor. This series commences with the two cere-monies of *yiko dano ma to* and *neko dyang me wi lyel* as described in the previous chapter. The *Etogo* do not appear at these first two ceremonies, and, should the *tipo* go through its transition period peaceably, their presence is only required at *achuban me gonyo tol* and at the *apuny* ceremony described in Chapter III (p. 63). But should the *tipo* prove its malevolence by bringing sickness upon its family, the *Etogo* has to be called in to perform other ceremonies in an endeavour to pacify it. The final extremity is reached when the *Etogo* dig up and burn the dead man's bones at the ceremony of *golo chogo*.

(*a*) **Achuban me gonyo tol.** Driberg has described the funeral ritual (*The Lango*, p. 167). The ceremony which he calls *achuban* or *mato kongo me wi lyel* I have already described under the name of *neko dyang me wi lyel*. The ceremony he calls *apuny me gonyo tol* I now describe as *achuban me gonyo tol*. It will be seen that Driberg's accounts are much the same as mine. He was not fully aware of the existence or functions of the *Etogo* nor of the serial nature of these Lango ceremonies. Ceremonies that are concerned with one particular subject, such as twins or funerals, are apt to be similar. The difference between them can only be realised when it is understood that one follows the other in a definite sequence. I believe that this has caused some confusion in the names that Driberg has used for the ceremonies, which he has none the less described accurately.

I saw *achuban me gonyo tol* (the December for loosening the string), also called *kongo me wi lyel* (the beer of the grave), at Ober near Bar, at Anwongi near Nabieso and at a village near Aboki.

The ceremony, which marks the end of mourning, takes place at the end of the November or the beginning of the December following the death, during the Lango month of *achuban*. Should the death occur in November, the ceremony is postponed till the following November. I was told at Anwongi that *achuban* marks the end of the agricultural year, and that it is therefore fitting that they should cease mourning for their dead brother and start the new year with renewed hope and gladness.

The ceremony lasts for three days. The members of the dead man's *Etogo* assemble on the first day, so that they may have time to brew beer from the beer flour (*moko kongo*) and fermenting agent (*bilo kongo*) of each widow. For each widow has to provide three large pots of beer, one for each meat division of the *Etogo*.

The clansmen line up in front of the dead man's house, holding spears with points towards the ground. The leader of the dead man's meat division sprinkles (*kiro*) them with water from a calabash (*agwata*) three times. If this is omitted the dead man's *tipo* will plague them, it is thought.

After this the *Etogo* members seize the man's widows and demand a goat and beer from each of them. They in their turn seize the men whose wives they wish to become, and these new husbands provide goats and beer. The beer is drunk by the *Etogo*, the leader of the dead man's meat division having first stirred it (see Plate VII at p. 124). A spell is laid (*gato*) on the grave and beer is poured over it. They dance into the night, finally throwing the ashes of the fire, on which the water for the beer has been heated, outside the village.

On the following day at dawn—I am now describing the actual ceremony witnessed at Ober—five goats and fifty chickens were killed. There were five widows and the goats had been provided by each widow's new husband. One of these widows, who was very old, had elected to remain under the protection of her son. Another had selected one of her co-wives' sons to be her husband. The others had chosen different men from their late husband's Clan. It was these men who provided the goats, which were killed by the leader of the dead man's meat division, who cut their throats in front of each widow's house. The chickens were brought by various members of the Clan and were also killed by the leader of the meat division, who beat their heads against the posts of the granaries, ten chickens for each widow. The goats were skinned and the chickens were plucked.

Each widow had a fire in front of her house and small pieces of goat's flesh were roasted there. The *Etogo* members then sat in their three meat divisions to eat this meat. The dead man's Clan did not eat with the *Etogo*, but were given pieces of meat by the eaters according to their meat divisions. Many friends of the dead man had also come and were given pieces of meat by the *Etogo*. A quarrel arose because one meat division had killed an extra chicken. They should have been divided on the basis of ten chickens for each meat division and twenty for the visitors. They said that the man who had killed the eleventh chicken for his meat division was very bad. He was told that another man of the Clan would die if he did that sort of thing. The chickens and most of the meat were placed in large pots to boil for each meat division, and were eaten later in the day.

Two of the dead man's chickens were produced. They were taken by the leader of his meat division. Many spears were leaning against the tree stump by the village fireplace (*otem me abila*). These belonged to the dead man and his sons. They were placed in a heap on the ground and the chickens were laid on their sides on top of the spear-heads, one chicken on top of the other. The leader of the meat division then placed a spear-point on the top chicken. All the dead man's sons grasped the shaft of this spear and together pushed it through the chicken. The leader of the meat division then picked the chickens up by the legs and beat them against the *otem*, the spears and the hunting nets, so that the blood fell on these things. This they called *lamo pacho* (blessing the village), 'because they wanted the whole village to be well and the spears and nets to catch many animals'.

The dead man's five widows now went off with the leader of his meat division to the marsh. They wore *lau* (leather tail) and *chip* (pubic fringe) only, and each carried a new *lau* and *chip* in her hand, together with some red-ochre powder and a water pot. Only the leader of the meat division might accompany them to the marsh, so I had to rely on a description of the episode there enacted. At the marsh they threw their old *lau* and *chip* into the water (*gonyo tol*: to loosen the string). The old man washed them in the marsh. They stained the new *lau* and *chip* with the red ochre moistened with water, put them on, filled their pots with water and returned to the village. The water was put on the fires to heat for beer. The leader of the meat division then shaved the heads of the widows, leaving a round unshaven patch on the top of each head.

The *Etogo*, who had come without their wives, had to do their own cooking and grind their own millet. For the wives of the dead man's Clan feared that, if they cooked for the *Etogo*, a member might become ill or they might quarrel with the Clan for cooking badly; then all the members of the Clan would become ill and die. So the *Etogo* set about cooking their food, while the others sat down to the beer pots drinking in groups according to their meat divisions. This beer, they said, was drunk 'for the ashes of yesterday's beer' which had been thrown outside the village.

I did not see the rest of the Ober proceedings, but I was told that they would be concluded in the usual way, which is as follows. They eat the remainder of the meat and chickens with the millet, which they have cooked. The *Etogo* then pour water on the fires to extinguish them and go home. But a few members of the dead man's meat division remain behind till the following morning, when a goat is killed and portions of it are eaten by the clansmen, sitting in their meat divisions. The *Etogo* members, who have remained behind, then clear up the village and deposit the ashes of the fire outside the village (*jobo bur*). If the ceremony is performed for a woman, the wife of a man of the dead woman's husband's meat division stays behind and sweeps out the dead woman's house thoroughly.

These *Etogo* members then leave the village and the clansmen arrange for the disposal of the dead man's property. His widows have already selected their new protectors and will abandon the old houses. The dead man's heir is his most capable son, usually the eldest, and he steps into his father's position as head and guardian of the family. After the ceremony at Ober, the dead man's possessions were brought out by the widows and the assembled clansmen decided how they were to be divided up. The heir, as head of the family, divided up the cattle so that his younger brothers would be assured of wives in due course. He said that he would sell what was saleable of the other goods so that he could send his younger brothers to school. Should a man leave minor children, his brother holds all the property in trust for them.

By this *achuban* ceremony the formal period of mourning is ended. It is important that the new year, marked by the sowing of the fields, should start in gladness. At the ceremony the heir is officially recognised, the division of the dead man's property is effected and his widows choose their new protectors. The *Etogo* group controls the proceedings and the leader of the dead man's meat division must kill the animals, stir the beer, sprinkle the clansmen with water and so on. The *Etogo* thus prevent the dead man's *tipo* from plaguing any of his clansmen. Besides the clansmen and *Etogo*, any of the dead man's friends may attend the ceremony. If he is a well-known figure, people may come from all over the country to pay their last respects to him.

(*b*) **Gato two.** I will describe the ceremony of *gato two* (laying a spell on sickness), also called *lamo kom dano* (purifying a man's body), which I saw at Akot near Aduku. I will describe it in detail as an example of my method of recording ceremonies in my field notebook.

I arrived at 7.45 a.m. when the people of the village were finishing off their last evening's meal. Soon after my arrival the old men who were to take part in the ceremony drifted in and sat talking to each other about various topics. Most of these men belonged to the *Etogo* of Obar, the sick man's *Etogo*, but there were others who merely came to assist in the ceremony and to drink beer. They discussed the sick man's symptoms. He said that once he was washing in a rain pool (*atapara*) near the village, when he became ill. After that, whenever he went near this pool, he felt ill. The *Etogo* all agreed that his

obanga (obanga mere) must be near the pool. The sick man then
said that his wife, who had died some time before, had been
buried near the pool. While washing himself there for the first
time, he had seen an eddy of air coming from her grave up to
the pool. This must have been the *yamo* (wind) of his wife, for
it gave him a bad headache. All agreed that this was the cause
and it was decided to take the sheep, that was to be killed, in
the direction of her grave. All this came out of the rather
casual discussion among the old men. It was confirmed by my
boy Okuja, whose note I reproduce with a word-for-word
translation:

'*Keny mumiyo yamo bange, en dako mere. Pien onwongo yam oyiko
chege kuno, dong pimeno ka en awoto i atapara meno etelwoko kome
iye etenwongo yamo me dako mere nu i atapara meno, otemiye two
twatwal. Kop mumiyo gitero romo kuno dang pi kop meno, tekopere
wi lyel tye kuno, doki atapara dang tye kuno.*'

'Keny (sick man's name) what-gave wind to-him, she wife
his. Because it-happened he-buried wife-his there, well therefore when he went into pool that and-he-washed his-body in-it
and-he-found the-wind of wife his that in pool that and-it-gave-
him sickness very-much. Reason which-gives that-they-take
the-sheep there also for reason this, it-signifies the-grave is there,
further the-pool also is there.'

Ogwal, who led the chant-chorus of the spell laying (*gato*),
said he did so because he was a respected man and the sick
man was like a son to him. Therefore the sick man had called
him to *gato* the *obanga* in his body. Ogwal was not a member
of the sick man's *Etogo*. The sick man's son refused to take any
part in the ceremony except to drink the beer. He said that he
had no desire to take part in it as he was a Christian. But he
thought that *obanga* would be pleased at the *Etogo* coming like
this and that his father would be cured. They waited for this
son's wife, and as she was long in coming an oldish *Etogo* man
said impatiently, 'The work of *obanga* requires people to arrive
punctually' (*nitimo obanga myero dano tuno piopio*). He then went
into the bush and brought back a thorn tree (*okuto*) four feet
high, and some grass.

At 9.30 a.m. the grass was laid out in front of the sick man's
house and the thorn tree was placed on it. The sick man's half-

brother then brought the brown sheep, that had been tied to the goat house, and laid it on the tree, the root end of which pointed into the house. The neck of the sheep was tied to the stem of the tree with the grass, its head pointing to the root end of the tree. The whole of its body was tightly enveloped in the tree, which was bound securely with the grass. A man then took the pole (*ayeb*), which is used for propping up the granary roof when taking out grain, and pressed the sheep with the forked end. Whenever I asked why they did all this, the invariable reply was, 'Work to do with *obanga*' (*tich kede obanga*).

By this time, 9.50 a.m., the son's wife had arrived with her children and the sick man went into his house with his grand-children and son's wives and all the women of the village. They sat on the ground in the centre of the circular house. The half-brother caught the thorn tree by the root end and dragged it into the house. He dragged it slowly round the house, encircling the people sitting there, while following it on the outside of the house went the old men with their spears, stabbing the wall of the house as they replied to the words of Ogwal. This process was termed *gato* or *lamo*. The words spoken and repeated many times were:

Ogwal	*Old Men*
'Let this sickness forget'	'Forget'
(*two ni wiye owil*)	(*owil*)
'If it goes, good'	'Good'
(*ka owoto, ber*)	(*ber*)
'If the village is at rest, good'	'Good'
(*ka pacho okwe, ber*)	(*ber*)
'May the dead forget'	'Forget'
(*wi jo ato owil*)	(*owil*)

Having encircled the house the sheep was dragged out again and laid at the door. They then came out of the house, walking so that the sheep passed between their legs. All then set off in single file into the bush, the sheep being dragged along in the middle. The *gato* chant-chorus was continued, led in turn by the half-brother, Ogwal and another *Etogo* man. The sentences were repeated time after time:

Leader	Old Men
'If you are Atim, if you are Ongu (dead wives of the sick man), let the people of the dead forget'	'Let the people of the dead forget'
(*ka in Atim, ka in Ongu, jo ato wigi owil*)	(*jo ato wigi owil*)
'If the village is at rest, good'	'Good'
(*ka pacho okwe, ber*)	(*ber*)
'May the sickness forget'	'Forget'
(*two, wiye owil*)	(*owil*)

No one was allowed to look back at the village as he went. They arrived at a clear space in the grass near the graves of Atim and Ongu and near the pool where the sick man had bathed. Here the people, who had been inside the house during the *gato* ritual, stood still while the old men went round them twice dragging the sheep. The sheep was then placed with its head pointing away from the village towards the east, from which direction they thought that the sickness had come. The people stood behind it. They were careful not to let it point towards a neighbouring village, for the sickness might go there. A calabash (*agwata*) of cold water had been brought from the village. Each man took some in his hand, spat into it and threw it on the sick man's grandchildren and their mothers, saying as he did so, 'Formerly the people were helped. Help the whole village to be at rest and keep well, and this leader of the village to rest well at peace.' Then the grandchildren and their mothers each spat into the sheep's mouth and returned to the village by another road, entering the village at the side opposite to the one from which they had gone out. Nor were they ever allowed to look behind them.

Meanwhile the other old men proceeded to kill the sheep. While it was still alive they cut the skin of the left front knee and broke the leg off at the knee. This they threw to the east, saying, 'Throw it to the east in case the sickness comes from there'. The stomach of the sheep was then slit open with a spear so that the entrails fell out, after which it was killed by cutting its throat with the spear. The body was then cut off the thorn tree, which was left with its crest pointing to the east. The carcase was tied to the fork of a nearby tree so that no animal would touch it, and a spear was placed point upwards against another tree to prevent kites from taking any of the meat. They then returned by the road that the grandchildren had taken, being careful not to look behind them, for the sick man would not recover if anyone did so. The grandchildren and their mothers were waiting in the village, and all went into the house. As they came out again the half-brother hit each person on the chest with an *epobo* twig once.

At 10.25 a.m. everyone crowded into the house and a small black pot of beer was placed in the centre. Ogwal and an *Etogo* man took turns in leading a *gato* chant-chorus of exactly the same words as before. The *Etogo* man poured cold water at the doorway, behind the pot and into the pot. Each old man then took cold water in his right hand, spat into it and flung it over the people in the house. Hot water was poured into the pot and the *Etogo* man stirred it and tasted it from a new calabash (*agwata kech*). They called this beer pot, *echol*, and they said that it was only used for *lamo kom dano*. The old men drank out of this calabash, but no young man was allowed to drink this beer. When they had finished the dregs were poured back into the pot, cold water was added and the half-brother took the pot outside. He poured some of the dregs at the edge of the village on the west side, where the people had returned, and then on the east where they had set out into the bush. Then he set the pot in the grass on the north side.

A large pot of beer was placed in the centre of the house. Cold water was poured into it and at the doorway to purify the pot (*me lamo gulu*). For the sickness had made this house its home and they wanted it to go away. 'So they poured out water to drive away the *tipo*s of the dead people who gave this man sickness' (*kun onyo pi me ryemo tipo me jo ato, mumiyo dano meno two*). Some hot water was poured into the pot and beer was decanted into a calabash (*agwata*). The half-brother and the *Etogo* man caught at the bubbles in the calabash with the finger and thumb of each hand and smeared (*juko*) the sick man and his grandchildren. The grandchildren and their mothers then drank out of the calabash. The young men were also allowed to drink this, but still without drinking tubes (*cheke*). At 10.55 a.m. the beer was decanted into pots and all settled down to drink it with drinking tubes.

At 11.45 a.m. the half-brother came out of the house with

a glowing stick from the fire. He took some grass from the thatch of the house and went into the bush towards the sheep. As he went he pointed out cow dung on the path and said that this was a very good sign. Another man followed with firewood. The half-brother cut the sheep from the tree and took out its entrails with a spear. He did not skin it but he cut through the ribs round the breast-bone and then along the stomach, cutting away the genital organs. This exposed the carcase inside and made it easy to roast the whole body. Meanwhile the other man made a fire and the carcase was placed on it. They also roasted the entrails and other pieces of meat separately on sticks. Various young men had come to help to do this.

The half-brother went back to call the old men. As each man came out of the house he took beer dregs and smeared (*juko*) them on the sick man. Then he would take some dregs in his hand, wave them round the sick man's head three times and throw them against the wall of the house in the direction of the graves. Then altogether they washed the outside of the beer pot and went off to the sheep. They were in a stupor from the beer. The half-brother brought the small black pot (*echol*) to the sheep. This would be taken away by an old man. It belonged to the *Etogo* and would be used again at the next *gato two* ceremony.

The *Etogo* sat round the sheep and ate the meat, which was distributed to each man according to his meat division. There was some quarrelling over the distribution. Several men, not of the *Etogo*, sat silently apart and were given some meat by the *Etogo*. They said that they would die if they approached any nearer the *Etogo* while they were eating. The sick man remained in the village, but the half-brother ate with the *Etogo*. At 1 p.m. they all went away.

By the ceremony of *gato two* sickness due to the visitation of a *tipo* is cured. It is believed that the *tipo* of a clansman or near relation can enter the body of a living man and make him ill. The sick man knows the culprit, for he continually dreams of the dead person. The visitation proves that the dead man's *tipo* is malevolent, that 'his head is bad' (*wiye rach*). The funeral ceremonies have not been sufficient to lay it to rest and so the *Etogo* must be called to deal with it.

Spirits of the dead can only enter the bodies of clansmen or very near relations, such as husband and wife, to afflict them. It is my hypothesis that by the *gato two* ceremony the *tipo* is first attracted into the body of the sheep. While in the sheep it is dragged away from the village towards the grave, which is its more ordinary dwelling-place. It is immanent in the flesh of the sheep, which is eaten by the *Etogo* men and so absorbed into their bodies. But it can do them no harm, since they are not of the same Clan or closely related to the dead person. The fact that in the ceremony just described several of the sick man's Clan did eat the sheep can be explained by the fact that the offending *tipo* was that of the sick man's wife, who was naturally not of their Clan and therefore could not trouble them. The sick man was not allowed to eat the meat, for he would then have reabsorbed the *tipo* of his wife, which was troubling him. (Cf. p. 113, where the dead man's Clan did not eat ritually with the *Etogo*, but were given pieces of meat to eat apart.)

(c) **Neko dyang me two.** It is usual for the victim of a *tipo* visitation to consult an *ajwaka* (medicine-man), and he may go to a specialist, who catches the *tipo* in a pot (p. 155), instead of summoning the *Etogo*. But the *ajwaka* is more likely to prescribe some stereotyped *Etogo* ceremony. He first asks whether the son of the dead man has killed a bull for his father (*neko dyang me wi lyel*, p. 108). If he has done so, then perhaps the *tipo* was not satisfied with the bull and another must be killed, *neko dyang me two* (killing a bull for sickness).

I will describe this ceremony as witnessed by me at Abonga-mola near Aduku.

The victim was a four-year-old girl. Her grandmother was an *ajwaka* and had discovered by means of her divining rattle that the *tipo* of the child's father's brother was responsible. She therefore prescribed the following ceremony.

At cockcrow two members of the *Etogo* arrived. Only these two had been invited besides the clansmen. They caught the bull and took it to the dead uncle's grave. They led it round the grave once and then one of the *Etogo* men stabbed it in the side with a spear and so killed it.

The slayer of the bull skinned it. A red spot on the tip of the heart was pointed out as being very auspicious. The entrails and kidneys were also good and they said that the village would be well. The main joints were cut up. The right front leg was taken off at the knee, and small pieces of meat from all parts of the animal were also cut off together with some chyme (*we*). These were wrapped up in leaves and put up in a tree away from the dogs. None of it could be brought into the village. The slayer of the bull had done all the skinning and directing. He then gave instructions about the division of the meat. He took pains to warn them not to quarrel over the division, for the sickness would become worse in the village if they did. The slayer of the bull was not allowed to enter the village. He went off with some meat and the head, which must not be brought into the village or everyone would become ill.

The clansmen then sat in three groups in the village dividing up the meat among themselves. There was a quarrel over the division (p. 45). They had finished doing this by 3 p.m. and the second *Etogo* man (he was the *nero*, mother's brother, of the dead man and had buried him), who had been allowed to enter the village, took the leg, meat and chyme down from the tree. He did not look back at the village, but went straight to the dead man's grave, being careful not to turn his eyes to right or left. He stood with his back to the grave and threw the leg, meat and chyme backwards on to it. Then he walked away, being very careful not to turn his head in the slightest degree to the left or right. He went home to his village and the ceremony was over.

(*d*) **Golo chogo.** I never saw *golo chogo* (digging up the bones) and this account is obtained from my informants. Driberg mentions it (*The Lango*, p. 168).

Digging up the bones of a dead man is a very dangerous task. The only person who dares to do it, or who is able to do it without hurt, is the chief old man of the dead man's *Etogo*. He does the actual exhuming. The bones are then burnt at the marsh and the ashes thrown into the marsh. A bull is killed and eaten by the *Etogo* on this occasion. The grave is sprinkled with medicine (*yat*) so that the spirit (always called *chyen* and not *tipo* on this occasion) will not kill them. The bull must be eaten at the marsh and not taken back to the village. It is eaten by the *Etogo* ritually in their meat divisions. The man, who does the exhuming, is paid two large heifers, and there must be no argument about this payment, as the work he has done is very dangerous and very important.

Golo chogo is the final and most drastic course, only taken if all other methods have failed to pacify the *tipo*. I believe that the word *chyen*, which is used of the dead man's spirit on this occasion, denotes that all hope of pacifying the jealousy of the *tipo*, and so translating it to the status of a helpful ancestor, has been given up. The burning of the bones extinguishes the malevolent and dangerous *chyen* and at the same time prevents it from entering the status of ancestor, which the funeral ceremonies tried to effect. Evidence that this is the correct interpretation of the *golo chogo* ceremony and the use of the term *chyen* will be found in *The Lango*, p. 241, where Driberg describes how an *ajok* (sorcerer) is burnt and his ashes buried in the marsh to avoid the 'machinations of the *chyen*'. The *tipo* of an *ajok* could not be helpful as an ancestor, and it is essential that the *ajok* should be cut out from the cycle of re-incarnation. The burning process is therefore applied to him immediately so that his *tipo*, whose jealous hatred would at once label it as *chyen*, cannot wreak the vengeance it would undoubtedly desire. The *chyen* is thus the spiritual counterpart of the *ajok*.

(*e*) **Rubo koti.** I saw the ceremony of *rubo koti* (mixing the seed) at Alipa and at Bung near Nabieso. The people feared that their millet would not grow if I saw this ceremony and my presence was tolerated only after much persuasion. Driberg was not aware of any such ceremony. The sowing of the millet is the most important task of the year, for life itself depends upon the crop, hence no doubt the concealment of the ceremony from outsiders.

In the ordinary course of events a man's mother and father mix his seeds for him. With the millet is sown sesame, peas and the other plants which serve as vegetable sauces (*dek*) to be eaten with the millet porridge (*kwon*). This mixing is done without any special ceremonial. The millet seed is placed in a heap, the other seeds—only a little of each—are poured on and then the family together mix them up with their hands. But should there have been a death in the family, or should any abnormal birth have taken place, a special ceremony has to be performed at the mixing and sowing of the grain. This is the *rubo koti* ceremony.

The ceremonies I witnessed were for dead women, and I will describe one of them just as it occurred.

The woman had died in November 1936 and the *rubo koti* ceremony was being performed for her in February 1937. I was told that, were it not performed, her *tipo* would cause the millet to die, for she would say, 'Why do you not do this for my grave so that I may sleep well?'

In the early morning the Clan of the dead woman's husband and some of his *Etogo* members assembled outside his house. On the ground was a basin of millet seed and calabashes of the various other vegetable seeds. A heap of the convolvulus *bomo* was lying near by. The dead woman's husband's brother caught a cockerel and someone else caught a pullet. The millet seed was poured on the ground in front of the husband's doorway, and the other seeds were poured on top of it by the husband's mother's co-wife. The clansmen and two men and a woman of the *Etogo*, who were also members of the husband's *Wang Tich* (cultivating group), all gathered round the heap of seeds. Some beer dough was brought out and they took lumps of it in their mouths. At a signal they spat this beer into the seed and mixed it up with their hands, stirring in the *bomo* as well (see Plate VII at p. 124). Then one of the *Etogo* men cut off the pullet's head with a spear on top of the seed (see Plate VIII at p. 136). It was allowed to flap about without its head and caused much laughter. The *Etogo* man then caught it again and allowed some blood to drop on to the seed, finally laying the body on top of the seed. Then he took the cockerel and beat it to death against a nearby tree stump. He laid the body near the seed. All the seed was put back into a large calabash (*wal*) with some *bomo*, while those who had mixed the seed put pieces of *bomo* on themselves, the husband putting it round his right wrist and ankle. The hand stone of the dead woman's grinding stone was laid near the calabash of seed. They all went into the house, where beer was poured into calabashes (*agwata*) and tasted, then it was drunk through drinking tubes (*cheke*).

The *Etogo* man cut the throat of a brown sheep at the edge of the village and skinned it. The cockerel was plucked and a small piece of meat was roasted and eaten by the *Etogo* men.

PLATE VII

Drinking beer at the ceremony of *kongo me wi lyel* at Anwongi

Mixing the seed at the ceremony of *rubo koti*

The rest of the meat was put in a pot with water to boil. I was told that no salt should be put with this meat or the dead woman's child would die.

A woman member of the *Etogo*, whose husband ate in the same meat division as the dead woman's husband, placed the calabash of seed with the unplucked pullet in it on a *bomo* pad on her head. They then went off to the field, which was about two miles from the village.

They went round the field marking off the two outside rows of cotton plants. These had to be left standing. Then the *Etogo* man and woman went to the centre of the field. They took seed in both hands and threw it on the ground saying, 'We want it to flower well' (*wamito tur maber*). Then they dug up the ground at this spot. They explained to me that the *Etogo* woman was identified with the dead woman, whose field this had been. In fact they said that the *Etogo* woman was the dead woman, though the use of the copula here probably has no more significance than 'stands for'. Were this ceremonial not carried out, they said that the dead woman's *tipo* would make her husband dream. The calabash of seed was left on the ground at the place where they had done the ritual sowing. The husband's brother then took the pullet and ran through the field, plucking out the feathers and 'sowing' them in the field.

They asked the two *Etogo* men what meat division they belonged to. One happened to belong to the same meat division as the husband, so he had to do the sowing. Meanwhile the remainder of the husband's *Wang Tich* (cultivating group) had arrived. They all went to one end of the field and started digging down the cotton plants, while the *Etogo* man went ahead sowing the seed. He refilled his calabash when empty from the calabash in the centre of the field. They were very careful to leave the two outer rows of cotton plants standing, as must always be done when digging the fields of someone who has died. They worked on till the field was finished and then returned to the village to drink beer. The *Etogo* then ate the sheep ritually, giving the *Wang Tich* some of the meat.

When a man dies the same ceremony is performed but more elaborately. Six chickens are killed, two for each meat division of the *Etogo*, and a large sheep. No ceremony is performed for a dead child. But if an abnormal birth occurs, a ceremony of a similar though modified nature is performed at the next sowing of the millet. If twins are born, the same ceremony as just described is performed with the addition of portions of the twin ritual, such as the anointing with *tanga* paste. But in neither of these cases do the *Etogo* take part.

The sowing of the millet is the most important annual event for the family. Should a shower cause the seed to germinate and then a few weeks of drought ensue, all their labours will have been in vain and they must re-sow. Their crops are at the mercy of the elements, forces which they cannot control empirically. The performance of economic magic, of which *rubo koti* is a good example, is therefore necessary either to calm anxieties or as an expression of man's desire to control his own destiny. Troubles come from other people's jealousy. Who is more likely to be jealous than a dead person bereft of his place on earth? Therefore it is particularly necessary to placate the dead person's spirit when digging what used to be his fields. Only the *Etogo* can control the *tipo* successfully, so the proceedings are entrusted to them. *Jok* power is manifested on the occurrence of abnormal births. The crops may be destroyed if this *jok* power is not recognised and controlled by the appropriate ceremony.

Conclusion. From a study of these *Etogo* ceremonies the nature of the *tipo* can be understood, and this is one of the most important premises of Lango eschatological belief.

The *tipo* is at first reluctant to leave the land of the living. It is jealous of the living and must be soothed by the funeral ceremonial, if it is to be translated to the status of a helpful ancestor. The transition rites are performed 'for the dead man'. He is told, 'Look at this beautiful bull we have killed for you! Look at the beer we have brewed for you!' But should the *tipo*'s jealousy be more than ordinary, the *Etogo* will have to put pressure upon it to constrain it to give up its malicious behaviour. Should even this fail, it becomes clear that the *tipo* is really a *chyen*, the spiritual counterpart of an *ajok* (sorcerer). A *chyen*, like an *ajok*, can never be of use to man. It is looked upon with horror and means must be found to destroy it utterly, and prevent it being re-incarnated through the status of ancestor. This is done by burning the bones of the dead man at the ceremony of *golo chogo*.

Chapter VI

CEREMONIES CONCERNING THE FAMILY

I have placed the following twelve ceremonies under the Family group, since they are most closely concerned with the individual as a member of his immediate Family. The first three ceremonies form a series associated with the avoidance of a man and his mother-in-law. The remainder are isolated ceremonies, performed as occasions arise. My evidence on these ceremonies is very meagre. I only witnessed four of them. I put very little trust in the details of ceremonies collected from informants. But their evidence indicates that such ceremonies do exist.

(a) *Kiro bang imat*. I never saw *kiro bang imat* (sprinkling at the mother-in-law's house), but it was explained to me in many parts of Lango.

One of the essential conditions for the successful production of children is that there shall be no quarrelling between the families of the husband and wife. The mother-in-law avoidance rule serves to prevent this. Any infringement of the avoidance rule is supposed to lead to the barrenness of the wife or the death of the children. But as soon as the productive process seems to have been assured, the avoidance rule appears to be a trifle unfriendly. It was designed in the first instance to prevent enmity arising between the mother-in-law and her daughter's husband. Later, with its prohibition against the son-in-law eating her food, it seems to signify enmity between them. Such a state of affairs must be ended—not by setting aside the avoidance rule, but by a ceremony which allows the son-in-law to eat her food and so demonstrate their good will to each other.

A boy must start avoiding his future mother-in-law as soon as he begins to court her daughter, and from henceforth he must not eat any of her food. Should he do so, he would die, or his children would die, or his wife would miscarry or become sterile. When three or four children have been born to the couple, the mother-in-law says to her daughter, 'Why are we such enemies that your husband does not eat my food?' So arrangements are made to 'sprinkle him with water', in order to absolve him from the prohibition against eating her food.

The mother-in-law prepares a great quantity of food and beer. The husband goes to her village with his Clan. She sits in the doorway of her house smoking a pipe, while he remains in the courtyard completely surrounded by his clansmen and with a skin or a winnowing mat on his head [in these days a large piece of cloth is generally used], so that he cannot see or be seen by his mother-in-law. She asks, 'what do you want?' (*imito ngo*), and he replies, 'I want good health' (*amito yot kom*). Then he asks, 'What do you want?' and she replies, 'I want good health'. Then she hands her pipe to his clansmen. It is handed through to him and he smokes it for a short time. [Not every Clan does this pipe episode.]

The husband goes off, still surrounded by his clansmen, to the house of his wife's brother. He sits in the entrance of the house and his wife's sister sprinkles (*kiro*) him with water by means of a head of grass. She then smears (*gwelo*) him with the food that has been prepared. She also takes some beer dough and waves it round his head before throwing it away. She takes a lump of millet porridge (*kwon*), dips it into the sauce (*dek*), and makes two passes at his mouth, putting it into his mouth at the third attempt. The food is then divided up and all present eat it and drink the beer. The husband continues to avoid his mother-in-law thereafter, just as he does throughout the ceremony, but he may in future eat her food.

The ceremony is an occasion for the Clan to come together and meet the other Clan bound to it by marriage, under conditions of general good will, emphasised by an excellent feast. In fact the ceremony might well have been assigned to the Clan group. I place it here on account of its serial association with the two ceremonies next described.

(*b*) **Yeyo moko me or.** I never saw *yeyo moko me or* (carrying flour to the son-in-law), but it was explained to me in many parts of Lango. It is unlikely for the ceremony to be performed unless *kiro bang imat* has previously been celebrated, though this is not an invariable rule.

When a man has had a few children, and if the families of the husband and wife are very friendly, the mother-in-law may decide to pay a visit to her son-in-law's village. She prepares beer flour (*moko kongo*) and, together with her family, carries it to her son-in-law's village. As usual the husband must avoid his mother-in-law all the time. They drink the beer and are entertained as guests. This visit may be paid any number of times according to the inclinations of the mother-in-law. But every time it is done she leaves the baskets or calabashes, in which the beer flour has been brought, behind, and the son-in-law has to take them back to her with a bull as a present. This is the reciprocal ceremony of *neko dyang me maro*, which I describe next.

(*c*) **Neko dyang me maro.** I only obtained verbal accounts of *neko dyang me maro* (killing a bull for the mother-in-law). It follows after each performance of *yeyo moko me or* as just described.

The mother-in-law leaves behind the receptacles used in *yeyo moko me or* and the son-in-law has to take them back to her. But 'he is filled with shame to take them back without a present for his mother-in-law'. So he calls two or three of his friends, who inform the mother-in-law of their prospective arrival. Then they all set off with a bull, a spear and a knife. One of the friends spears the bull in front of the mother-in-law's house. The meat is divided up and she eats it with the knife that they have brought.

This ceremony may be performed even if no *yeyo moko me or* ceremony has been celebrated. If the husband is on good terms with his wife's family, his father may say, 'I see that our friends over there are very good, and I suggest that we go there to cook for them'. Word will be sent to the mother-in-law, who will tell the women of her village to prepare beer for the occasion. The bull is taken, together with a spear, salt and a knife. It is speared in the village pasturage and presented to the wife's father or mother. She complains that it is a very small bull and quarrels with the visitors, but is finally pacified by the other people present. On the following morning the bull's loins are produced and the husband's mother, together with his wife and the women of her father's Clan, place their hands in the loins, saying, 'We want good health' (*wamito yot kom*). Then the wife's people give them a bull, the necessary gift for distinguished visitors. This is taken home in pieces. A leg and a shoulder are given to the *Jo Doggola*, the other shoulder to the girls of the Clan and the remainder is kept by the husband's family.

(d) **Birth.** I arrived soon after several births, but only saw one actual delivery. This was at Amya near Aduku. I will describe it rather fully, as it shows the laxness that now prevails in these ceremonies, owing to proximity to modern conditions. The birth that took place in Moroto, when I was there, followed the general lines cited by Driberg (*The Lango*, pp. 138–42). But in no other ceremony do the details vary so much from Clan to Clan as at birth. Moreover, there is much variation according to whether it is the first or a subsequent child, or a child born after previous deaths, and as to the particular practices of the different midwives. So that neither Driberg's observations nor mine are in any way comprehensive on the subject of birth ritual.

The labour pangs of the mother at Amya started at 5 a.m., when the husband immediately came to tell me. I arrived at 9.30 a.m. The house was full of the women of the village with their children. They objected to my boy coming into the house, but not to me. The husband stayed in the house all the time, except when the cord was cut and the name given.

The mother sat on her legs in a kneeling position with knees spread apart. She sat on the bare floor of the house with her back to the fire. At each labour pang she sighed aloud 'o, i'. This was her fifth child.

Soon after my arrival the midwife, who had come from a neighbouring village, took some sesame oil in her hands, spat into it and rubbed (*wiro*) the mother's stomach with it. They said that clarified butter (*mo dyang*) should have been used. She then shook the stomach violently with both hands.

After twenty minutes, during which the women chattered unceasingly, the child was born. The midwife rushed over to the mother to help her and the women gathered round talking a lot. The midwife caught the child in her hands. It was a perfect delivery. She placed it on the mother's knees. It was a boy. The mother bent down and sucked the child's nose and mouth to clean them. She spat this on the floor. She smiled and looked very pleased. The blood and fluid flowed over the ground.

After a five-minute wait the midwife sprinkled some cold water on the child's stomach. It burst out crying and the women slapped the mother hard on the back, scolding her as if it were she who was crying.

Twenty minutes later the midwife shook the mother's stomach violently to help out the after-birth. By that time the after-birth had slipped on to the ground between the mother's knees. The mother held the child on her lap all the time.

They now set about cutting the umbilical cord. They called for some string, but none could be found. Thread would do, but there was none. So the husband's god-daughter (they were Christians), who had come to help the mother run the household, tore off a thin strip of rag and twisted this on her thighs. The midwife moulded it between her finger and thumb. The god-daughter tied four pieces of this twisted cloth at inch intervals along the umbilical cord, starting at the navel end. They asked the mother what had been used on previous occasions for cutting the cord. She was not sure. A spear was produced, but eventually they decided to use a sliver stripped off a thick dried stem of *rau* grass.

The midwife cut through the cord between the two last strings on the placental side. She held the severed cord between finger and thumb and with the cut end she touched the mother's breast-bone, the child's breast-bone, the child's forehead, the mother's forehead. Then she let it drop while the mother moved slightly so that the whole after-birth lay a little to her right. It was covered with an old piece of cloth.

The midwife made two scratches in the ground at the doorway with a piece of wood. They said that this was to prevent anyone from coming into the house and stealing the blood from the ground. Should anyone do so the mother would not bear again. No unauthorised person could enter the house once the scratches had been made. When I asked what would happen to anyone who did enter and steal the blood, my suggestion seemed preposterous, as no one would dare to do such a thing once the scratches had been made.

The god-daughter brought in a winnowing mat with a heap of dust on it, which she spread over the blood and fluid. A piece of potsherd was brought and the placenta placed on it by the midwife. It was covered with a piece of old cloth and placed near the wall.

The midwife washed the mother's nipples with water and they asked me to give the child a name (*chako nying*). I suggested my native name, Malakwang. So they offered the child the breast and said, 'Suck, Bwanamalakwang' (*dot Bwanamala-kwang*). The breast was pushed into its mouth so that it was forced to suck. Its name therefore became Bwanamalakwang and as such it was duly registered in the *Jago*'s book on the following morning. I was always referred to as its 'guardian' (*wonere*) after this.

The midwife threw water once into the air, once towards the door and once into the fire. She sprinkled some in play over the child. She washed her hands with soap in the remainder of the water which was in the basin, and then poured it on each side of the after-birth and in front of it. The after-birth would be thrown into the bush secretly on the following day by the mother. The door of the house was shut when I left, leaving the mother and child alone there. She would wash herself later in the day. The husband said that he would give the midwife four shillings as her reward when the mother next bore a child. If no further child were born the midwife would receive nothing. It was clear that they believed that the mother would only be able to bear again if the midwife carried out her share of the work properly.

The mother and child were secluded in the house for three days. Had it been a girl, four days' seclusion would have been necessary. During this period only unsalted gruel (*nyuka*) was eaten by the mother. This she cooked herself. She had washed herself daily, but the child was to be washed for the first time on the day of *donyo oko* (coming out). No fence had been put round the house. It was not necessary, they said, since the door of the house had been kept closed.

On the third day after the birth the mother and child came

out of the house and the *donyo oko* (coming out) ceremony was performed. I arrived at 11 a.m. The midwife was summoned and came with her daughter-in-law. The mother came out (*donyo oko*) with the child and sat under the granary in front of the house. She smeared millet flour round the midwife's forehead and cheeks. The midwife repeated the performance on the mother, child and daughter-in-law.

After twenty minutes the midwife and her daughter-in-law went away. The mother went back to her house. She collected all the ashes from the fire on to her winnowing mat and also the refuse of the house, which she swept. She emptied all this into the grass about twenty yards away. Returning to the house with some leaves of *nege*, she squeezed their juice on to the child's navel to help the remnant of cord, still tied with the strings, to wither off. The mother complained that her stomach hurt, and I think that was why she did not eat anything then, for it is usual to eat at *donyo oko*. Whenever the child defecated, the mother let it do so on her own clothes, wiping it off afterwards with a piece of cloth kept for the purpose. Warm water was brought into the house and the mother washed the child with soap for the first time since the birth.

I arrived at 9.30 a.m. on the following day. The mother was washing the child in the house. When she had finished, she emptied the basin on the floor of the house. She said that she could not throw the water outside until the child's head had been shaved and it had been washed in the open. The remnant of the umbilical cord had fallen off by now. The midwife arrived at 10.45 a.m. The mother and child had already come out of the house. A basin of water was produced and the midwife sharpened her razor, made from a piece of hoop iron, on a spear. Holding the child in her lap, she cut some hair off and placed it in the child's left hand, closing the hand up. This she said was to prevent it from crying. The mother then took the child on to her lap, while the midwife shaved its head, letting the hair fall on to the ground. They said that the child would not remain well for long if its head were not shaved. They carried out all these actions 'on account of the ritual observance'. A tuft of hair was left in the centre of the child's head.

The mother washed her hair with soap and the midwife then

shaved it. A child threw all the hair into the grass outside the village. Meanwhile the husband's god-daughter had cooked millet porridge (*kwon*) and vegetable sauce (*dek apena* and *nino*) with salt. She swept a space in front of the doorway and the mother sat there with the child on her lap and with her legs straight outstretched. The midwife anointed (*gwelo*) the mother and child with the *dek*. Then she took a lump of *kwon*, filled it with *dek* and put it into the mother's mouth. After this they all sat down and finished off the food.

The midwife went away. She said that they should flutter (*buko*) a chicken at 6 p.m. if one could be found. They added that, as the child had accepted my name, it was my duty to provide the chicken and also soap for washing the child. On making inquiries elsewhere I found that this was quite true, and in addition I should drink the beer that the mother would provide.

When I returned at 6 p.m. I found that the mother had placed twisted strings of cloth (not of the usual *kworo* bark) round her own neck and round the child's waist, neck, wrists and ankles (see drawing, Plate V, 4 at p. 98). This she said was to make the child grow strong.

I had brought a cockerel with me, but they said that a pullet must be used for a boy and a cockerel for a girl. The husband could not use one of his chickens, but if I exchanged my cockerel for one of his pullets, all would be well, as the pullet would no longer belong to him.

The mother sat in front of the doorway with legs outstretched and with the child on her lap. The midwife fluttered the pullet, grasping it by the leg and swinging it round the mother's head twice. Then she stood it on the mother's head. After this it was allowed to go free. It would not be killed. Should it be killed accidentally it would not matter very much, but the child might become ill as a result. In the event of the chicken's death, the old men would eat it. I did not ask whether these old men had to be the *Etogo*. The chicken would be fluttered by the midwife every new moon until the child was big. *Rwot* Ogwalajungu told me that, when a midwife flutters a chicken round a child at the new moon, she says, 'When you rise, may you rise with this child. When you go over to the east, go alone, may you leave this child well and may no sickness come upon him' (*Ka ipor, ipor ki ngadi. Ka idok kidi, idok keni, iwek ngadi bed makome yot, two moro owek bedo i kome*). I visited Amya a month later and the child was in a carrying sling of cloth, which had been bought at an Indian shop. The child's head had been shaved again. It had to be kept short with the patch in the middle (a Clan custom) till the child was strong enough to fend for itself.

The changes that have taken place in birth ceremonial since Driberg's time cannot be estimated very accurately owing to Clan variations in ritual. The tendency to build square houses with hedge fences round them has made it unnecessary to rope off the mother's courtyard (*The Lango*, p. 139). But in the more remote villages the roping off is still done, especially when the birth has been difficult. The new social value of cloth, arising from the adoption of clothes, is well brought out in the ceremony recorded, where cloth instead of *kworo* string was tied round the umbilical cord and the wrists, ankles, neck and waist of the child. A cloth carrying sling was also used instead of the traditional and ritually constructed skin. But at the *donyo oko* ceremony I saw at Orumo an elaborate ceremonial was carried out in which the *okeo* of the mother's husband struck her with *epobo*, for it was the mother's first child. When the mother suffers any misfortune in the reproductive processes, the ceremonies are performed with careful solemnity.

(*e*) **Atin akwer.** If there has been a succession of infant deaths, the parents may decide to 'refuse grief' (*kwero jul*) and make the next child an *atin akwer* (ritual child). Chronic malaria is responsible for a high infant mortality rate in Lango (according to the medical authorities), so that the ceremony of *atin akwer* is very common. I will describe the ceremony I saw at Bungakelalyek near Ngai.

The ceremony is usually performed by a woman of another Clan, who is noted for her knowledge of this ritual. The child is not given a name in the usual way on birth, so that the jealous Clan *tipo* or the malevolent *jok* power, which must be causing the deaths, is deceived. On the day of *donyo oko* the old woman shaves the child's head, leaving a narrow strip round the base of the crown after the manner of twins. The left ear lobe of a boy, or the upper lip of a girl, is pierced and a blue bead threaded on a brass wire is worn there. The mother and child are wreathed with *bomo*. The old woman plants a cutting of *candelabrum euphorbia* (*apongpong*) in front of the mother's doorway, together with *modo* grass and other plants, and places a *tuk* (termites' nest) there (see Plate VIII at p. 136). She then gives the child a name usual in her own Clan and not in use in the child's Clan.

There is much more ritual, which will be apparent in the following description. But the ceremony I will now record was performed by the sister of Odok, the interpreter of the famous Atworo manifestation of *jok* power (p. 162). The ceremony was performed at Odok's village, and therefore the planting of euphorbia as just described was omitted.

The mother had brought her two months' old child from a village about ten miles away. A serval cat carrying skin was made for the child. The woman, who did the ritual, held the child under the granary outside her house, and Odok's wife took it from the left side of the woman, thus drawing it under the granary (cf. *The Lango*, p. 58). The mother then sat with her back to the granary holding the child, and she and the child were washed by the woman with water from a calabash (*agwata*). A cockerel and a pullet were fluttered (*buko*) round her head. The woman plucked a feather from one of the birds and planted it in the ground at the right-hand front support of the granary. Some beer was brought in a small calabash (*agwata*). The woman and Odok's wife took mouthfuls of this beer, spat it at the mother's chest and emptied the dregs on each side of the granary. The woman then took the mother by the hand and led her up from the granary with a formal attempt at the *jira* cry of victory.

The mother now sat in front of Odok's wife's house and the child was again washed well. The mother washed herself. The woman held the child and asked me to give it a name (*chako nying*). I suggested Malakwang and the woman said, 'Bwana-malakwang, suck'. The child was forced to suck the woman's breast and so that became its name.

They placed the child on its mother's back, and fastened it

PLATE VIII

Killing a chicken at the ceremony of *rubo koti*

Atin akwer's euphorbia tree

there with the new carrying skin. The woman placed a spurtle for stirring beer (*lot kongo*) and one for stirring millet porridge (*lot kwon*) in front of the doorway. The mother, in a crouching position, and with the child on her back, jumped over these. They were placed in front of her again and she stepped over them the second and third times, 'because the child was a boy'. Had it been a girl it would have been done four times. The mother turned at the doorway and was led away again with a formal *jira* cry by the woman.

This ended the proceedings and the family went home. They said that they would plant a euphorbia tree (*apongpong*) with *modo* grass and a *tuk* on the following day at their village. They said that when other children had been born to the mother, the woman would be repaid for her services by a bull killed at her village and a cow for her to keep for herself. The hair of the child would not be cut until it was about eight years old.

The misfortune of a succession of infant deaths is attributed to the jealousy of the spirits of the dead (*jo ma to*), or to *jok* power, or to someone using magic (*yat*). The ceremony of *atin akwer* is supposed to obstruct their attentions. The giving of a name provides a handle by which these malignant forces can work upon the child. It is therefore not named on birth in the usual way. Moreover, it is only the Clan *tipo* which can afflict the child, so when it is finally named at the *atin akwer* ceremony, it is given a name appropriate to some other Clan, so that the *tipo* of its own Clan will be further confused. Or it may be given a derogatory name such as 'Dung' to avert the jealousy of the malignant forces. All subsequent children are also considered to be *atin akwer*.

(*f*) **Kiro dano.** This account of *kiro dano* (sprinkling a man) is drawn from verbal sources. It is essentially a purifying ceremony, which is performed on various occasions: 1. If a man has returned from a long journey. 2. If he has just been let out of prison. 3. If two brothers quarrel and then make it up. 4. When a man returns to his Clan after binding himself as a pawn under the old institution of *chaporo*.

The man's mother brews a large quantity of beer. The man does not enter the village until the beer is ready. He stays in a

nearby hut. When it is ready he goes into the village and is
sprinkled with water from a calabash (*agwata*) with a piece
of *modo* grass. The water is sprinkled about the village also.
A goat is killed and he is smeared (*juko*) with its chyme (*we*).
A necklet of its skin is put round his neck (*tumo*). He is smeared
(*gwelo*) with food, and then all present eat the food and drink
the beer.

If a man quarrels with his brother, he may say, 'I will never
eat your food again'. The brother will reply that he too will
not eat the other's food. Should by chance the wives mix up
their foods so that one of the brother's family eat the food of the
other brother, he will become ill and die, unless the *kiro dano*
ceremony is performed. This ceremony absolves the brothers
from their observance, and puts an end to the quarrel. In
practice, as soon as a member of one of the quarrelling families
becomes ill, they go to an *ajwaka* (medicine-man). He will
know of the quarrel, or will soon find out from questions, and
will put the illness down to this cause. He will order the brothers
to put an end to their quarrel by means of the *kiro* ceremony.

(*g*) **Neko dyang me woro papo.** During a ceremony at
Achaba *neko dyang me woro papo* (killing a bull to honour one's
father) was resorted to, because the father refused to kill a bull
for his guests.

Each son and daughter once in their lives may kill one of their
father's bulls for him to eat. This will be done if the Family and
Jo Doggola have not had any meat to eat for some time. It is
an emergency means of obtaining meat when there has been
no ceremony for a long time. I first heard of this custom when
trying to prove to certain Christians that the Lango ceremonies,
to which they objected, were a means of providing the people
with meat, and that if they were abolished it would be difficult
to have bulls killed. They replied that this was false because
the meat supply would be assured by the custom of *neko dyang
me woro papo*.

The son goes to two or three of his friends and says to them,
'Tomorrow I am going to cook for my father, I would like
you to kill the bull'. At dawn on the following day his friends
kill one of the bulls without his father knowing. They skin it

and bring the meat to the village. One of them says to the father, 'Here is the relish which your child has killed to honour you' (*dek eno ma atin ni oneki me wori*). The father pretends to be very angry, saying, 'Why does he spoil my cattle? What will he marry with?' But the friends soothe him, saying that his son has done it in his honour, and so the father proceeds to divide up the meat among the *Jo Doggola*.

Should a daughter wish to carry out this custom, she goes to her brother or father's brother and he kills the bull. Her father must not be angry, but he says, 'If she gets into debt like this, who will pay up?' The meat is then divided.

(*h*) **Migrating to a new house.** If a man has lived in a certain spot for about ten years or so, the place will have become dirty and the fields played out, and he will want to migrate. Or if there have been deaths in the house, an *ajwaka* may order a migration.

He must first find a good spot. This will be on the crest of a rising, as it is bad to build in a valley. Formerly he would have gone to an *ajwaka*, who would have told him what tests to carry out to ensure that the new place would be lucky. Or he might know of the tests himself. Thus he might put a chicken and beer on the spot over night. If a merekat takes the chicken or a jackal drinks the beer, he knows that it is a bad spot.

When he has built his house, he kills a goat and three chickens and brews three pots of beer. Then he calls the old men and women to the village. The chief old man will 'spread out the road of migration to his house' (*peti yo me dak i ot mere*). He breaks off *olwedo* leaves, which the man carries. By the entrance of the new house *olwedo* leaves and grass will have been spread out. The old women and men go into the house, and when they have come out the boys and girls go in. If an *ajwaka* is present, he sprinkles the family with water by means of an *olwedo* branch. Everyone then takes beer in his mouth and spits it on the chests of the migrating family, saying, 'Good if you keep well. We want good health in this house. May all the children be well.' Then they drink the beer and eat the meat.

(*i*) **First fruits.** This is performed when the first fruits of the harvest have been gathered each year. Each family cooks a little of all the new foods. They sit in front of the doorway of their house and the father smears (*gwelo*) them with this food.

(*j*) **Sterility and impotency.** Marriage is not complete until the wife has borne a child. In fact the real marriage ceremony, *tweyo lau* (p. 83), was not performed until she was pregnant. All the Clan ritual observances and ceremonies were designed to produce and protect babies. It is a woman's greatest shame to be barren.

A barren woman goes to an *ajwaka*, who gives her a special medicine, or tells her to carry out a ceremony such as *myel arut* (p. 97) or *yeyo lyeto* (p. 88), which they hope will make her pregnant on the sympathetic principle.

Two reasons are given for impotency in a man. Either he has been badly handled at birth, so that his testicles have been injured, or a *tipo* of a dead relation, usually his father, has caused him to be impotent, has in fact castrated him through jealousy.

In the first case the whole of the birth ceremony is re-enacted. The fully grown man remains in his mother's house for three days, as at the time of seclusion after birth. He cries like a baby, sucks his mother's breasts and defecates in the house, just as if he were a baby. The *donyo oko* ceremony (p. 133) is then performed, and it is hoped that the damage done in childhood will thus be repaired.

Rwot Ogwalajungu described a ceremony that might be performed for an impotent man. A small grass hut, four feet high and three feet in diameter, was built. It was called an *abila*. The man entered by an opening which was then covered with grass. He broke through at some other point head first as soon as an old man set fire to the house at the opposite end. This appears to be a sort of rebirth ceremony. The *Rwot* said that it was never performed in these days and I had no other information on the subject. (But compare the dissolution of the blood-brotherhood pact, p. 105.)

If, after divining (*tyeto*) at an *ajwaka*'s village, the cause of impotency is discovered to be a *tipo*, the *ajwaka* will prescribe some ceremony. I saw the following examples of this:

1. Near Alito a man had built a small hut (*abila*) about

eighteen inches high in the courtyard by the fire (*otem*). He said that he had suddenly become impotent, and as he knew that his father had once built an *abila*, he did so too. Now, he was no longer impotent.

2. At Abier near Amaich a policeman, who failed to emit semen during intercourse, was told by the *ajwaka*, whom he consulted, that he should build an *abila*. In the previous February he had built a conical-shaped *abila* on top of a twin house (*ot rudi*). At that time he had also killed a black goat and was smeared (*juko*) with its chyme (*we*).

3. At Angwechibunge near Dokolo an *abila* had been built the day before I arrived by the father of the man concerned. The man had been able to copulate successfully formerly, but now, though he could still copulate, he failed to eject semen. An *ajwaka* had divined and told him to build the *abila*, as it was clear that his dead uncle had castrated (*diyo*) him. They knew it was his uncle's *tipo* that had castrated him, because it had brought him dreams. All the people of the village had assembled when the *abila* was built, and a man of the *Etogo* had killed two chickens. Beer had been brewed in a two-mouthed pot (*dogaryo*), the necks of which were wreathed with *bomo*, and it was placed near the *abila*, where it was when I arrived.

(k) **Gato le.** According to all my informants, after the killing of any of the large and dangerous animals such as buffalo, elephant, lion, rhinoceros, leopard, and also the roan antelope, a person in the slayer's family corresponding in age and sex to the animal killed will contract the disease of *jok orongo*. This is a form of madness, the person afflicted talking incoherently. But it will not occur if the ceremony of *gato le* (laying a spell on an animal) is performed. I saw such a performance at Akwon near Ngai for a roan antelope, which had been killed a week previously at a hunt in which I took part near Ngai. A lion was also killed at this hunt and a reliable informant sent me an account of the *gato* ceremony carried out for it. I will describe the ceremony I saw.

The roan (*ochwil*) was killed by mistake. No one would kill a roan intentionally. The meat was divided in the ordinary way. But the horns were cut off the head, which was left where the animal had fallen in the bush. They said that the head of the animal brought *jok orongo*, therefore it must not be brought into the village. There was some disagreement as to whether these animals, which brought *jok orongo*, possessed *tipo* or not. Apparently medicine (*yat*) for *gato ochwil* is only known to the Ochukuru Clan. Perhaps such was only the case for this district. The man who performed the ceremony was referred to as *won agat*.

The *won agat* and his brother arrived at 9.30 a.m., carrying various leaves with them. They plaited a grass rope (*akedi*) and with it they tied a small black chicken on to the bundle of leaves, which consisted of: *okuto, olwedo*, a *yago* fruit, *ogali, mida, acher, ibeli, epobo* and *obia* grass.

The *won agat* put some medicine (*yat*) in a calabash of cold water. He waved the mixture round the first spearer's head, throwing some behind him and saying, 'Go back into the bush' (*dok i tim*). His brother did the same. The second spearer had some of the water put on his head and the remainder was poured on the thatch over the doorway of the first spearer's father's house, in which the ceremony was performed. The two horns of the roan were filled with grass and laid by the side of the bundle of leaves.

The members of the first spearer's Clan crowded into his father's house, men, women and children. They sat there while the old men waited outside. The *won agat* then dragged the bundle of leaves round inside the house, while the old men followed outside, stabbing the house with their spears on repeating the last word of the chant-chorus spoken by the *won agat* (cf. *gato two*, p. 117). This was to the effect that the roan should go back to the bush and stay with the leopards and hyaenas and not trouble the village. As the *won agat* finished the circuit of the house, he dragged the bundle out of the doorway and all those inside followed him. They went in a long line out of the village to a tall tree surrounded by undergrowth about five hundred yards away. No one was allowed to look back towards the village. As they neared the tree, the women and children branched off towards the left and took a circuitous route back to the village, not looking behind them. The *won agat* and his brother then killed the chicken under the tree with the spear, with further exhortations to the roan not to plague them. They had done the *gato* chant-chorus all the way to the tree. The bundle of leaves and the dead chicken were left there. Everyone went back by the road taken by the women and children, being very careful not to look behind him.

At the village the animal's skin, which had been resting on a twin house (*ot rudi*), was produced. The breast-bone, liver and other portions of the meat, which had all been smoked, and the ears of the roan were tied up in the skin and taken off by a boy to the village of the *won agat*, in addition to the horns and the tail. The tail would be thrown secretly into the bush, they said.

Everyone crowded into the house. The *won agat*'s brother cut the thorns off two stout thorn sticks, each about a foot long. Two pots of beer were placed in the centre and their mouths were covered with calabashes (*apoko*). The *won agat* poured cold water over the pots and into the beer. He and his brother then sprinkled everyone in the house with cold water, as did the first spearer's father. The *won agat* put one of the sticks into one of the pots. The first spearer and his father, the second spearer, the *won agat* and his brother together held the stick and stirred the beer. The same was done with the other pot. The *won agat* and his brother then bowed down their heads, the *won agat* holding one of the sticks pressed into the grass ring on which the pot rested. In this position they again did the *gato* chorus. Among other things they said, 'May the people of the dead (*jo ma to*) not trouble us'. After working himself up to a high pitch of concentration, the *won agat* threw the stick between his legs out of the doorway. They all sat perfectly silent for a few moments, being careful to see that everyone had his fingers bent. Then they continued the *gato* chant-chorus, the *won agat* shaking an *olwedo* branch as if it were a rattle (*aja*).

They settled down to drink the beer. When this was finished they did the *gato* chant-chorus again, using the second thorn stick in the same way as they had done the first. Then they went home. The *won agat* and his brother demanded as their fee two shillings, a chicken and the meat and skin that had already been taken to their village. The beer dregs would be poured into the bush on the following day.

(*l*) **Lamo tong me two.** I saw the latter half of *lamo tong me two* (blessing a spear for sickness) at Oget near Orumo. For the remainder I had to rely on verbal evidence. The *ajwaka* may prescribe this ceremony for a sick man. It is very similar to the *gato le* ceremony just recorded.

The performer of the ceremony, an old man or an *ajwaka*, takes a black chicken, a kigelia fruit (*yago*), a thorn tree (*okuto*), and *ogudo* leaves, and lays them in front of the sick man's house, while the sick man sits in the doorway. The performer then takes an old spear and does the *lamo* ceremony. He says, 'I draw you right out, a a, right out into the bush. I lay a spell on you with my *ogudo*, with my thorn tree, with my kigelia, with my chicken. I take you right away; leave the body of my embryo (child) that it may be well. I cast a spell on you with the spear with which our ancestors formerly cast spells on sickness, a a, you come right out' (*Akwanyi i kan oko, a a, oko i kan i tim man. Alami ki ogudona, ki okutona, ki yagona, ki gwenona. Akwanyi kan oko iwek kom nyodona obed aber, alami ki tong ma yam kwarowa lamo ki two, a a, i kan oko*).

The performer then takes the spear and makes three cutting motions with it, one on each side of the doorway, and one in the centre in front of the sick man. He makes the motions away from the house. Then he gathers the leaves, chicken and other articles together and takes them off into the bush, either to a patch of forest, or to a large tree, or to a rain-water pool (*atapara*). Here they are left. The sick man is never allowed to pass this spot or he will become ill again.

CHAPTER VII

CEREMONIES CONCERNING TERRITORIAL GROUPS

Before British administration the Lango Clans lived together in a loose, almost anarchic state with no central authority. A local leader by his prowess in war would dominate the Clans in his neighbourhood. These Clans would ally themselves under him for self-protection and he was called *Jago*. A *Jago* who had outstanding successes in warfare would exert an influence over a still wider sphere, and neighbouring *Jagi* would acknowledge their subservience to him, styling him as their *Rwot*. The *Twon Lwak* (bull of the crowd) was a temporary commander-in-chief over several *Rwodi* when, after the festival of *ewor* (p. 71), the Lango would for a short period achieve sufficient tribal unity to organise a raid upon a neighbouring Tribe. It was a military system designed for a Tribe of warriors.

Driberg asserts that this organisation was unrelated to the Clan system. I find this hard to believe. The Clan was the focus of the individual's aspirations. Each Clan had a duly consecrated chief (p. 103), whose duty it was to lead the Clan's team of warriors in battle. It is therefore most unlikely that *Jagi* and *Rwodi* should not at the same time be the chiefs of their respective Clans. I was told repeatedly by my informants that such was the case. They said that the chief of the strongest Clan of a locality became a *Rwot* and appointed as *Jagi* under him the Clan chiefs of the stronger Clans within his sphere of influence, the lesser Clan chiefs being appointed as village guardians. But I think that this is an inaccuracy due to confusion with the modern system. British administration, centralised at Lira, has demarcated the District into twelve *sazas* (counties) under *Rwodi*; each *saza* is divided into a number of *gombololas* (parishes) under *Jagi*; each *gombolola* is split up into divisions under *Wegi Amagoro* (guardians of the waste); under each *Won Amagoro* there are a number of *Wegi Pachi* (guardians of the village).

The difference between the old and the new system is that the new is based on a geographical demarcation of boundaries, while the old was based on self-preservation, local groups of people giving their allegiance to the *Jago* best able to protect them from raids and to lead them on successful expeditions. According to the fortunes of the *Jago* or *Rwot*, so he gained or lost followers.

By virtue of their positions as leaders the *Jago* and *Rwot* would settle inter-Clan quarrels within their spheres of influence. The bonds linking together the members of these spheres of influence were therefore the functions of the chief as arbitrator in disputes and leader in battle. I have found no ceremonies which could be considered as enhancing these links, save the ceremony of consecrating the Clan chief (p. 103). Nor is this to be expected where the territorial group in question was constantly changing its boundaries and was based on the personality of the leader.

The village communities were the more stable territorial groups. The daily work in the fields, the beer drinking and dancing made unifying ceremonies unnecessary. But Driberg records two ceremonies which have a purely village emphasis. The *jo awi dyong* had a ceremony and the ritual associated with the hunt served to link villages.

(*a*) **When lightning strikes a house.** The following is quoted from Driberg's *The Lango* (p. 261):

'The following ritual is observed if a village or any of its inhabitants or property has been struck by lightning, fatally or otherwise. All the spears in the village are rubbed with ashes and at once stuck through the roofs of the houses from the inside, the blades projecting above, in order to threaten the rain and to deter it from further malpractices of this nature. The roots of the erythrina tree are cut up, pounded and mixed with water, which is sprinkled over the village. The houses are also tied to one another with a grass rope. The whole village then dances a bell dance in the village pasturage, accompanied by one drum, the *atimu*, and singing the fire song. The rope and spears are so left until the next new moon, when the inhabitants of a neighbouring village come and take the rope from the houses and remove it to a stream or swamp. Here a he-goat is killed, and the flesh cooked and eaten, except the flesh of the head. The rope, the head of the goat, its bones and skin, are

PLATE IX

The *Jago*'s *Lukiko* at Orumo

Invoking the good will of the bush before the hunt at Chiawanti

buried deep in the marsh. The villagers then remove their spears from the roof.'

I have quoted this in full as all my evidence on the subject did little more than confirm Driberg's account. I saw one village that had been struck a few months previously in Moroto. The grass rope was still up and hanging on it was a small calabash, which was pointed out to me as being important. The whole of this section of the village had been abandoned. The old men of the village said that they had killed a red-coloured chicken at the marsh and left it there. They also said that, should a man be killed by lightning, they bury him in the ordinary way in his sleeping mat in the marsh, all his goods and food being thrown in after him.

On the day following my arrival at Lira a hut in the hospital was struck and a man killed. The hut was never again occupied, and all the patients living in the neighbouring huts fled back to their villages. There is a great fear of lightning, and to swear by lightning is the most solemn oath, for, if a lie is told, it is believed that the perjurer will be killed by lightning.

(b) **Ryemo two.** The following is quoted from Driberg's *The Lango* (p. 56):

'The ceremony known as *ryemo two*, or the driving away of disease, takes place every June, when the millet is ripening, and also at other times on the outbreak of sickness. The ceremony is carried out village by village. In the evening two branches of the tree, *okango*, are cut and placed in the *otem*, or outdoor fireplace. Next evening, just after sunset, the whole village assembles and everyone takes a torch of grass from the thatch of his porch and lights it at the fireplace in his house. Holding the lighted torch in his hand he takes a hide in the other, preferably the hide on which his baby sleeps, as it is thought that the baby's urine with which it is impregnated is a good antitoxin. If there is no baby in the family, any old worn skin (*adwel* as contrasted with *pyen*) may be used. After the ceremony, the hide is returned to the house. Each man beats his hide soundly in his house, waving his torch into all the nooks and crannies. The noise and the lighted torches have in this way frightened the disease out of all the houses in the village, and the whole village escorts it, raising the cry of victory and beating the hides, till it is driven into a river or swamp, from which it cannot return. Ashes from the house fireplace are put in potsherds and calabashes and are left there at the river's brink, and there the next morning the two branches of *okango* are planted. The potsherds and calabashes are sometimes deliberately broken, but are usually left whole. If there is no convenient river, the ceremony may conclude at a crossroads, as the disease will not know which road to take in order to return to the village.'

Again I quote Driberg because any inquiries I made on this question merely substantiated his account. One witness said that, when his village heard of the ceremony being performed in the neighbouring village, they also started the performance, and so the news spread, each village performing the ceremony in turn. But the ceremony is no longer performed annually. It is only resorted to when some epidemic, such as small-pox, comes upon the country.

(*c*) **When opening a new *awi dyang*.** My evidence here is verbal. I once saw chicken feathers hanging over the entrance to a new *awi dyang* (cattle kraal). On making inquiries I was told that, when the cattle first enter a new *awi dyang*, a chicken is killed at the entrance. The *echach* stick belonging to the Clan of the *Won awi dyang* (guardian of the cattle kraal) is placed across the entrance so that the cows step over it when entering the *awi*. All the *jo awi dyang* (people of the kraal) are present at this ceremony.

(*d*) **The hunt.** I record only the ritual details of one of the hunts, in which I took part, and not the actual organisation of the hunt, which does not belong to the sphere of ceremonial. This seems the appropriate place for recording the evidence, since the people of a locality take part in the hunt and it is one of the influences linking members of territorial groups. But the ritual duties of the *Won arum* (guardian of the hunting area) almost place him in the category of medicine-men (*ajwaka*), who are considered in the following chapter.

The country is divided into hunting areas (*arum*). The Lango say that this division was made when the Lango first entered the country. The leaders, who first occupied a locality, claimed it as their *arum*. Each claimant was called the *Won arum* (guardian of the *arum*). The office was hereditary and the *arum* remained the property of the Clan. The functions of the *Won arum* were magical and administrative. But his magical qualifications are more important than his administrative duties. For he alone has magical control over the *arum*. This was brought out very clearly by Philipo Lawottim of Ngai: 'When the British sent a new *Jago* (chief) to rule over the Lango at Ngai, the *Jago* said, "I am *Jago* here and so there cannot be a *Won arum* who is more important than I in the hunt". But when the people went to hunt with the *Jago*, they killed no animals. Then the people complained to the government that they could not kill animals if the *Jago* refused to recognise the *Won arum*. The District Commissioner said that the *Wegi arum* must remain in the positions they had always enjoyed in the land.'

On the night before the hunt the *Won arum* may not have sexual intercourse with his wife. The *Etogo* of the *Won arum* help him in his magical duties by *gato winyo* (laying a spell on luck) on the night before the hunt, when beer is drunk.

I arrived at the house of the *Won arum* of the great Chiawanti hunt when the sun was rising at 6 a.m. The *Won arum* came in from the bush with an *ogudo* root, which he had just dug up. He put it on the fire, by the side of which there were laid five bundles of sticks and leaves. These consisted of: 1. Animal droppings collected on the previous evening and wrapped up in *olwedo* leaves. 2. Sticks for drilling fire. 3. *Rau* grass and an *acher* shrub. 4. An *acher* shrub and an *akalakiu* shrub. 5. A bundle of a shrub called *aleokato* (overcomer of animals).

A boy started to beat a drum to inform the nearby villages that the hunt was about to begin. I went with the *Won arum* to the village of the neighbouring *ajwaka*. We went into his house. He put some cold water into a calabash (*agwata*). Placing another *agwata* on the ground inverted, he sprinkled it with water, spat on it twice and then balanced the calabash of water on it. He squatted in the corner with his back towards us and started to shake his rattle (*aja*). After half a minute resounding noises came from the corner. These were like the sounds from a toy siren. The *ajwaka* obviously made them with his mouth. Between each boom of noise a voice spoke giving instructions to the *Won arum* in jerky, gruff tones, the rattling sounding all the time. The *Won arum* was told to dig up two small *olwedo* plants and two *enwewe* plants, and to take these with him on the hunt. When the hunt was over the *Won arum* must bring a large shoulder of meat for the *ajwaka*, then many animals would be killed. The *ajwaka* had himself spoken all this in a gruff staccato voice, which was supposed to be the voice of *jok*. When he had finished, he turned round and repeated *jok*'s instructions, reminding the *Won arum* to bring a large shoulder of meat. We then went back to the *Won arum*'s village.

The *Won arum* collected some water from his house in a long-necked calabash (*apoko*). He gave the five bundles, described above, to a man to carry and we set off. As we went the *Won arum* collected the two *olwedo* and *enwewe* plants. He also added two *lot kwon* saplings. A boy beat a drum to inform the surrounding villages. The *Won arum* continually ran aside off the path to collect plants. These were all plants which were particularly favoured by animals as food. A man was sent on a short detour to collect earth from a salt lick, which they said was used by the animals of the *arum*.

We met the party coming from the opposite direction at the traditional place under a large *atek* tree. A friend of the *Won arum* took the earth obtained from the salt lick and moistened it with water from the *apoko* calabash. Then, breaking off a piece, he fashioned a lion out of it. Taking this lion carefully between finger and thumb, he went with the *Won arum* and another old man in the direction opposite to that in which the hunters were to advance. He carefully placed the lion model underneath a clump of grass facing away from the hunt. The three of them said, 'Run, run over there. We don't want you in the hunt to spoil it'. They told me that now we were certain not to meet any lion in the hunt.

Returning to the *atek* tree, the man made a ball out of the remainder of the salt lick mud. He placed it on the ground and covered it with *ogudo* leaves. Some of the thorn tree (*okuto*) was placed near by. They said that we must now wait till the other hunters arrived. Groups of men arrived continually and soon the same old man and the *Won arum* went back to the

CEREMONIES CONCERNING TERRITORIAL GROUPS 151

mud ball. They moulded out of the mud a man and a woman, and then all the animals likely to be met in the hunt—*alop, atil, akal, amor*, etc. Two rhino were also fashioned. Each animal had a calf. These figures were placed facing in the direction of the hunt with the man and woman behind 'to drive them'. Taking a piece of dry grass stalk, an old man violently stabbed the rhino pair, saying, 'Thus shall you die'. He placed them on their sides in front of the other animals, leaving the grass 'spears' in them. All those who had helped to model the animals now sat in a circle with spears on the ground pointing to the centre of the circle, where the mud animals were. The bundle of game droppings covered with *olwedo* leaves was put in front of the models and was opened up slightly in the direction in which the hunt was to proceed.

All the hunters now lined up behind the animals, facing in the direction of the hunt with spears pointing forwards. An old man proceeded to lay a spell over the hunt or bush (*gato dwar, gato tim*). This consisted of sentences spoken by the leader, the last words of which would be repeated in chorus by the company, as occurs at all *gato* ceremonies. The old man shouted towards the area that was to be hunted sentences of the following nature: 'Bush be peaceful. . . . If there is much slaughter, good.' (Chorus) 'Good' (see Plate IX at p. 146). This continued for about ten minutes. Meanwhile the *Won arum* went up and down the line of hunters, who lunged forward with their spears at each chorus. He touched their spear-points with the other four bundles of leaves and sticks. Another man touched the spear-heads with a branch of *okuto* thorn tree and the men on the flanks of the hunt were given pieces of *okuto* with which to touch the spears of late-comers.

The *Won arum* and his friend gave instructions where everyone was to go and the direction in which to proceed. The plan was to form a semicircle, about two miles or more in circumference, and drive the animals into a large marsh where most of the killing would be done. We then set off with much excitement and the blowing of hunting whistles. Those in the middle of the line, and anyone else who wished, stepped over the mud animals and speared an animal with a piece of grass as they passed. During this performance a man covered the figures of the man and woman with his hands to prevent their being speared accidentally. They said that the models of the man and woman were made and protected in this way so that no one would be speared accidentally in the hunt. They said that, if this had been the first hunt in the season, they would have done a ceremony with a grass rope. The rope would be held by the line of hunters and at a command each man would cut it with his spear and carry off his severed section with him to the hunt (cf. *The Lango*, p. 113). The animals would not be able to pierce the cordon after this ceremony.

The *Won arum* and others had strings round their necks with a number of small sticks strung on. These were their private hunting charms (*yat me dwar*). One boy had some *bomo* round his wrist 'for the hunt', though he was not a twin nor had his mother borne twins. One old man had *tanga* paste on his chest 'for the hunt'. He was the father of twins. The *apoko* calabash of water, previously mentioned, was carefully corked up with leaves and a man carried it all through the hunt. They said that rain would not fall during the hunt if this was done. But at the end of the hunt the water was poured out carefully into the lake, so that the rain would come to water their crops at the correct time. Were they to pour the water out carelessly anywhere, the rains would be sure to fail.

The details of this ritual illustrate the important part played in Lango religion by sympathetic magic. The symbolic spearing of the animals, the symbolic expulsion of the lion, the symbolic protecting of the man and woman, and the symbolic cordon of grass rope are religious actions very typical of Lango psychology.

CHAPTER VIII

CEREMONIES CONCERNING MEDICINE-MEN

The ceremonies I have described in the foregoing chapters are all of a stereotyped nature. They comprise certain set ritual forms constructed from the elements of magical ritual.

The *ajwaka*, or medicine-man, can use these ritual elements with greater freedom and by this means he can create impromptu and involved ceremonies, which at the same time conform to the logic of Lango ceremonial structure. Some of the ceremonies I witnessed are too long and tedious to be described minutely and I will give mere summaries of them. Where detailed description seems necessary I will record the proceedings exactly as I saw them.

Whereas the ceremonies already described serve to maintain the social structure of the Lango groups, the ceremonies of the *ajwaka* are essentially of a magical nature. As such they are even more important as evidence of the interpretation of Lango religion which I have given in Chapter I.

(a) **Exorcising of *jok nam*.** Atim, who lived at Awei near Aduku, suffered from fits which were diagnosed as a *jok* disease. The *ajwaka*, Odur, had previously been cured of the same disease by a Munyoro man from the lake and therefore he knew the technique of *jok nam*. The rambling ceremony which he performed lasted for two days.

Atim, clad in serval skins and wreathed with *bomo*, went with the *ajwaka* and his women helpers to an ant-hill, in which Atim always found good grinding stones. No one else was able to find such stones there, which proved that Atim's *jok* power was associated with the ant-hill in some manner. Here they started chanting endless songs to the monotonous rhythm of rattles (*aja*). This was continued in front of Atim's doorway, the singers sitting in a semicircle while she sat in the centre. The monotony of the rhythm produced an hypnotic effect on Atim, who began to jerk her body about in time to it. Then she began to make hoarse grunting noises in her chest. Suddenly she fell over and lay straight outstretched. The singing and rattling stopped and they all said, 'Her *obanga* comes' (*obanga mere obino*). The state of dissociation into which she had fallen signified to the onlookers that she was now possessed by her *jok* power. [They used the terms *obanga* and *jok* indiscriminately.] The *ajwaka*'s chief helper, who was referred to as *atin jok* (child of *jok*), also became dissociated, or pretended to be so, and the two of them continued to shuffle about and do absurd things for some time, including a fight underneath a blanket (see Plate X at p. 154).

The *ajwaka* demonstrated his control over *jok* power by causing two shilling pieces to stick to the vertical wall of Atim's house. 'Look, Bwana,' he cried, 'this is my work. I love my work. By putting these shillings like this I earn much money. By this means I have bought this wife of mine and I will buy another.' I tried to put the shillings on the wall, but failed. The people said, '*Jok* does not like him, he does not accept him'. Then they said, '*Jok*, why do you not accept Bwana? We ask you to accept him.' The *ajwaka* said, 'It is because I have not held his hands'. Enclosing my hands in his, he said, '*Jok* will accept you now'. By this time I had discovered the trick, which was to balance the coin on some small fibre projecting from the wall. I did this and they shouted, 'Look, *jok* accepts him'. The *ajwaka* then proceeded to divine the future by throwing cowrie shells.

Part of the twin ceremonial was performed in front of the twin house (*ot rudi*), for Atim had borne twins and it was thought that the *jok* power of the twins might have caused her fits.

Dissociated states were again induced in Atim and another woman by means of rattling and chanting. This was done inside the house, which the *ajwaka* filled with an incense-like smoke by burning some herbs on a potsherd. Atim first started to jerk her body to the rhythm, but suddenly the other woman howled and fell to the ground. '*Jok* is killing her', whispered the *Won amagoro* to me. She shook and moaned and hopped about. The *ajwaka* bent the woman's head from side to side. She put her hand to her mouth several times and ate some beer dough that was handed her in a calabash. Atim then started

PLATE X

At Atim's exorcising ceremony

Omara preparing pots for catching *tipo*s

the same performance. From now on these two women were the principal actors. Some herbs were rubbed on the woman's neck and she asked for the *ajwaka*'s helper's necklaces. These she put round the *Won amagoro*'s neck, saying that the *Won amagoro* was the darling of her *jok*. She asked for water to be brought. With this she washed the *Won amagoro*'s legs and face. Then she started to abuse the people, saying, 'Semen in your mother's ears'. This is a very bad term of abuse and always leads to a fight. The women asked, 'Why does she abuse us?' and she replied, 'It is the *jok* that is abusing you'. Then Atim suddenly began to talk. 'Listen you people, listen. I am alone and in poverty, in great poverty' (*winyunu, winyunu. An abedo keno kedi chan, kedi chan madwong*). She wept and huge tears fell down her cheek. Later they asked her her name and she gave a name. They asked the name of the husband and child. Okuja, my boy, recorded this in his notebook as follows. 'The *ajwaka* asked the *jok* in the body of Atim in this manner, "What is the name of your husband?" Atim said, "The wind in my body says that his name is Okomo". The *ajwaka* cried out, "See, see. Thank you, thank you very much."'

The whole of this scene was exactly like a spiritualist séance, the identity of the spirit in possession of Atim being established by asking its name and the names of its husband and child. It is significant that the term *tipo* was never used in connection with this controlling spirit, which was referred to as her *jok*, although it was obviously the spirit of someone who had been alive and was known to those present. But Atim did refer to it as the 'wind in her body' (*yamo i kome*).

On the following day some more twin ceremonial was performed, chiefly in connection with the killing of a goat.

It was clear that Atim had had much of this type of ceremonial performed on her before, and that she was already practising as an *ajwaka*. Odur had obviously initiated her, and soon she would become a full-blown *ajwaka* of *jok nam*.

(*b*) **Mako tipo.** I saw the *ajwaka*, Omara, give two elaborate performances of *mako tipo* (catching a *tipo*), also known as *umo tipo* (covering a *tipo*), at Achungi near Aduku. Driberg also mentions it (*The Lango*, p. 232).

If a man is ill as a result of what he believes to be a *tipo* visitation, instead of summoning the *Etogo* (Chapter v), he may engage the services of an *ajwaka* to entrap the spirit in a pot. Most *ajwaka* know how to perform the ceremony, but certain of them tend to specialise in it, as was the case with Omara. Besides being rewarded for his services, the *ajwaka* and his Clan receive the meat of the bull which is killed on this occasion. The lure of the meat attracts women to the ceremony, especially the *ajwaka*'s female helpers (*otino jogi* = children of *jok*).

First it is necessary to discover whose *tipo* has entered the patient's body, has 'seized' his body. This information is obtained by exactly the same technique as in the ceremony just recorded. A state of semi-dissociation is induced in the patient by means of endless chanting to the monotonous rhythm of rattles, the house being filled with incense-like fumes from burning herbs. This is done by the *ajwaka*'s helpers. The patient begins to jerk his body to the rhythm and then blurts out the name of a dead relation, whose *tipo* is thus branded as the culprit. In one of the ceremonies I witnessed the patient started to speak in a gruff voice, saying, 'I am very angry. I want meat.' The people assured the *tipo*, who had spoken through the sick man's lips, that there would be meat in plenty and beer and dancing, but first he must tell them his name, as many people had died recently in the village and they wanted to know whose *tipo* was causing all the trouble. There was a pause for fifteen minutes and then the sick man, making loud groaning noises, croaked out three names. His sister, who was also being treated, called out one name. The *ajwaka* said that the man had three *tipo*s in him and the woman one. I believe that this process is similar to the technique of the psycho-analyst. The dead relation is on the patient's mind, either as a result of grief or through a bad conscience due to a quarrel with him during life. His name is brought up in much the same manner as a free association. Dreams of a dead relation are a sure sign that this relation's *tipo* is the cause of the dreamer's illness.

After ascertaining the name or names of the *tipo* or *tipo*s in the patient there is a pause, during which small pots according to the number of *tipo*s are prepared for trapping them (see Plate X at p. 154). A sheep or goat's skin is stretched over the mouth of the pot, leaving a flap of skin sufficient to cover the pot a second time, and a hole about two inches in diameter is cut in the first layer of skin. Mud from the marsh is mixed with grass and plastered round the pot, and a mud cover is made.

A bull is killed and bits of meat and beer are placed in the pot to attract the *tipo*, which is very suspicious and yet very greedy. Dried banana leaves are put in the pot, the crackling of which will show that the *tipo* is dancing about inside the pot and so is securely caught.

The rattling and singing again induce a state of semi-dissociation in the patient, who, at the climax of his excitement, bends down and expectorates the *tipo* through his lips into the pot through the hole in the skin. The skin flap and the cover are clapped over the hole, while the patient's mouth, nose and ears are stopped up to prevent the *tipo* from jumping back at the last moment. The patient is carried in a state of collapse to the granary, where he is revived with cold water.

The cover of the pot is then plastered on securely with marsh mud. The pot is placed near the doorway and a plume of grass is stuck into the top of it. The rattling and singing recommence to encourage the *tipo* to dance in the pot. This is denoted by the grass moving, which is usually effected by a convenient gust of wind.

The *ajwaka* buries the pot secretly in the bush. The *tipo* is thus finally trapped and will not afflict the living any further.

(c) **Kwanyo.** It is a most common belief in Lango that pains in any part of the body are due to some substance, such as a piece of charcoal, wood, stone, a nail, that has been 'thrown' into the body of the sufferer by an *ajok* (sorcerer). It is further believed that the *ajwaka* can cure this pain by extracting (*kwanyo*) the offending object. He does this by cutting the place and sucking out the object, or by extracting it with his hand, or in some other miraculous manner. He then rubs the juice of some root or herb into the cuts. This is painful and is clearly a counter-irritant, which detracts from the pain of the swollen part. I saw many performances of this, but will describe only a few of the more striking cases. It is clear that the display of magical power by the *ajwaka* in extracting the foreign body sets up a powerful auto-suggestion in the patient. But some other herbal remedy is also given internally or externally.

1. *Curing of earache.* At A'auroga near Nabieso a female *ajwaka* named Atala was treating a woman for earache. This woman had been treated before, but not having recovered had returned for a longer treatment. They said that she had a 'bird in her ears' (*winyo i ite*), which buzzed in her head all the time. Twice a day the *ajwaka* carried out the healing process, which she proceeded to show me.

The *ajwaka* fetched something from the granary. She gave some roots to a child together with some instructions. Then, preceded by her patient, who carried an aluminium pot of water and a calabash (*wal*), she went off to her ant-hill about three hundred yards from the village.

She took two *ochoga* leaves that had been placed in a tree stump and told the patient to sit near a hole that had been dug in the ant-hill. Pouring water into the calabash she began to wash the patient's ear. She threw water into the ear and slapped it with her hand. Then she began to blow into the ear, softly at first and then harder and harder. Her right hand was round the patient's ear and her left hand supported the patient's head. Suddenly she let go of the patient's head and produced a piece of charcoal from the patient's ear. It was an inch long and a quarter of an inch thick and broad. She held it between the thumb and index finger of her right hand. She squeezed it well and then laid it on one of the *ochoga* leaves.

The same process was carried out on the other ear. It was clear to me that the pieces of charcoal had been in her mouth and that she spat them into her hand when blowing into the patient's ear. She had probably placed them in her mouth in the village when she went to the granary. It was well done and I did not see the charcoal pass from her mouth to her hand, though my boy, Okuja, said that he did see this. The two bits of charcoal were thrown into the hole in the ant-hill. She called the bits of charcoal 'birds' (*winyo*). Then she washed the patient's ears well with the *ochoga* leaves. The patient washed her own face in the water and we went back to the village.

The patient returned to the village with reluctance and the reason soon became apparent. The child brought a leaf, which he had twisted into the shape of a funnel. The pounded root was in the funnel. Water was added and the child squeezed it into the patient's ear. The first ear did not trouble her much, but the second gave her great pain and she continued to howl for half an hour. This process was carried out twice a day, so the patient must have suffered considerably.

When the girl was healed her husband would bring a goat and ten shillings as payment. But if he were a rich man, he might bring as much as forty shillings. The goat is killed and eaten by the *ajwaka* and the patient together with their husbands, and a necklace of the skin is placed round the patient's neck.

2. *Curing of stomach-ache.* Akau of Anwongi near Nabieso was a female *ajwaka*. She was referred to as a 'great *ajwaka*' (*ajwaka madwong*) and also as 'mother of *jok* power' (*min jok*: probably this is best rendered as 'source of *jok* power').

She took some medicine (*yat*) consisting of a powdery substance wrapped up in a banana leaf, some water in an aluminium pot and a calabash (*wal*). All these she placed outside the village at the spot where her last house had stood. She also had a small broom about nine inches long. She asked me to hold the medicine.

The patient was an infant suffering from some form of stomach-ache. It had been taken to the Aduku dispensary without being cured, and so the mother had now brought it to Akau.

The mother held the baby on her lap while the *ajwaka* made eight cuts in its stomach with a sharp knife, drawing blood in the process. She filled the calabash with water and told me to drop the medicine into it. Then she splashed the mixture with her broom all over the child. When it was finished she pointed to jelly-like substances that covered the body of mother and child. These, she said, had come out of the infant's stomach through the cuts.

The *ajwaka*, who had been a mother of twins, said that she had learnt this method of curing from the 'wind' (*yamo*) that came into her body. This happened sometime before when she was very ill and nearly died. She dreamed at that time that, if she cut her body and treated it with this medicine, she would be saved. Since then she has been able to save anyone who had a disease characterised by stomach-ache.

I returned to her village again that evening and found that she had a woman and two babies to treat in the same manner. She cut the heads and bodies of the infants and the woman with her knife, put the medicine in the water and started her splashing. I managed to steal some of the medicine. The bodies of the patients again became covered with jelly-like globules which seemed to me to be frog-spawn. On returning home I placed the medicine in water and the small black seeds immediately swelled up into globules. [I had thought that the *ajwaka* collected frog-spawn, dried it in the sun and mixed it with other herbs to make her medicine, the dried eggs swelling up again when placed in water. But I have since discovered in India a type of hollyhock seed which swells up in this manner, and is used as a poultice and internally as a cure for dysentry. I now believe that some such seed was used by Akau.] The *ajwaka* says that the globules have come out of the patient's body through the cuts, and that they are the cause of the pain. It is interesting to note that the globules were thought to come out of the mother, who was not ill, as well as her infant. This is another illustration of the fact that a mother and baby are thought to be one person (p. 131).

After this preliminary conjuring trick I went with the *ajwaka* to find some more medicine. This was real medicine, which had to be eaten by the patients. When she found the plant, she told me to hold the hoe in my hands while she did the first stroke of the digging. This was for my good health (*kom yot*). Then she dug up the roots of the plant. She told me to chew these roots, which I was told was done by all Lango when suffering from stomach-ache. She also dug up a bulb, which is used by the Lango to rub into cuts on the body for healing purposes, especially for headaches. These roots and bulbs were given to the patients. The mothers chewed the roots, which they would also pound up and mix with water to give to their babies.

All those present were loud in their praises of the *ajwaka*. They said that she effected thousands of cures, and she said to me, 'This may seem a simple process to you, but I *do* cure many people by it and they come to me from all over Lango'. The *ajwaka* would be paid six shillings for this piece of work when the patient had recovered, but nothing if the patient did not recover. She said that the healing process I had witnessed was a very small affair and that she did much bigger cures. She spoke always with a pronounced air of authority. When she wanted the patients to come to her, she sent someone to call them, saying, 'Tell them that I, the *ajwaka*, call them'.

3. *Curing pain in the knee.* Achen, who lived at Agwichiri near Chiawanti, was referred to as 'mother of *jok* power' (*min jok*). She was a twin and had been born with one breast. She did not even have a nipple on the right side.

A man with a painful knee was produced. The *ajwaka* put water into a calabash. With this she washed out her mouth and washed the patient's knee. She made the patient throw some water over her. Then she made two cuts in his knee with a small sharp knife. She sucked these cuts, and on lifting her mouth there were two pieces of charcoal resting on the cuts, which she said she had sucked out. She did this three times, on each occasion producing two pieces of charcoal from the cuts.

The *ajwaka* said that these things got into a person through an *ajok* (sorcerer) throwing (*bolo*) them into him. It was very painful and could only be cured by this process of *kwanyo*.

About half a mile from this *ajwaka*'s house there lived another female *ajwaka* also called Achen. She was not a twin, but had once given birth to premature twins. She had only one eye and her teeth protruded in a repellent manner.

She carried out exactly the same process as that just described on another man's knee. She said that she always demanded immediate payment, her fee being six shillings. If a person stayed with her for a long time to undergo treatment and was finally cured, her fee might be thirty shillings.

4. *Curing sore throat.* A female *ajwaka* at Abiloro near Nabieso cut slits in her patient's throat and sucked out pieces of stone in the same manner as already described. She said that her fee was one shilling in the first instance, with a further six shillings when the person was cured. This *ajwaka* was a mother of twins.

In all these cases the *ajwaka* must have been well aware of the deception practised on the patients. In the sucking processes it was clear to me that the *ajwaka* had concealed the objects in her mouth. This was very obvious, but *Rwot* Ogwalajungu said to me that he knew very well when an *ajwaka* was tricking them, for she would not wash out her mouth properly before starting. It was obvious, he said, that these women who had demonstrated to us did not deceive us by concealing things in their mouths, for they had washed out their mouths so carefully.

Though the *ajwaka* knows that he is deceiving his patient with the conjuring trick, he also regards this conjuring trick as an essential part of the cure. This is indeed so, for the chief aspect of native cures is the psychological. It is only in modern times that the *ajwaka* has tended to demand payment before the cure, so it cannot be said that he practised his deceit purely for gain.

Driberg pointed out to me that fire is associated with *jok* power and hence no doubt the use of charcoal (dead fire) in these cases. This is a point well worth noting.

(*d*) **Visits to the villages of Atworo and Oming.** Bunga-kelalyek near Ngai is the village of an *ajwaka* named Odok. When people refer to this place, they talk of the great *ajwaka* or *min jok* Atworo, Odok being considered merely as the interpreter of Atworo. No one has seen the body of Atworo and they do not know if it is male or female.

Odok took me into his house, which was arranged as in Plate XI at p. 162. Odok squatted in the corner marked ×. I sat at the spot marked *A* and Philipo Lawottim and the other man, who accompanied me, sat at *B* and *C*. The rest of the people sat in the part of the house marked with dots, so that they could not see Odok sitting in his corner, as the L-shaped wall intervened.

Sitting in his corner with his back towards us, Odok began to call out at the wall, 'Atworo, Atworo great one' many times. Then he said, 'Come quickly, Atworo, for the people want to go away'. After a quarter of an hour of these preliminaries Atworo began to speak. It was clearly Odok speaking in a gruff, staccato voice. He spoke very fast, always starting with 'i, i' or 'ai, ai'. Atworo would say, 'i, i, you come to me?' and the people would reply, 'Yes, we come'. Odok's whole body shook with the effort of speaking in the assumed voice,

PLATE XI

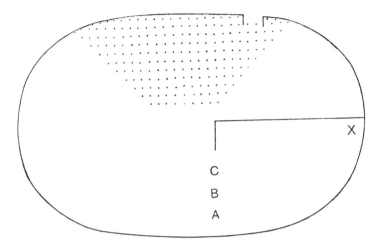

Ground plan of the houses of Atworo and Oming

Cleaning cotton in the village

though there was no attempt at ventriloquism. Philipo Lawottim mentioned this to me, saying that it was obviously Odok speaking. But the people could not see Odok, because of the L-shaped wall, and it appeared to 'them to be another person talking.

The people assembled in the house now began to put questions to Atworo. One man said that his wife's children died one after the other, and that she had aborted twins. He wanted to know what to do. The man said that he had previously been to Oming, but had not benefited. Atworo asked for full details and having received them said that the disease from which the man's wife was suffering was like plague. He told him to come another time and he would tell him what to do. Another man said that his sister's daughter suffered from a disease which made all her body shiver. Atworo told the man to tell her husband to come to him and he would give him medicine. Another man asked why rain never fell on his fields, while it fell on his neighbours' fields. Atworo asked whether the man had brought any presents for him, for if he had not, Atworo would not send him any rain. The man said that he would bring some sesame later. I then asked if the hunt on the following day would be successful. Atworo said that many animals would be killed, but rain would wet us all. Atworo said that he would now go with us to visit Oming.

The people said that Atworo lived in the bush and only came when called by Odok. He had been there for many years, but was only known through Odok. In other words Odok had started the cult of Atworo. Odok was about forty-five years old. Under the *olam* tree in the *otem* of Odok's village there were an *abila*, an *ot rudi*, and the skull of a hartebeest. The *abila* had been built long ago, they said, for success in the hunt. [After this the ceremony of *atin akwer* was performed as described above (p. 135).]

Oming's village was about six miles from Atworo's. Oming held exactly the same position as Atworo and the *ajwaka* who interpreted him was a man named Gira.

Gira consented to call up Oming for me. The plan of his house and the whole performance were exactly the same as those in the case of Atworo, so that it is not necessary for me to repeat them.

The diagram (Plate XI, p. 162) of the house is identical for the two *ajwaka*s. Oming, having been called up by Gira, spoke in the same staccato voice. I asked whether my mother was well. Oming said that she was very well and was at peace in her village in England. She happened to be having a very serious operation and was in Ceylon at the time. I then asked if the hunt on the following day would be successful. Oming said that we should kill many animals and also a large lion, but that no one would be hurt by the lion. [This actually occurred on the following day and, having speared the lion, the hunters thanked me for having gained the help of Oming.]

The people said that Oming spoke from the ground. He usually lived in a tree in the forest. But often he just remained anywhere in the forest or in the wind. They said that at Inomo near Aduku there used to be a very great Atworo (*Atworo madwong*). This Atworo heard that there was no *ajwaka* at Ngai. So he sent for Onyang, who was an ancestor of his. Onyang came to Atworo with food and Atworo sent his two sons, Atworo and Oming, to Ngai with Onyang. This is how Oming and Atworo came to be there. The two *jok*s announced their names in the first instance through their interpreters. Before Gira's time his mother, Angwen, did the interpreting. But Odok was the first to start Atworo. They said that Atworo and Oming were nothing to do with ancestors. Each one was a *jok*.

I had heard great stories about Oming from all parts of Lango. Each informant had said that Oming was a very great *ajwaka*, for he spoke from the ground and no one had seen his body. I had suspected ventriloquism. Gira was never mentioned in connection with Oming, and they did not seem to think that he was very important.

Philipo Lawottim said that he did not believe in Atworo or Oming. But he said that Gira undoubtedly knew a great number of medicines which cured people. 'They are just like your doctors, who sometimes cure us and at other times are unsuccessful.'

It seemed to me that Oming had existed for many years, probably beyond the memory of any living person, as they said that Oming had always been there. Atworo was an upstart. Odok had either bought the secret from Gira, or had discovered the secret and copied him. Both Gira and Odok were very rich men as a result of their practices.

(e) **Curing by means of jok nam.** I was going from Ngai to Achaba to see a ceremony, when I heard that they were 'singing for jok' (*wawero jok*) at Abonyamomkato. I went to the village and found the husband of one of the initiates building the framework of a beehive hut. It had two doorways, one facing the man's house and the other facing into the bush. He said that they were singing for *jok nam* or *jok abani* (*wawero jok abani*). The two women concerned were having their heads shaved by the *ajwaka* at the marsh. They said that I could not go to see this process.

I went on to Achaba and returned in the evening. A special kind of dance was going on. The two initiates and the other women, who were dancing, wore serval skins and held spears pointing towards the ground. The necks of these spears had spiral twists. The dancers gazed at the ground all the time and never looked up.

The beehive hut had been completely thatched in the Bantu manner. The entrance that faced into the village had a porch over it, but not the one facing the bush. They called it *ot jok* (house of *jok*). A goat and a chicken had been killed at each entrance. Grass was spread on the floor inside. Parts of the goat and the plucked chicken were placed over each doorway.

At the end of each dance the women would dash into the *ot jok*. The two initiates would sit on the laps of the women who were instructing. The initiates were called *otino jogi* (children of *jok*), while the instructors were called *wayo jok* (drawers out of *jok*). The female *ajwaka*, who was directing the whole performance, was called *min jok*.

I returned to the village on the following morning. They were singing and dancing to the rhythm of rattles. This was the same as on the previous evening, and they would dash into the *ot jok* in the same manner. Then they lined up in a kneeling position in front of the *ot jok* and blankets were put over their heads. In this state they jerked about to the rhythm. I was told that this was the dance for *jok obanga*, while the spear dance had been for *jok odudi*. The entrance of the *ot jok* which faced inwards was for *jok odudi*, the other was for *jok obanga*. They said that *jok odudi* was a sickness that attacks the back and neck, while *jok obanga* attacks the chest.

They had started this dancing six days before. This was the last day of the ceremony and the *ajwaka* together with her helpers (*wayo jok*) would go home. The *wayo jok* were women who had already been cured by the *ajwaka*. In a year's time the two initiates would be able to divine (*tyeto*) like the *ajwaka*. A spear (*tong jok*) was left in the *ot jok*, and the two initiates would sleep in the *ot jok* until the full moon was out in about a fortnight's time. The *ot jok* will always be kept in good repair.

They said that the two initiates were not ill. They had ceased to bear children and, having divined at the *ajwaka's* (*tyeto bang ajwaka*), they were told that *jok nam* was preventing them from bearing. Therefore they were undergoing this ceremony, which was to draw the *jok* power out of them and so give them control over it. One of the initiates had borne twins some time back, and so the ceremony was finished off with a twin dance and anointing with *tanga* paste at the *ot rudi*.

(*f*) **Curing by means of *jok lango*.**   I saw this at Abonya-momkato directly after the proceedings just recorded. It took place in the house of one of the initiates. In her house there was a structure just like the *ot rudi* and similarly built of *okango* wood erected near the wall. It was called *peto okango* (*okango* spread out), and was for *jok lango*. She said that the disease of *jok lango* was recognised chiefly by pains in the stomach. The same *ajwaka* had initiated this woman into the mysteries of *jok lango*.

On the structure there were some beer dough and one of the chickens that had been killed in the previous ceremony. The woman then agreed to divine (*tyeto*) for me. She took from the structure a calabash containing a number of pencil-shaped pieces of wood, about eight inches long, and four solid round cylinders of wood, two inches in diameter and four inches high. She made these wet and then balanced the sticks in four clumps on the four cylinders of wood. One stick fell off, and they said that this signified that a man would die. The *ajwaka* broke this stick in half and threw it away. The sticks balanced as a result of their shape. Each stick tapered into a point and was so shaped that a bunch of them formed a cone-like mass that balanced comparatively easily. But the effect was fairly remarkable.

The woman then swept all round the structure. Her husband placed a calabash on the ground with the rounded side uppermost. He balanced another calabash of water on top of this. Then he explained that if the sticks refused to balance, the disease of the inquirer was *jok nam*, which was represented by the calabashes. If the calabashes refused to balance, the disease was that of *jok lango*, as represented by the sticks.

The woman, on account of her inexperience, was too shy to divine in front of me. The *ajwaka* chided her and then took the rattle (*aja*) herself. She turned her back on us and rattled by the *jok lango* structure. She soon began to speak in an assumed voice, which they said was the voice of *jok lango*. The *ajwaka* said that this *jok* lived in the earth of the wall of the house.

(g) **Some other ajwakas.** 1. *Akelo of Kibuji*. Akelo lived near the Kibuji ginnery. She was referred to as *min jok* and was very famous. When I arrived there were many people assembled in her courtyard from as far away as Lira. She was in particular a specialist in curing sterility.

I sat down in her house and she sat on the ground in front of me. She then started to belch very loudly, which impressed the spectators. She shouted out questions at me in a very loud voice. She said that my wife had miscarried some time ago and had previously borne twins, and that my brother had been put into prison through the chief's jealousy at his success in his work.

A woman then came in and was treated for childbirth. Her previous child had miscarried. Akelo dipped *olwedo* leaves in water and sprinkled the woman with it. Akelo questioned her all the time and then smeared her with ashes. Then she made the woman smear ashes on herself, Akelo. When the next child was born, the woman was to bring Akelo thirty shillings as payment. She was also given some medicine to drink.

Throughout the proceedings with me and the woman, Akelo constantly divined by throwing a pair of sandals into the air and reading the result from the positions they adopted on the ground.

2. Min jok *at Ayala.* As I passed Ayala I saw a crowd of people dancing. I was told that they were dancing for a sick man. The man was produced and it looked as if he was suffering from pneumonia.

In the village there was an *ot abani.* This consisted of a bee-hive structure with flounced thatching and with two doors, each having a porch. An *ajwaka* was in charge of affairs. She was new to the job but was referred to as *min jok.* She said that the door of the *ot abani* which faced into the village was the door by which the *jok* inside the sick man entered the *ot abani,* while the door facing into the bush was the one by which the *jok* went out into the bush and so left the man.

The *ajwaka* said that *jok orongo* had seized the man as his brother had killed a leopard recently. She said that all the fierce animals and large-sized buck could send their *tipos* to give you *jok orongo,* if you killed them. Yet the people said that they were singing for *jok nam (wawero jok nam).* The whole ceremony was also obviously to do with *jok nam—ot abani,* serval skins, etc. [This shows that there is much looseness in ceremonies, for *jok nam* is here used to exorcise *jok orongo,* which was everywhere said to be a manifestation of *jok lango.* Whether this looseness belongs to the new conditions and the decay of the old Lango culture, or whether it is an example of a principle which I have not fully understood, I am not able to say. The people, when questioned more closely, said that *jok orongo* was *jok nam.* I never heard this anywhere else in Lango, and Driberg agreed with me that it is impossible.]

There was a two-mouthed pot (*dogaryo*) in the *ot abani.* The dancing and singing continued from 5 p.m. to 8 p.m. It recommenced on the following day at dawn and was to continue for the whole day, I was told. At the end of the day the *ajwaka* with some of her helpers would drive the disease away with their spears. The dancers wore serval skins, but they did not dance with spears. The sick man would pay the dancers ten shillings each when he recovered.

3. Ajwaka *at Alito.* I was taken to see an *abila* near Alito. The man who had built the *abila* said that he had once been

very ill. He had called a *min jok* to help him. She said that the *tipo*s of his father and brother had seized his body. So she built an *abila* for him of *odugo* wood, and in his house she built a *jok lango* structure of *okango* wood. He is now able to divine (*tyeto*) at this structure and *jok* speaks to him from the ground telling him what cures to give to the people who consult him.

(*h*) **Dreams.** 1. *The* Jago *of Nabieso.* Philipo Oruro, *Jago* of Nabieso, used to record his dreams in writing and used to interpret them. *Rwot* Ogwalajungu told me that some day the *Jago* would become a famous *ajwaka*, because the interpretation of his dreams always came true. This proved that he had the elements of an *ajwaka* in his head.

The *Jago* gave me some indications of the principles which he followed in interpreting dreams. He said that, if you wanted something to happen, you would not dream that it had happened. For instance, if you wanted very much to go to Kampala, you would not dream about it directly, but you would dream of some incident that would happen to you on the way to Kampala. If you dream that something happens to you, this means that it will happen to someone else. But if you dream of it happening to someone else, this means that it will happen to you. While I was waiting outside my sleeping quarters at Achaba near Nabieso, a summons was brought to the *Jago*. It was for a debt of twenty shillings due to a bicycle repairer at Lira. The *Jago* said that he had already paid the bill and held the receipt for it. Then he said, 'I know that I will win this case, for last night I dreamed that an elephant came and trod on my house to break it. But I escaped with a clean body. This dream refers to this case and so I know that I will escape it.' The *Jago* then said that when a person goes to sleep, his *tipo* goes to *obanga*, who tells it things, and these are the dreams that come to him.

The *Jago* is a very intelligent man. He is well educated and a Christian. It seems to me that his interpretations are based on analogy. Intelligence consists largely in being able to see the analogy between two different circumstances. Joseph's power in Egypt was based on this ability. The psycho-analysts work on very similar principles.

I have the full text of the *Jago*'s dreams, but they are not of very much value, except as showing how heavily the affairs of administration and fear of the District Commissioner hang upon the mind of a native chief. Should any reader wish to see these dreams I will willingly lend him my notes.

2. *Rodia of Aloro.* Rodia was an old woman who gave me much information at Aloro. She said that she often dreamed that she flew up into the air and saw the ground miles below her. Then she would start to fall and she felt terrified. But she always woke up before hitting the ground. She said that people think this to be a good dream. It is bad to dream of raw meat. It is good to dream of sweet potatoes. If you dream that you are pregnant, it refers to someone else. If you dream of someone who is dead, you yourself will die, for this is his *tipo* seizing your body. Sometimes a man dreams that the *tipo* of his ancestor is speaking to him from a tree and tells him to build an *abila*. When an *ajok* (sorcerer) dances outside your house, you dream about it. His body swells up and all you can do is to cry out in your sleep as you lie in bed.

3. *Philipo Lawottim of Ngai.* The following points about dreams were given to me by Philipo Lawottim of Ngai. Two other men were present and confirmed what he said:

1. If you dream that you kill a man, you will kill an animal in the hunt.

2. If you dream that you kill an animal, a relation will die.

3. If you dream of sorghum, you will kill an animal in the hunt.

4. If you dream of sweet potato mounds, a relation will die.

5. If you dream that you are swimming in water, rain will fall.

6. If you dream of meat, you will see a new-born baby.

7. If you dream that you go down into a deep hole, someone will die.

8. If you dream that you eat honey, a relation or you yourself will contract yaws.

9. If you dream of a woman carrying water in a pot, this woman will become pregnant.

10. Often a man dreams that he soils his body while defecating. This denotes the chyme (*we*) of an animal that he will kill in the hunt.

11. If you dream that you dig up potatoes, or that someone puts a pile of potatoes in your house, it means that someone wants to kill you by means of black magic.

12. If you dream of a black cow, this is the *chyen* of a dead relation that is coming to afflict you.

13. If you dream of a dead relation, this is his *tipo* which will make you very ill.

14. If you dream that you fly up into the air, it is very good.

15. If an *ajok* dances outside your house, he will fall to the ground and his body will swell up. You are asleep in your house and you dream of all this. Then you shout and raise the alarm cry, but no one will be able to hear you. They only hear you groaning in your sleep.

16. The most common dream of Lango men is that of sleeping with other women.

4. *Some other dreamers.* My boy, Okelo, used to tell me his dreams. He said that he often dreamed that he climbed up a very tall tree and then fell down slowly. He was terrified as he thought that he was going to die. But he never reached the bottom. One day he dreamed that he was pregnant and swelled up. This made him furious (his wife was expecting a baby at the time). He dreamed that he came into the rest house while I was asleep. I was very frightened and said, 'Okelo, come here'. I then gave him my torch as a present. [Okelo always coveted that torch of mine.]

My other boy, Okuja, also told me his dreams. He dreamed that he was a child at the Mission station at Boroboro. The Missionary put him on his shoulders and took him far away. He then threw Okuja into a deep hole, and so he died. On another occasion he dreamed that he was in his house at Awelo. His father came in and said, 'Why haven't you gone to Bwana [referring to me], he is waiting for you?' His father was very angry. Okuja immediately rose to cross the lake, but on the way across he was attacked by two hundred hippos. One bit him in the side and he died. Okuja said that if you dream of water or snakes, it signifies graves and someone will die.

A certain woman said that she often dreamed of raw meat. She took the meat, cooked it and ate it. This information was given me during a ceremony, and the other women present said that they often dreamed of meat. This is not surprising considering their great craving for meat. The woman said that people dreamed chiefly about death (*to*). The people who were dead (*jo ma to*) sent the dream and then the dreamer would die also.

(*i*) **Magic against fire.** There was a big bush fire near the Aduku rest-house. I watched a man trying to keep the fire away from his houses. He carried a hoe and a spear. He frantically dug up the grass near his houses with the hoe. The whole time he spoke to himself and to the fire. He would point his spear threateningly at the oncoming fire and say, 'Go over there, fire, go over there. Go to the lake where there is much water, or to the jungle where you will find many animals to kill. Oh, so you want to burn my house? It does not matter, I do not mind. I have another house, so you can burn this one if you want to.' Then he would take a torch of grass and set fire to the grass round the threatened house. The heat from the main fire caused a draught in its direction, which drew the artificially created fires in towards the main fire and away from the house. A patch of burnt grass therefore protected the house. The man also carried a leafy branch with which he would beat out any fires caused by flying sparks.

He saved his houses and when all was over said, 'Those people over there will have had their houses burnt unless they know how to keep the fire away like me'.

The women and children also held sharp sticks or spears pointing at the fire whenever it threatened. The women caused the spears to wave slightly all the time. The object of this was obviously to frighten the fire away from the house.

This is a very good illustration of the fact that magic is ineffective without hard work as well. The acts of talking to the fire and threatening it with the spears were of a magical nature, although no specific magical ceremony was performed. It illustrates well the attitude of mind that lies behind the more ritualistic magical practices, and I record it in this chapter for want of a better place.

(*j*) **The *abila* and the house of *jok*.** Driberg describes the *abila* (*The Lango*, p. 219). They seem to have been frequent in his day. But now, in most parts of Lango, it is very difficult to find them, and they are rarely put up for the *tipo* of an ancestor (see Plate IV. 7 at p. 95). The house of *jok* (*ot jok*, also referred to as *ot abani*) is a beehive structure as described in the *jok nam* ceremonies (p. 165). It is undoubtedly an importation from the west, being associated with *jok nam*. The *ot rudi, ot abani* and *abila* are all referred to as *ot jok*, which seems to be a generic term denoting the association of each of these structures with *jok* power.

I could not combine my information on the *abila* into a generalisation. I therefore give a list of all the occasions on which I saw these or similar structures.

1. About six miles from Ngai I passed through a village in which there were a four-foot-high *abila*, an *ot abani* and an *ot peru*. A man in the village said that the *abila* had been built by an old man for their ancestors, but was rather vague about it. The *ot jok*, he said, was for *jok abani* or *jok nam*. In the beer season some Jopaluo from Minakulu come to divine (*tyeto*) in this *ot jok*. There were two spears (*tong jok*) within, and it was built of grass laid on a wooden framework with a nilotic type of doorway. What they termed an *ot peru* was a wooden structure covered with grass but having no walls. The term *peru* seems to be applied to any building that has no walls. It was also called an *ot jok nam*. The Jopaluo had gone home, since the beer season was over and beer was the medium in which they were paid for their services.

2. In the village of Akweredidi near Aboki I found an *abila*. The woodwork was of *okango* and was constructed just like a miniature *ot rudi*. Sticks of *okango* were laid out on top of the four-posted structure instead of the grass of the *ot rudi*; this was called *apeta*. A conical thatched roof covered the structure so that only the four posts were visible. Underneath there was a spray of thorn tree with which to bless spears (*lamo tong*). The old man who had built the *abila* said that his ancestors had built a similar one and so he had imitated them to enable him to kill animals in the hunt. He said that if a person was ill through a *tipo* visitation, an *abila* might be built. If the *abila* is for a *tipo*, some meat and beer are placed in a calabash underneath for the *tipo*. If the *abila* is for success in the hunt,

the meat of animals killed is laid by it. When it is built, a chicken is fluttered (*buko*) over the *abila*.

3. In a village near Akweredidi I found an *etoba* tree and *oligo* (euphorbia) planted together in the *otem*. Stuck into the ground next to them were two dead branches of *olwedo* and *okango*. They called this cluster an *abila*, because it was situated in the *otem*. It had been planted there for success in the hunt.

4. In a village near Achaba I found an *abila*. It was not built like an *ot rudi*, for it merely had four posts which supported the conical thatched roof. Planted near it were *apongpong*, *oligo*, *etoba*, *kore*, *yatchakdyang*, *okango*, *olwedo*. The owner said that he had built this *abila* for success in the hunt. They had fluttered and killed two chickens when building it and some meat and beer were put under it. He said that the Acholi built *abila* for the dead, but the Lango built them for success in the hunt.

5. There was an *abila* at Oja near Kibuji. The owner had built it for success in the hunt, as he had not killed any animals for a long time. He had built it because he remembered that long before his father had built one. He had placed a small calabash of beer under it. It was built of *okango*. Near by was a small *ot abani*. This was for his wife, who, when young, had been possessed by *jok abani*, which had been exorcised. The man was emphatic that no one would ever build an *abila* unless an ancestor had built one in the past.

6. A woman at Kibuji told me that an *abila* might be built for a *tipo* and food would then be put under it for the *tipo*.

7. At Abier near Amaich there was an *abila* constructed on top of an *ot rudi*. It had been built for impotency (p. 141).

8. At Angwechibunge near Dokolo there was an *abila* which had been built for impotency (p. 141).

9. Near Alito a man had built an *abila* for impotency (p. 140).

10. Philipo Lawottim of Ngai said that the custom of building *abila* came from the Acholi. I found the majority of *abila* on the land bordering the Acholi. He said that an *abila* would only be built if the man's ancestor had previously built one for some reason. The *abila* would be built if one of the man's family became ill. But *abila*s were not built as shrines for *tipo*s. If a man killed an animal which might give him *jok orongo*, he would build an *abila* so that his luck should not desert him in the future.

11. Rodia of Aloro said that a man may dream that the *tipo* of an ancestor comes to him in the night and tells him to build an *abila*, which he would proceed to do. People still built *abila* in the *otem*. Most of my informants on the subject of the *abila* said that they were built for sickness, for success in the hunt, for impotency. If a man suffers any of these misfortunes, he goes to an *ajwaka*, who may advise him to build an *abila*. The *abila* seems to be a magical structure by which these misfortunes can be cured. But it is dying out rapidly. It is only to be found in the remote villages, and there is only a meagre amount of evidence to show that it served the purpose of a shrine for the spirit of an ancestor as described by Driberg (*The Lango*, p. 231).

(*k*) **Miscellaneous magical beliefs.** Driberg gives a list of magical beliefs (*The Lango*, p. 267). I add a few that I discovered.

1. If a man has sores on his body which will not heal, he catches a lizard, spits into its mouth, drags it over the sores and then lets it go.

2. A certain species of owl is an *ajok* (sorcerer). If it sits on the roof of a man's house at night, he will die.

3. If a jackal or merekat calls continually round the village, someone in the village will die.

4. I saw a man with a partial albinism of the legs. I was told that, if you were to kill a man with such an affliction, your brother or child would contract a similar defect. You yourself would be untouched.

5. If you have some task to perform, the cry of the woodpecker, *atetel*, if he cries with clear notes in succession, is good. If he screeches, it is a bad omen.

6. Lightning is greatly feared by all Lango. To swear by lightning is the gravest oath that can be taken—for perjury will be visited by death through lightning.

7. When clearing out a spring, the people are careful to replace the mud fish found in it. They say that, if this is not done, the spring will dry up. The effect of this belief is to ensure a constant supply of fish, which are eaten.

8. If a bat hits against you, it is very good luck; you will live long and be happy.

9. I once saw an old man at a ceremony, who had a down-turned nose and continually chewed. He looked like a rhino-ceros. He said that he had become like this because he had once killed a rhino. I was told by those present that this is always the case. If a man kills a rhino, either he chews like this for the rest of his life, or his body swells up. There was a medicine that the *ajwaka* could give such a person to make him better.

10. When a man hiccoughs, it is because someone has mentioned his name.

11. If you throw something at someone and he catches it, it means that you like him very much.

12. The chameleon is greatly feared. If one bites you in the dry weather when the sun is strong, it will not affect you much. But should it bite you during the rains, the place will swell up enormously, so the Lango say.

13. People fear to stand under a tree called *awilakot* (ery-thrina) while it is raining, for they will be struck by lightning if they do. This tree has scarlet flowers at the top and is very tall. The root of this tree is used for counteracting lightning (*The Lango*, p. 262).

INDEX AND GLOSSARY OF LANGO TERMS AND MATERIAL CULTURE

178   INDEX

Adwel (p. 147). An old, worn-out hide or skin.

Adyebepar (p. 44). A wild plant subject to certain prohibitions in Clan ritual observances.

Adyeda (p. 91). A village about 5 miles north of Aloro.

After-birth (pp. 97, 98, 102, 131–2).

Age Grades (pp. 14, 38, 39, 40, 47, 50, 51, 60–3, 65, 66, 71, 72, 73, 74, 75, 79).

Age Groups (p. 38). See also Age Grades and Status Groups.

Age Sets (p. 61).

Agents (pp. 71, 75, 80).

Agnates (p. 52).

Agwata (p. 68). *Gombolola* headquarters in Dokolo *saza*.

Agwata (pp. 79, 85, 97, 98, 101, 112, 118, 119, 136, 138, 149). The Lango term for the shell of half a calabash. The *apoko* has a long neck but the *agwata* has a short neck. It is a good receptacle for flour, etc. An old *agwata* is called '*agwata atok*' and a new one '*agwata kech*'. I found one old woman making these calabashes in her village. She said that she would sell each calabash for the amount of millet flour that it contained. A drawing of an *agwata* will be found facing p. 98 (Plate V, drawing 5). See also *Apoko, Keno, Obuto, Wal*.

Agwata kech (pp. 79, 98, 119). A new *agwata*.

Agwichiri (p. 161). A village near Chiawanti.

Air (pp. 18, 116). The spirit of a man is likened to air. See also *Yamo*.

Aja (pp. 14, 25, 121, 143, 149, 153, 156, 165, 167). The 'rattle' used by the *ajwaka* when divining (*tyeto*) and in other ceremonies. It is made from an *apoko* calabash by inserting some large seeds through a hole in the bottom, which is then corked up. The *aja* is held by the neck when shaken and it produces a monotonous, hypnotic rhythm. See Plate V, drawing 3 at p. 98 and Plate X at p. 154.

Ajok (pp. 3, 12–14, 16, 18, 19, 22, 29–30, 33, 34, 106, 107, 123, 126, 157, 161, 170, 171, 175). Sorcerer or witch. One who practises black magic.

Ajwaka (p. 1, 4, 5, 7, 8, 9–10, 11, 14, 21, 22, 23–9, 31, 33, 34, 46, 77, 79, 82, 95, 107, 110, 121, 138–41, 144, 148, 149, 150, 153–69, 175–6). Medicine

man or woman. One who practises white magic.

Akal (p. 151). Reedbuck.

Akalakiu (p. 149). A shrub used for magical control over animals.

Akalu (pp. 11, 68). *Gombolola* headquarters in Eruti *saza*.

Akau (pp. 159, 160). A medicine-woman of Anwongi.

Akedi (p. 142). Lango term for a type of plaited grass rope.

Akelo (pp. 25, 167). A medicine-woman of Kibuji.

Akeo (p. 56). Relationship term; sister's daughter.

Akoreloke (pp. 74, 76). Lingo's village, about 3 miles south of Aduku.

Akot (pp. 18, 115). A village about 6 miles north-east of Aduku.

Akweredidi (pp. 173, 174). A village near Aboki.

Akwon (p. 91). A village about 8 miles south of Aduku.

— (p. 141). A village about 6 miles east of Ngai.

Alai. A village about 3 miles north-west of Orumo. See Plate I at p. 58.

Albinism (p. 175).

Aleokato (p. 149). A shrub used for magical control over animals.

Alibor (p. 69).

Alipa (pp. 68, 123). A locality about 7 miles east of Nabieso.

Alira (p. 97). A village near Aduku.

Alito (pp. 79, 140, 168, 174). *Gombolola* headquarters in Koli *saza*.

Aloi (p. 68). *Gombolola* headquarters in Eruti *saza*.

Alop (pp. 67, 151, 163). Hartebeest.

Aloro (pp. 9, 13, 79, 91, 110, 170, 175). Headquarters of Atura *saza*.

Alur (pp. 36, 80). A nilotic tribe living to the north of Lake Albert.

Amagoro. See *Won amagoro*.

Amaich (pp. 4, 65, 68, 72, 79, 141, 174). *Gombolola* headquarters in Eruti *saza*.

Amiayta (p. 74). Lingo's father's village, about 4 miles south of Aduku.

Amor (pp. 43, 151). Duiker, small deer.

Amorung (pp. 61, 67, 68, 70, 72, 73). Rhinoceros, but this term is used only in rain ceremonies and as the name of an Age Grade.

Amugo (p. 68). *Gombolola* headquarters in Moroto *saza*.

Amya (pp. 130, 135). A village about 6 miles south-west of Aduku.

Atimu (pp. 98, 99, 100, 146). A long narrow drum about three feet in length. It is hollow all through. The diameter is about seven inches at the base and ten inches at the drumhead, over which is stretched tightly the skin of a monitor lizard, which is held in place by means of small wooden pegs driven into the outer rim. This drum is of the same shape as the mortar (*pany*) used by women for pounding food-stuffs. The *atimu* is used in twin ceremonies, where it is indispensable. It used also to be used in the old type of Lango band (see *The Lango*, p. 125), which is now obsolete. It is slung by a leather thong over the neck and clasped between the knees. The performer beats it rapidly with the flats of his hands. It has a high note. See Plate IV, drawing 2, at p. 95 and Plate VI at p. 102.

Atin akwer (pp. 17, 42, 53, 135, 137, 163). Ritual child.

Atin jok (pp. 154, 156, 165). Child of *Jok*; plural, *otino jogi*. An *ajwaka* usually has a few of them attached to him as helpers.

Atura (pp. 79, 105). Name of the northeast *saza* of Lango.

Atworo (pp. 79, 136, 162–4). A manifestation of *jok* power. Odok, the interpreter of Atworo, lives at Bungakelalyek near Ngai.

Auto-suggestion (p. 158).

Avoidance (pp. 82, 83, 127–9).

Awalu (p. 68). Crested crane.

Awei (pp. 14, 153). A village about 4 miles south-east of Aduku.

Awele (p. 68). Pigeon.

Awelo (pp. 7, 8, 9, 33, 41, 68, 79, 171). Headquarters of Kyoga *saza*.

Aweno (p. 68). Guinea-fowl.

Awi dyang (pp. 38,44,53,59,60,93,146, 148). Cattle kraal. It is a circular stockade about ten feet high, made by planting rough, stout poles several feet in the earth and weaving other branches between them. There is a narrow entrance which is closed by means of logs. A mound with a tree is usually enclosed by the stockade. This provides an island of dry land for the cattle when the rest of the kraal is a sea of black wet mud. The tree affords shade.

Awilakot (pp. 146, 176). Erythrina tree.

Awobi (pp. 68–70). Boys. Applied to candidates for initiation at the Age Grade ceremonies.

Aworon (p. 66). Initiation festival.

Awurunguru (pp. 32, 33). Small squirrel-like animal used for purposes of black magic.

Axe (p. 98).

Ayala (p. 168). A village about 5 miles south-west of Alito.

Ayeb (p. 117). A long pole, forked at one end, which is used for propping up the roof of the granary (*dero*) when taking anything out. At the *gato two* ceremony the sheep was pressed with the *ayeb*, showing that it has a certain ritual importance.

Bachelor's hut. See *Otogo*.

Bad luck (pp. 5,6, 33, 34). See also Good luck.

Baganda (pp. 6, 39–40, 71, 80). A Bantu tribe living between Lakes Kwania, Kyoga, Salisbury and Lake Victoria.

Bagishu (p. 32). A tribe living on Mount Elgon.

Bakenyi (pp. 7, 40). They were water gypsies living on the lakes south of Lango. They have now been compelled to settle on the lake shores.

Bantu (pp. 39, 40, 165).

Banyara (p. 40).

Banyoro (pp. 7, 39–40, 80). A Bantu tribe living to the east of Lake Albert.

Bar (pp. 68, 112). *Gombolola* headquarters in Eruti *saza*.

Bar (p. 68). Pasturage.

Bari (p. 37). A Sudanese tribe living on the Nile well to the north of Lango.

Barrenness (pp. 12, 28, 29, 97, 127, 140).

Baruli (pp. 7, 40). A Bantu tribe living to the south-west of Lango.

Basis of group membership (pp. 36, 39, 40–1, 48, 52, 53, 54, 56, 58, 59, 60, 61).

Bat (pp. 5, 175). *Olik*.

Bata (p. 68). *Gombolola* headquarters in Dokolo *saza*.

Bateson (pp. 28, 35, 36).

Battle (pp. 15, 42, 43, 57, 145, 146). See also Fighting and Warfare.

Beating with *epobo* (pp. 55, 86, 93, 94, 119, 135).

Beer (pp. 6, 32, 33, 49, 58, 59, 68, 70, 75, 79, 82, 84, 85, 86, 87, 89, 90, 91, 93, 94, 96–7, 99–100, 101, 102, 104,

Bride price. See Marriage goods.
Bringing ornaments (pp. 44, 47, 88). *Yeyo lyeto.*
British administration. See Administration.
Broom (pp. 95, 159).
Buffalo (pp. 15, 61, 65, 67, 141). *Jobi.*
Buko (pp. 32, 98, 134, 136, 174). This word is used to describe the process whereby a chicken is fluttered round a person's head, or over an *abila*, an *ot rudi*, a hunting net, etc. The chicken is held by a wing or a leg and is swung fluttering round the person's head. The subsequent fate of the person, usually a child, is associated to some extent with the fate of the chicken. It may well be that this process of *buko* brings good luck upon the person or thing treated in the same way as the pennant-winged nightjar if it flies round a person's head (p. 5). On this analogy the process of *buko* would convey *winyo* (q.v.) to the person. I have no proof of this, however, and cite it merely as a suggestion.
Bull of the Clan (pp. 42, 98, 99). *Twon me atekere.*
Bull of the crowd (pp. 57, 71, 145). *Twon lwak.*
Bung (p. 123). A village near Nabieso.
Bungakelalyek (pp. 135, 162). The *ajwaka*, Odok's, village about 5 miles north-east of Ngai.
Burial (pp. 44, 53, 63, 76, 99, 102, 106, 107, 108, 116, 122, 123, 147).
Burning a dead man's bones (pp. 21, 123, 126).
Bushbuck (pp. 43, 85). *Aroda, Aderi.*
Bushman digging-stick weight (pp. 4, 79).
Butter. See *Mo dyang.*

Calabash (pp. 14, 75, 76, 77, 79, 85, 86, 88, 90, 92, 96, 97, 98, 99, 100–1, 102, 112, 118, 119, 124–5, 129, 136, 138, 142, 143, 147, 148, 149, 150, 152, 154, 158, 159, 161, 166, 167, 173, 174). See *Agwata.*
Candelabrum euphorbia. See *Apongpong.*
Carrying flour (pp. 53, 128). *Yeyo moko.*
Carrying skin. See *Abeno.*
Cassava (pp. 66, 72, 74).
Castration (pp. 21, 140, 141).
Catching a tipo. See *Mako tipo.*
Catholics (p. 33).

Cattle (pp. 20, 38, 40–1, 46–7, 51, 55, 58, 59, 60, 82, 83, 93, 115, 139, 148).
Cattle kraal. See *Awi dyang.*
Caves (pp. 4, 79).
Cerebral cortex (p. 18).
Ceremonial (pp. 2, 3–4, 8, 9, 10, 12–25, 27, 28, 34, 35–6, 39–55, 56–8, 60–6, 69–76, 79–112, 114–16, 120–30, 133, 135–49, 150–4, 155–7, 163–5, 166, 168, 171, 172, 176).
Ceremonial structure (p. 153).
Chako nying (pp. 132, 136). Giving a child a name.
Chakwara (p. 68). A locality about 6 miles south-west of Awelo.
Cham. Food. It refers to the staple food, usually *kwon*. The verb 'to eat' is *chamo*. This verb is also used of a man holding office (*echamo won pacho*, he holds the office of *won pacho*), of debt (*echamo banya*, he is in debt, or, he is granted credit), of a man's salary (*echamo ochoro adi?* what is his salary?), of conquest (*echamo piny duchu*, he conquers the whole country). See also Diet for a list of the various types of food.
Chameleon (p. 176).
Chant and chorus (pp. 6, 14, 78, 116, 117, 119, 142, 143, 151).
Chaporo (p. 137). The institution of *chaporo* is now a thing of the past. It meant, 'To engage oneself as a pawn to someone'. Should a boy have been so poor that he had no means of obtaining a wife, and neither his clansmen nor his mother's brother's family (*Neo*) could help him, there was only one recourse left to him, that of *chaporo*. The boy would go to a man and bind himself as a pawn to him. Several coils of iron wire were twisted round his neck as a sign of his condition and he would be made to work very hard for a year or two. All my witnesses emphasised the arduous nature of the work the boy would have to perform. After this his master, if satisfied with him, would give him a cow. The boy would take the wire off his neck and go home. On his arrival home his clansmen would assemble and perform the ceremony of *kiro* (sprinkling with water) to purify him. The cow would be put in the cattle kraal and form the nucleus of a herd with which he would be able to marry later.

Chaporo (*contd.*)

This institution was very common in the past and its abandonment is due to the new means by which wealth can be obtained as a result of the introduction of a money economy. The new recourse open to a boy who cannot obtain a cow from his clansmen or *Neo* is to earn money by means of hawking or wage labour. With the modern economic system the Lango father is becoming progressively less inclined to help members of his Clan, other than his own sons, to find wives by providing them with cattle or money. The result is that there are many more individuals than formerly who must build up their own resources without the help of clansmen or *Neo*.

The abandonment of the *chaporo* institution and the rise of a group of traders and wage-earners in its place is a striking result of the new economic system. (See 'Wage Labour and the desire for wives among the Lango' in *The Uganda Journal*, vol. VIII, No. I, September 1940.) The two systems may not appear to be similar, and the change is certainly not apparent to those who are most affected by it—the Europeans and Indians who require indigenous labour. The connection between *chaporo* and wage-earning or trading is that of incentive. In both cases a great amount of economic work is produced, and in both cases it is the desire for a wife that provides the incentive. As soon as that desire is satisfied, the worker leaves his arduous duties for the more congenial life of a married farmer. There are some who find the work they have adopted as a temporary expedient sufficiently satisfying for them to keep to it permanently, but this is rather exceptional. It may be pointed out here that attempts to prevent the size of the marriage goods from increasing will further restrict the reservoir of wage labourers, unless new wants are created which the individual prefers to satisfy by working for a wage.

Charcoal (pp. 4, 157, 158, 161, 162).

Chastity (p. 82).

Chege (p. 55). Spouse.

Cheke (pp. 85, 99, 102, 119, 124). The drinking tube through which *kongo* (beer) is sucked up. These drinking tubes are made out of dried grass stems or a special type of reed. They have wicker or metal strainers attached to the ends so that the dregs of the *kongo* do not pass up through the tube. Old men often carry them in a hole hollowed out of their walking-sticks. There are rarely sufficient *cheke* for all those sitting round a pot of *kongo*, so it is customary to suck up a few mouthfuls and then hand the *cheke* to one's neighbour. The host always has the first suck through the *cheke*. This shows that he has no evil intentions. For an *ajok* will put poison (*yat*) in the *cheke* to kill an enemy. *Cheke* are not used when *kongo* is to be drunk ritually (p. 119). See Plate V, drawing 6 at p. 98 and Plate VII at p. 124.

Cherry (p. 43).

Chiawanti (pp. 10, 68, 78, 149, 161). *Gombolola* headquarters in Kwania *saza*.

Chibo adit me atekere (pp. 43, 44, 56, 103, 105). Ceremony of installation for a new Clan chief.

Chicken (pp. 32, 48, 54, 59, 95, 98, 107, 108, 112–14, 124, 125, 134, 136, 139, 141, 142, 143, 144, 147, 148, 165, 166, 174).

Chiefs (pp. 9, 13, 65, 71, 74, 77, 78, 80, 83, 102, 103–4, 105, 108, 145–6, 149, 167, 170).

Child of Jok. See *Atin jok.*

Children (pp. 8, 11–14, 16, 17, 19, 29, 35, 37, 41, 44–6, 47–9, 52, 53, 54, 55, 56, 60, 61, 64, 69, 81, 82, 83–4, 86, 87, 88, 89, 90–6, 97, 106–9, 115, 117, 125, 127, 129, 130, 131, 132–6, 137, 139–40, 142, 143, 144, 155, 156, 159–60, 163, 166, 167, 171, 172, 175).

Chinese 'stream-of-life' theory (p. 19).

Chip (pp. 83, 84, 89, 90, 114). A cotton fringe worn by girls over the pudenda. The fringe is attached to a thin leather girdle (*del*), which is fastened behind and twisted into a horizontal, stick-like projection about nine inches long. The *chip* is only worn on certain ceremonial occasions by the modern woman who wears clothes. See Plate I at p. 58.

Chogo. Bones, q.v.

Christian (pp. 5, 9, 11, 13, 18, 22, 27, 31, 65, 80, 83, 87, 94, 108, 109, 110, 116, 131, 138, 169).

Papo	Father.
	Father's brother.
Toto	Mother.
	Father's wife.
	Mother's sister.
	Father's brother's wife.
Tato	Father's mother.
	Mother's mother.
	Husband's mother.
	Husband's father's sister.
Kwaro	Father's father.
	Mother's father.
	Husband's father.
	Husband's father's brother.
Nero	Mother's brother.
Omin	Brother.
	Father's wife's son.
	Father's brother's son.
Amin	Sister.
	Father's wife's daughter.
	Father's brother's daughter.
Wot	Son.
	Brother's son.
	Co-wife's son.
	Husband's brother's son.
	Father's brother's son's son.
Nya	Daughter.
	Brother's daughter.
	Husband's brother's daughter.
	Co-wife's daughter.
	Father's brother's son's daughter.
Owayo	Father's sister (w.s.).
	Brother's wife (w.s.).
Okeo	Sister's son (m.s.).
	Father's sister's son.
	Father's brother's daughter's son.
Akeo	Sister's daughter (m.s.).
	Father's sister's daughter.
	Father's brother's daughter's daughter.
Omaro	Wife's sister's husband.
	Mother's sister's son.
	Mother's sister's husband.
Amaro	Mother's sister's daughter.
Oro	Daughter's husband.
	Sister's husband (m.s.).
	Wife's father.
	Wife's brother.
Maro	Wife's mother.
Amu	Wife's sister.
	Sister's husband (w.s.).
	Wife's brother's wife.
	Husband's sister's husband.
	Husband's brother.
	Brother's wife (m.s.).
Okwaro	Son's son.
	Daughter's son.
Akwaro	Son's daughter.
	Daughter's daughter.
Chwaro	Husband.

Dero *(contd.)*

top of the mud wall and which is propped up by means of a forked pole *(ayeb)* when anything is to be taken out of the granary. The whole *dero* is raised about a foot off the ground by a platform of logs which rests on four stone supports. A projection of sun-dried mud acts as a step so that the woman can easily reach the things which she stores in the *dero*. The *dero* is usually built in front of the door of the house on the opposite side of the courtyard *(dyekal)*. It has a diameter of from four to six feet and is about five or six feet high. See Plate II at p. 66.

Diagnosis (pp. 8, 25, 26, 153).

Didinga (p. 43). A nilo-hamitic tribe living to the north of the Acholi.

Diet. The staple and favourite food of the Lango is millet, ground into a flour *(moko kwon)*, moistened with water and cooked until a thick glutinous mass *(kwon)*. It is continually stirred with a stick to prevent burning as it is cooked. Millet is also made into beer *(kongo)*, as is sorghum *(bel)*. Other less liked staples are sweet potatoes, cassava, and, very occasionally on the shores of the lakes, bananas. Cassava is a famine reserve which has been introduced and encouraged by the British. With these foods is eaten *dek*, which consists of any form of vegetable, meat, herbs, ground-nuts, flying termites, etc. The staple is taken in the hand and rolled into a ball. A depression is made in it with the thumb and the *dek* gravy is thus scooped up. They will not eat *kwon* without *dek* as it is a most unappetising food without anything to help it down.

I did not have time to obtain sufficient dietary statistics, but the following foods are eaten. The wife tries to arrange a varied diet.

A. ***Cham.*** ('Food.' Carbohydrates.)
1. Millet (*Eleusine coracana*).
2. Sorghum (*Sorghum vulgare*).
3. Sweet potatoes.
4. Cassava (*Manihot utilissima*).
5. Maize. Only a very little eaten.
6. Bananas. Only a very little eaten.
7. Yams. Only a very little eaten.
8. Chiefs and other wealthy people may eat rice bought from the Indians.

B. ***Dek.*** ('Sauce' or 'relishes' to be eaten with *Cham*.)

(*a*) **Albuminoids:**
1. Pigeon peas.
2. Ground-nuts.
3. Cow peas.
4. Various types of *Phaseolus* spp.

(*b*) **Fats:**
1. Sesame.
2. Ground-nuts.
3. Shea-butter nuts.
4. Milk and its derivatives.

(*c*) **Green vegetables:**
1. Leaves and pods of all beans, peas and legumes.
2. Leaves of *Hibiscus* spp.
3. Fruit of *Hibiscus* spp.
4. Cucurbita of various types.
5. Various uncultivated herbs such as *Amomum* spp.
6. Chillies.

(*d*) **Fruits:**
1. Wild plum.
2. Aluter.
3. Wild figs.
4. Tamarind.
5. Wild cherry.
6. Wild grape.
7. Bananas.
8. And others, with a growing desire for mangoes, pineapples and lemons where they can be got.

(*e*) **Meat:**
1. Sheep.
2. Goat.
3. Beef.
4. All clean eating birds.
5. All game.
6. Fish.
7. Fried flying termites (*aripa*) and a number of insects.

The diet of the people remains much as it has been with the addition of shop-bought salt and sugar. The sweet potato is a comparatively recent acquisition from Buganda, and cassava has been introduced as a famine reserve by the British. The richer classes consume great quantities of 'tea' (*chai*), which consists of a weak infusion of Kenya tea mixed with

Eagle of Baganda kings (p. 6).
Earache (p. 158).
Ebibi (p. 64). Milk supplier to the C.M.S. station at Boroboro.
Echach (pp. 84, 89, 92, 104, 148). A stick of wood, four or five feet long, which is the property of the Clan and is only produced on certain ceremonial occasions. It is part of the Clan ritual observances (*kwer me atekere*). I saw the *echach* stick used in most of the ceremonies associated with the Clan. I was told that when a new cattle kraal (*awi dyang*) was made, a ceremony was held during which the cows passed into the kraal stepping over the *echach* stick. In the ceremonies the *echach* stick was usually leant against the woman's shoulder. If she was anointed (*wiro*) with *mo dyang*, some of the *echach* was first scraped off into it. The *echach* stick was also used when the Clan chief was being installed by the ceremony of *chibo adit me atekere*, while he was at the same time anointed (*wiro*) with *mo dyang*.
Echau jok (pp. 60, 92). Duodenum.
Echol (pp. 119, 120). Small black pot used in the ceremony of *lamo kom dano*.
Economic crops (p. 59).
Economic magic (pp. 125, 126).
Economic organisation (pp. 35, 58, 59).
Education (pp. 31, 53, 62, 87, 103, 109, 169).
Egypt (pp. 6, 169).
Eidos (pp. 28, 29).
Ekori. See *Jo ekori.*
Ektu (p. 67). Zebra.
Ekwaro (p. 67). Serval.
Ekwera (p. 68). In Dokolo *saza.*
Ekwinkwin (pp. 8, 9). Epilepsy.
Elephant (pp. 15, 61, 67, 68, 70, 72–3, 141, 169). *Lyech.*
Elgon (p. 32). Mountain on the boundary between Kenya and Uganda.
Emotions (pp. 2, 11, 34, 48, 51, 53).
Endogamy (p. 40).
Engato. See Lion.
Entrails (pp. 92, 95, 118, 120, 122).
Enwewe (p. 150). A plant giving magical control over animals.
Epidemics (pp. 60, 148).
Epilepsy. See *Ekwinkwin.*
Epobo (pp. 28, 29, 55, 63, 64, 69, 86, 93, 119, 135, 142). Elder tree.
Erythrina. See *Awilakot.*

Esoteric knowledge (pp. 34, 71, 75).
Etek (p. 78). Species of tree, used at the rain dance.
Etoba (p. 174). Species of tree, grown near the *abila.*
Etogo (pp. 6, 12, 17–18, 20–1, 23, 27, 38, 39, 40, 42, 45, 46, 47–51, 57, 61, 63–6, 71, 72, 76, 80, 81, 108, 111–23, 124–5, 126, 134, 141, 149, 156). Religious group.
Euphorbia. See *Apongpong* and *Oligo.*
Europeans (pp. 37, 80).
Evans-Pritchard (p. 52).
Ewor (pp. 13, 21, 39, 47, 57, 61, 63, 65, 66–73, 75, 80, 145). Quinquennial initiation ceremony.
Exhumation. See *Golo chogo.*
Exogamy (pp. 41–2, 45, 47, 48, 54, 81).
Exorcism (pp. 14, 16, 153, 168, 174).

Faeces (pp. 29, 33).
Faith healers (p. 27).
Falcon of Egyptian kings (p. 6).
Family (pp. 16–17, 19, 20, 27, 38, 47, 48, 49, 53–6, 58, 81, 82, 88, 94, 99, 106–7, 108, 109, 111, 115, 123, 126, 127, 129–30, 137, 138, 139, 141, 147, 174).
Famine (pp. 38, 40, 46, 63, 66, 72, 80, 109).
Feeding a person ritually (p. 101). See Ritual eating.
Feet presentation (p. 3).
Fertility (pp. 28, 85).
Fetish objects (p. 4).
Fig (pp. 43, 44, 85).
Fighting (pp. 5, 15, 34, 37, 40, 48, 61, 62, 68, 71, 72, 80, 99, 100, 104, 154, 155). See also Battle and Warfare.
Fire magic (pp. 33, 172).
Fire-making (pp. 85, 88, 92, 94, 95, 101).
Fireplace (pp. 5, 85, 86, 88, 92, 93, 104, 105, 113, 141, 147, 148). See *Otem.*
Fire song (p. 146).
Fire-sticks (pp. 85, 88, 92, 149).
First fruits (pp. 53, 139).
Flour (pp. 53, 70, 98, 128, 133). *Moko.*
Flour for beer. See *Moko kongo.*
Flying (pp. 79, 171).
Food prohibitions (pp. 43, 127).
Frog-spawn (pp. 4, 160).
Function (pp. 23, 25, 35, 40, 48, 50, 51, 53, 57, 62, 110, 111, 146, 149). See also Value of groups.

Keny (p. 116). Man on whom the cere-
mony of *gato two* was performed.
Kenya (p. 97).
Kibuji (pp. 68, 72, 167, 174). Head-
quarters of Maruzi *saza*.
Kide atyeng (p. 97). A stone used in
a ceremony for curing a child's sore
eyes.
Kide jok (pp. 4, 79). A stone imbued
with *jok* power.
Kide kot. See Rain stones.
Kidneys (p. 122).
Kigelia (p. 144).
Killing a bull (pp. 91, 105, 122, 137,
139, 157).
Killing a bull for sickness. See *Neko
dyang me two*.
Killing a bull for the grave. See *Neko
dyang me wi lyel*.
Killing a bull for the wife's mother.
See *Neko dyang me maro*.
Killing a bull to honour one's father.
See *Neko dyang me woro papo*.
Killing a goat (pp. 44, 47, 138, 141,
155).
Kinga. A method of dressing the hair
of twins. All the hair is shaved off save
for a thin strip round the crown.
Kiro (pp. 69, 101, 112, 128, 137, 138). To
sprinkle. The sprinkling is done cere-
monially with water from a calabash
(*wal* or *agwata*), and usually with a
head of *modo* grass, though *olwedo* leaves
may be used, as in the rain dance.
Kiro bang imat (pp. 53, 127, 128).
Sprinkling at the wife's mother's.
Kiro dako (pp. 81, 87, 88, 92, 96, 99).
Sprinkling the wife.
Kiro wang atin (p. 96). Sprinkling a
child's eyes.
Kite me kwer. Custom of the ritual
observance. See also *Kwer*.
Kodi (p. 69).
Kom yot. See *Yot kom*.
Kongo (see also Beer). Lango beer,
which is made in the following manner.
    Millet (*kal*) is threshed and left on
the ground or in a jar for three days
in a moist state. At the end of the three
days it will have germinated slightly
and is then spread out in the sun to
dry on the ground in front of the house
(*dyekal*), the space having been carefully swept clean. As soon as it is dry
it is ground into flour. This flour is
moistened until it becomes firm, and
it is then sealed up with mud in a large

earthenware jar, or in a kerosene tin,
or merely in a hole in the ground, for
two or three weeks. It is then taken
out and roasted for about seven hours
over a fire, being carefully stirred all
the time with a spurtle (*lot kongo*) to
prevent burning. Now it is spread out
once more to dry in the sun. The dried
flour that results is called beer flour
(*moko kongo*), and it can be kept in this
state for many months without de-
teriorating. Most families keep a
reserve of this *moko kongo* always in
readiness in case *kongo* should suddenly be required for a ceremony. If
a woman requires beer but has no
moko kongo, she will buy it from a neighbour. *Moko kongo* is also sold in the
market at Lira.
    Kongo cannot be brewed from *moko
kongo* alone. A reserve must therefore
be kept of what is known as 'the taste
of beer' (*bilo kongo*). A small quantity
of millet is left for three days in a moist
state so that it germinates slightly. It
is then dried in the sun, whereupon
germination ceases. It can be stored
in this state and keeps for many
months.
    When *kongo* is required, the *bilo
kongo* is ground into flour, only a very
small quantity being required. It is
placed in a pot together with the *moko
kongo*, water is poured in and the mixture is stirred. The *bilo kongo* ferments
the mixture, which is ready for drinking
in three days. It is clear therefore that
three days is the minimum time required for the preparation of *kongo* for
any purpose. *Kongo* has to be drunk
on various ceremonial occasions, such
as after birth and death at the *donyo
oko* ceremonies. On both of these
occasions the birth and death are relatively unexpected occurrences and
kongo is immediately prepared. But it
will not be fit to drink for three days.
This, I think, accounts for the fact that
the period of seclusion in the house
between birth or death and the *donyo
oko* ceremony extends for three days.
    Before drinking the *kongo* warm
water slightly hotter than blood tem-
perature is poured into the pot up to
the brim. Before this is done those
present take a little *kongo* dough into
their mouths and spit it out cere-

Kongo (*contd.*)

monially. This will have been noticed in the ceremonies already described, as will have been the continual ceremonial use of *kongo*, the drinking of which probably heightens suggestibility. *Kongo* is sucked up out of the pot through long drinking tubes called *cheke*. But when drunk ritually it is decanted into calabashes and drunk with the lips, *cheke* (see Plate VII at p. 124) not being allowed.

Kongo may also be made from sorghum (*bel*), but this is not liked as much as millet beer. *Kongo* is very sustaining and very refreshing after a long day in the sun. I found it to be mildly intoxicating, but the Lango contrive to be affected by it and brawls leading to death sometimes occur after a good night's drinking. Hot water is added to the *kongo* until it becomes tasteless. The dregs of the *kongo* may be eaten later. They used to be sold as food in times of famine.

Kongo me wi lyel (pp. 111, 112). Beer of the grave.

Kore (p. 174). A plant.

Kot. See Rain.

Kul (p. 67). Wart-hog.

Kumam (pp. 33, 39, 40, 71, 72). A tribe living to the contiguous southeast of the Lango.

Kwach or Kwaich. See Leopard.

Kwanyo (pp. 157, 161). Process of extracting supposed stones, etc., which have been 'thrown' into a person by a sorcerer.

Kwer (pp. 2, 43, 95). I have translated this word by 'ritual observance'. *Kwer me atekere* then becomes 'Clan ritual observance'. Driberg suggested to me that this was preferable to the use of the word 'taboo'. These are the Clan prohibitions enumerated on pp. 43-4. It is not so easy to translate the verbal form *kwero*, which means literally 'to refuse'. When used in the expression *kwero dako* or *kwero atin*, it means 'to place the woman, or child, under the influence of the ritual observances'. The ceremony of *tweyo lau* is also called *kwero dako*, for the woman has in future to pay regard to the ritual observances of her husband's Clan. When a child has gone through the ceremony of *atin akwer* (ritual child), it might be

said of it, 'They have placed the child under the influence of the ritual observances' (*gityeko kwero atin*). At the same time on the occasion of this ceremony the mother might be asked, 'So you are refusing grief to-day?' (*ikwero jul tin*).

Kwero jul (p. 135). To refuse grief; referring to the ceremony of *atin akwer*.

Kwon (pp. 86, 89, 90, 93, 123, 128, 134, 137). Millet porridge, the staple food of the Lango. Millet is stored in mud granaries (*dero*) in the ear. When it is required for eating it is pounded in the mortar (*pany*), and winnowed on a winnowing mat (*oderu*). Then it is ground on the grinding stone (*kide*) into a flour (*moko kwon*). It is mixed with water and boiled in a pot or aluminium saucepan. The cooking has to be done carefully. The *kwon* has to be stirred vigorously all the time with a spurtle (*lot kwon*) to prevent burning. When cooked it forms a slightly glutinous mass with a sandy taste. A lump of *kwon* is taken in the hand, it is moulded into a ball, a depression is made in it with the thumb, it is dipped in *dek* sauce and then it is eaten. See also Diet.

Kwong (p. 70).

Kworo (pp. 134, 135). The bark of the *kworo* tree is chewed and twisted on the thigh to form a string, which is then tied round the wrists of a baby at the *donyo oko* ceremony. See Plate V, drawing 4 at p. 98.

Lake Albert (p. 37).

Lake Kwania (p. 38).

Lake Rudolph (pp. 36, 37).

Lamo (pp. 117, 119, 144). It might be translated as 'to bless', or 'to purify', or 'to cleanse'. The thing or person who is the object of the *lamo* ceremony is liked by the performers. He has fallen into misfortune and they by the *lamo* ceremony try to reinstate him in his old prosperity. The *lamo* ceremony is like a collective blessing which has great potency as a result of its utterance by the company of old men. The ceremony described on p. 115 can be called either 'purifying the body of a man' (*lamo kom dano*) or 'cursing the sickness in a man' (*gato two*). See also Gato.

PLATE XII

The old type of Lango house—Nilotic style

The type of house usually built in Lango to-day

Otogo (*contd.*)

The *otogo* is functionally obsolete now, though twenty years ago it was still part of the tribal culture. I devote so much space to it, not because I consider it of any great importance, but because there have been various theories as to its significance and I wish tentatively to suggest another possibility, which may be of interest to those with psycho-analytical leanings.

First, it is necessary to examine four explanations of the *otogo* as cited by Driberg:

1. **Sexual segregation.** The Elders, by spreading ashes round the *otogo* at night, would know if the unmarried men were visiting girl friends. As Driberg points out, this is absurd. But a Lango told me that in the old days a married man could find out who was sleeping with his wife by listening at the *otogo*. Should an *otogo* be empty, he knew that the owner was the culprit and so could decide whether to spear him at once, or wait and demand compensation. On the other hand a Lango told me that they loved the *otogo* because each man could take his girl there and make love with impunity.

2. **Security.** In the insecure pre-Administration days the bachelors in their *otogin* were in a safe position if the village was raided. Driberg points out, however, that the cumbersome mode of egress would put the occupants at the mercy of any raiders. But the Lango told me that the danger in the old days came from personal enemies. A man lying in a drunken sleep was likely to be speared by anyone who had a grudge against him. The *otogo* made this impossible.

3. **Warmth and mosquitoes.** The old men tell me that they sleep in the *otogo* because it is warm and mosquitoes cannot enter through the covered doorway. As the young men did not carry fire-wood, it is likely that the *otogo* served a useful function before the advent of blankets.

4. **Magic.** Finally Driberg agrees with Professor Seligman that the *otogo* 'was originally built to prevent the boys being "magiced" at a particularly susceptible period of their lives'.

Though put rather vaguely I think this hypothesis is nearer the truth.

An item of culture will have a number of functions. For this reason I believe that protection from the cold night air and mosquitoes, and from being stabbed when incapacitated by beer, were functions of the *otogo*, and it was a means of indicating the sexual proclivities of the occupant. [This is especially likely since its disappearance is associated with the advent of clothes and blankets and political order. The Lango say that entering the *otogo* spoilt their clothes and so they stopped using it. The influence of the Administration and the Schools were also responsible for abolishing these unhygienic houses.] But all these ends could be achieved without the aid of the grotesque *otogo*.

It was the very grotesqueness of the structure that first drew my attention to the fact that it was extraordinarily like an enlarged womb, which I had once seen preserved in spirits in a hospital. The significance of the *otogo* may rest on its representation of a woman giving birth. The Lango is not conscious of the similarity of the *otogo* to female organs of reproduction. If I am right, its significance would be symbolical and would form part of the latent content which acts by this process of symbolisation as a psychological backing to the manifest content of the *otogo*. I will not elaborate this idea of latent and manifest contents of culture, which is borrowed from Rivers's similar division of dreams (*Conflict and Dream*, by W. H. R. Rivers), for my meaning will be obvious to every psychologist.

The *otogo* was associated with two ideas—Fertility magic and Rebirth. These two elements were interdependent and inseparable. I consider that life in the *otogo* represented rebirth from the status of child to that of man. The boy built himself an *otogo* at puberty. He remained in it till the birth of his first child. Every time he came out of his *otogo*—head first with face pointing to the underside of the entrance—he enacted a perfect birth. But the change of status was not completed till the man had a child of his own. Social maturity differs from biological maturity. Puberty merely indicated that the boy was 'ripening' towards manhood; he would soon be a father. While he was enacting his own rebirth, he was also enacting the birth of his child. By a process of sympathetic magic his wife was sure to bear him a child so that his maturity would be complete. The desire for children was one of the ruling motives of the Lango's life.

Man and wife lived in the *otogo* until the first child was born. Sexual intercourse had to take place in the *otogo*. It was considered very dangerous for a man to have intercourse with a girl anywhere in the open, as it was thought that she would become barren and they would both become ill and might even die. The first pregnancy took place in the *otogo*, and would be noticed when the wife had difficulty in entering the narrow opening. As soon as the child was born the father built a proper house, the symbol of his new status as a mature man.

It must be understood that no Lango has explicitly stated that the *otogo* had these two significances. I take care to point out that these ideas lie latent in the whole *otogo* complex.

In different parts of the country I suggested that it would be easier for a man to come out of the *otogo* backwards. The idea was greeted with horror. They said that if a boy did so he would be called an *ajok* (sorcerer) and would be beaten by the old men. Besides, if he had a wife, she would never be able to bear a child again. A child born feet first is always looked upon with horror and is called an *ajok*, as is the case with all abnormal births. It is believed that a mother will not bear again after an abnormal birth unless special precautions are taken, such as the building of an *ot arut* or *ot rudi*. I suggest that a boy coming out of his *otogo* backwards would be symbolising the tragedy of an abnormal birth. The fact stressed by my witnesses was that as a result of coming out backwards the boy would not be able to beget a child. The old men questioned were definitely

filled with horror at the suggestion. But a younger man put forward the more mundane and obvious suggestion that no one would have gone out of the *otogo* backwards for fear of being speared in the back by an enemy. It is considered bad to come out of any house backwards, unless to fetch something which is then carried out backwards.

Another fact that lends weight to my suggestion that the *otogo* is a model of a pregnant womb is that the earthen wall above the narrow, round hole of the entrance is decorated in a manner very reminiscent of pubic hairs; the conical thatched roof of the *otogo* adds to this illusion.

I had compiled a paragraph of evidence based on linguistic usages, showing how, like the word *etogo* (p. 51), *otogo* might be derived from the word *tego* (to ripen), as being the house in which the boy 'ripened' or 'matured' into the status of manhood. But such linguistic evidence is dangerous and so I exclude it.

house. It consists of a platform about two feet high by three feet long and two feet broad, made of *okango* wood. The four corner-posts are embedded in the ground. They have forked ends on which cross-pieces are laid, and then sticks of *okango* are placed lengthways across these cross-pieces. Grass is spread on top, and underneath are placed one or more termites mounds (*tuk*), together with a pot containing the umbilical cords of the twins. According to Driberg this structure used to be called a *peru jok*, but I never heard it so called. However, the word *peru* is used of any building which has no walls, and therefore it would be correct to use it of the *ot rudi*, which is also called *ot arut* or *ot jok*.

The *ot rudi* was built: 1. On the birth of twins, when the umbilical cords of the twins were placed in a single pot balanced on three *tuk* underneath the platform. Should one of the twins have died, its body would have been placed in another pot which would have been propped against the

Ot rudi (*contd.*)

pot containing the cords. 2. On the death of twins, the body of the twin would be placed in a pot under the platform. 3. On the occasion of an abnormal birth, such as feet presentation. 4. On any occasion that might be fraught with danger to one of the twins or at any ceremony specifically concerning a twin.

The structure built in the house of an *ajwaka* of *Jok lango* (p. 166) was called *apeta kango* (*okango*, spread out), and was a platform made of *okango* wood and identical in design to the *ot rudi*. See Plate VI at p. 102.

Otuke (p. 37). A hill in Karamoja to the north-east of Lango.

Owinyakulo (p. 42). The aged *Rwot* of Atura *saza*.

Owls (p. 175).

Ownership of water (p. 58).

Pacho. See Village.

Pany (p. 85). Mortar. Anything that requires crushing is pounded up by means of the mortar and pestle (*alek*). It is about eighteen inches high, but more elaborate *pany* may be as high as three feet. It is made by hollowing out a log of wood. I have already noted the resemblance between the *pany* and the *atimu* drum. See Plate IV, drawing 6 at p. 95.

Papo (pp. 64, 67). Father.

Parenthood (p. 60).

Pars pro toto (pp. 23, 29).

Pastors (p. 80).

Pasturage (pp. 63, 64, 68). *Bar.*

Patriliny (p. 41).

Pattern of culture (pp. 1, 13, 36, 38, 40, 60, 61).

Pawn (p. 137).

Pax Britannica (pp. 80, 109).

Payments (pp. 132, 159, 160, 161, 162).

Peace (pp. 66, 71, 151).

Penis (pp. 43, 55).

Pennant-winged nightjar (p. 5). *Achulany.*

People of the cattle kraal. See *Jo awi dyang.*

People of the dead. See *Jo ma to.*

People of the doorway. See *Jo doggola.*

People of the Lake. See *Jo Nam.*

Peru jok (pp. 98, 173). See also *Ot jok* and *Ot rudi*.

Pestle (pp. 85, 92). *Alek.*

Peto okango (p. 166).

Philipo Ebi (p. 77). A bogus *ajwaka*.

Philipo Lawottim (pp. 9, 10, 96, 149, 162, 163, 164, 170, 174). A useful informant living at Ngai.

Philipo Oruro (pp. 22, 24, 169). *Jago* of Nabieso, who recorded his dreams.

Photographs (pp. 31, 32).

Physiological system (p. 18).

Pigeons (p. 68). *Awele.*

Pisé de terre. This method of building is being recommended by the Government for the natives of Uganda. A demonstration of building and the finished *pisé de terre* houses was given at the Lango Show of 1936. The following account is an extract from the pamphlet issued by the Government Medical Department.

'Construction in *pisé de terre* is of special advantage in areas where timber is scarce. There is evidence that well-constructed *pisé* buildings will often last as long as buildings of burnt brick, and in support of this statement one may mention the Moorish houses in Spain and the Great Wall of China, which are standing after many centuries. By reason of its cheapness, relative ease of construction, its durability and its rat-resisting character, *pisé de terre* is well adapted to become the most popular and suitable type of building in Uganda.

'*Pisé* construction is not difficult and it is believed that African labour should become sufficiently skilled after a short period of instruction to carry out simple buildings in this material.

'Any soil with the exception of clay, ant-hill and sandy earth is suitable for *pisé de terre* construction. Clay and ant-hill are not recommended as they are liable to extensive cracking during the drying process, but in areas where other kinds of soil are not plentiful these materials can be used if mixed with earth of a different character.

'Having collected the earth, remove all visible vegetable matter. With blocks of wood or hammers beat the earth so as to crush stones and lumps of greater size than three-eighths of an inch cubes. All lumps or pieces which cannot be broken up into pieces of this size should be removed. Sprinkle the beaten earth with a small amount

PLATE XIII

Otogo near Orumo

Pisé de terre smallholding at the Lango Show

Pisé de terre (*contd.*)
of water and thoroughly mix. The amount of water added should not be greater than is necessary to make a mixture that will adhere together when tightly squeezed in the hand. The earth will then be ready for use in building.

'In all wall construction it is essential that the walls should be perpendicular and each course laid in true horizontal alignment. To attain this object certain devices have been incorporated in the design of the wooden mould now recommended.

'No building can be expected to stand unless it is placed on good foundations. If the surface soil on the site is only loose earth, an excavation for the foundations should be made up to a depth of at least one foot, care being taken to remove all roots that might damage the building at a later date. The trench should then be filled with stones to a height of four inches above the level of the surface of the ground. Where stone is not available, the construction of the *pisé* wall can, however, begin from the bottom of the trench.

'The mould should be placed in position and filled with the prepared earth mixture to a depth of three inches, which should then be rammed. Ramming should continue until the earth does not rise round the hammer when it is brought down with force. The mould is now ready to be filled to a further depth of three inches but, before any more earth is put in, the top of the preceding layer should be pitted with a sharp instrument so as to provide a rough surface to which the next layer will adhere. The ramming of three-inch layers continues until the mould is full. The mould can then be removed and refixed for the making of the next block. In this way the wall is gradually built up out of blocks of hard earth.

'The majority of Africans build their houses during their leisure hours, and it is quite common for the work to extend over a lengthy period and to be suspended completely during the wet weather. For this reason it is recommended that the roof be entirely

erected before work on the walls is commenced.' See Plate XIII at p. 200.
Placenta. See After-birth.
Plague (pp. 7, 8, 163).
Poison (p. 31). *Yat.*
Political system (pp. 46, 56, 57, 146).
Potatoes (pp. 170, 171).
Pot of the *lau.* See *Gulu lau.*
Pots (pp. 14, 21, 29, 31, 49, 70, 74, 75, 76, 78, 84, 85, 86, 88, 90, 92–3, 96–9, 101, 102, 112, 113–14, 119–21, 125, 139, 143, 148, 156, 157, 158, 159, 170). See also *Gulu.*
Prayer (pp. 78, 108).
Pregnancy (pp. 44, 81, 83, 140, 170–1).
Premature birth (pp. 99, 102, 103, 161).
Premise (pp. 2, 3, 6, 11, 15, 23, 28, 33, 36, 126).
Pre-nuptial chastity (p. 82).
Preservation (pp. 35, 40, 46, 48, 53, 58, 81).
Priest (p. 23).
Prison. See Jail.
Private parts. See Genital organs.
Privileged relationship. See Joking relationship.
Prohibitions (pp. 12, 13, 43, 44, 65, 68–9, 70, 84, 85, 93, 99, 100, 101, 127, 128, 149).
Prostitution (p. 12).
Psychic disturbances (pp. 6–11).
Psycho-analysis (pp. 11, 156, 169).
Psychological aspect of healing (pp. 11, 25, 27, 162).
Puberty (pp. 12, 17, 60, 61, 64, 68).
Pubic fringe. See *Chip.*
Pubic hairs (p. 55).
Public opinion (p. 54).
Pyen (p. 147). A new skin.

Quarrel (pp. 15, 16, 20, 24, 25, 32, 41, 43, 45, 46, 49, 51, 52, 57, 58, 59, 60, 65, 66, 92, 94, 105, 107, 113, 114, 120, 122, 127, 129, 137, 138, 146, 156).
Quinquennial festival. See *Ewor.*

Radcliffe-Brown (p. 19).
Raids (pp. 14, 40, 41, 57–8, 60, 71, 74, 145, 146).
Rain (pp. 6, 14, 34, 39, 40, 61–3, 65–7, 71–9, 80, 146, 152, 163, 170, 176).
Rain dance. See *Myel akot.*
Rain guardians. See *Won kot.*
Rain-making (pp. 4, 18, 21, 39, 40, 43, 47, 50, 51, 57, 61–3, 66, 67, 68, 74, 75, 76, 111).

Twon (*contd.*)

war leader under whom several *Rwodi* used to combine. The expression *twon me atekere* (bull of the Clan) is used for the famous ancestors who were supposed to have founded the Clan. The names of these persons are known together with their prowess and incidents associated with them. These names and incidents form a Clan cry (p. 42) which is shouted out by clansmen on joyful or victorious occasions, such as in battle or at the twin ceremonies. *Gwongo twon* means to shout the Clan cry. When I used to ask a man what the *twon* of his *atekere* was, he would say, 'Do you mean the bull which they invoke?' (*twon ma gigwongo*). Driberg says that the term for the Clan cry is *gwong* and that the expression is *gwong ma gigwongo*. This may be true, though I never noticed it, but the expression *twon ma gigwongo* is certainly used also.

Twon lwak. See Bull of the crowd and *Twon.*

Twon me atekere. See Bull of the Clan and *Twon.*

Tyeto (pp. 10, 140, 166, 169, 173). Usually translated as 'to divine', but this is not satisfactory. By the process of *tyeto* the *ajwaka* discovers, through *jok* power, what is wrong with an inquirer, the cause of his misfortune and the remedy for it. This is done by means of a rattle (*aja*) which the *ajwaka* shakes. The voice of the local manifestation of *jok* power which the *ajwaka* controls is heard speaking through the sound of the rattle. This is really the *ajwaka* speaking in an assumed voice.

Tying on the marriage skin. See *Tweyo lau.*

Tying up the rain (pp. 14, 29, 65).

Tying up the wind (p. 78).

Umbilical cord (pp. 97, 130, 131, 133, 135).

Umo tipo. See *Mako tipo.* Covering a *tipo.*

Unity of groups (pp. 36, 39–40, 41, 42, 50, 52, 53, 54, 56, 57, 58, 59, 60, 61, 66, 145, 146).

Urine (pp. 14, 29, 147).

Valleys (p. 139).

Value of groups (pp. 36, 40, 48, 51, 52, 53, 54, 55, 56, 57, 58, 59, 60, 62).

Variations in ceremonial (pp. 41, 42, 43, 45).

Vegetable marrow (p. 43).

Vegetables (pp. 76, 85, 123, 124, 134).

Ventriloquism (pp. 26, 163, 164).

Victory cry. See *Jira.*

Village (pp. 15, 24, 31, 32, 38, 45, 53, 56, 58–60, 63, 68–71, 74, 75, 76, 77, 78, 79, 82, 83, 86, 87, 88, 89, 92, 93–4, 95, 96, 97, 98, 99, 100, 102–4, 106–8, 111, 112, 113–14, 115, 117–19, 120, 121, 122, 124, 125, 128, 129, 130, 134, 135–9, 140–2, 143, 145–8, 149–50, 156, 158–60, 162, 163, 164, 165, 168, 173, 174, 175). *Pacho.*

Viscera (pp. 49, 65, 92, 93).

Voice of *jok* (p. 150).

Vulture (pp. 68, 107).

Wailing (pp. 106, 107, 108).

Wal (pp. 76, 124, 158, 159). A calabash receptacle made by cutting vertically in half a large round calabash (*keno*). Beer is sometimes drunk out of a *wal*. A large *wal* is used for covering the baby to protect it from the sun when slung on the back. This is called *wal wich* (*wal* for the head). See also *Agwata, Apoko, Keno, Obuto*; also Plate I at p. 58.

Wal wich (p. 90). See also *Wal.*

Wang tich (pp. 38, 53, 58, 59, 124, 125). Work group.

Warfare (pp. 18, 37, 39, 40, 72, 74, 98, 104, 105, 109, 111, 145). See also Battle, Fighting.

Warriors (pp. 104, 105, 145).

Wart-hog (p. 67).

Washing (pp. 69, 75, 79, 84, 85, 92, 93, 95, 101, 114, 116, 120, 132, 133, 134, 136, 155, 158, 161, 162).

Washing the child's eyes. See *Lwoko wang atin.*

Washing the pot. See *Lwoko gulu.*

Wat (pp. 38, 54). Group of relatives.

Waterbuck (pp. 43, 67). *Apoli.*

Water gypsies (p. 40).

Wayo (p. 56). *Okeo*'s mother.

Wayo jok (pp. 165, 166).

We (pp. 69, 93, 95, 122, 138, 141, 170). The intestinal dung, or chyme, found in the stomach of a slaughtered animal. It is much used in ceremonial, when the people concerned are anointed (*juko*) with it.

Wedding ring (p. 83).
Whistling (p. 30).
White Magic (pp. 2, 3, 22, 23, 27, 31, 33, 34).
Widow (pp. 55, 63, 66, 106–8, 112, 113, 114–15).
Wife (pp. 12, 14, 18, 20, 29, 41, 46, 47, 53, 55, 64, 74, 81, 82, 83, 84, 85, 86, 87, 88, 99–104, 112, 114, 116, 117, 121, 127–30, 136, 140, 149, 154, 163, 167, 174). See also Wives.
Wild cherry (p. 43).
Wild fig (pp. 43, 85).
Wi lyel. See Grave.
Wind. See *Yamo.*
Winnowing mat. See *Oderu.*
Winyo (pp. 5–6, 15, 158). Bird, used for describing luck.
Wire (pp. 65, 105, 136).
Wiro (pp. 84, 92, 104, 130). Best translated as 'to anoint', but the anointing is done in the following way: Only *mo dyang* or *mo nino* oil is used. The performer faces the person and takes the oil in both hands. Starting from the back of the shoulders it is smeared over the shoulders and down over the breasts. After this it is also smeared over the stomach, starting from the small of the back. See also *Gwelo* and *Juko.*
Witch. See *Ajok.*
Witchcraft. See Black Magic.
Wives (pp. 43, 44, 45–7, 54, 84, 85, 86, 87, 100, 114, 115, 117, 138). *Mon.* See also Wife.
Won. See Guardian. This is usually translated as owner, much misunderstanding being caused thereby. It would be more accurately rendered as 'One who has influence over the object'. The words 'Guardian', 'Protector' or 'Trustee' might sometimes be adequate translations. The word 'owner' should be avoided, though the modern meaning of *won* is tending towards the idea of owner in our sense of the word as a result of the new economic system with its emphasis on individual ownership.
Won agat (pp. 142–3). Leader of the *gato* chant-chorus.
Won amagoro (pp. 102, 145, 154, 155). A lesser chief. See also *Saza.*
Won arum (pp. 6, 12, 148–52). Guardian of the hunting area.

Won awi dyang (pp. 59, 60, 148). Guardian of the cattle kraal.
Won dok (p. 46). Guardian of the cattle.
Won kot (pp. 23, 24, 65, 72, 74, 75, 76, 77, 78). Rain guardian.
Won pacho (pp. 108, 145). Village chief. See also *Saza.*
Won wang tich (pp. 58, 59). Guardian of the work group.
Woodpecker (p. 175).
Work group. See *Wang tich.*

Yago (pp. 142, 144). Kigelia.
Yamo (pp. 18, 78, 116, 155, 157, 159, 164). Wind. *Jok* power is described as being 'like moving wind' (*bala yamo muwoto*). *Yamo* becomes then practically a synonym for *tipo.* It was said, 'Keny's wife has given him her wind', meaning that Keny was suffering from a *tipo* visitation (p. 116). The presence of a *tipo* is denoted in eddies of air (p. 116). But it is clear that the eddy of air is not identified with the *tipo*, for it was said in a *mako tipo* ceremony, 'The wind of the *tipo* prevents him from walking', and in the same ceremony the *ajwaka* said that there was always wind when the *tipo* danced. Atim when possessed by *jok* power said, 'The wind in my body says that his name is Okomo' (p. 155).
Yamo is also used with the meaning 'to flirt'. When a boy talks in secret to a girl he is said to *yamo* with her. It is interesting to note that the word *chodo*, originally used of flirting (see *The Lango*, p. 155), is now definitely used for sexual intercourse, whereas the term *yamo* is used in the same sense as the old use of *chodo.* This is illustrative of the significant change that has taken place in courting etiquette, trial intercourse being substituted for the old form of platonic courting. (See 'Changes in Lango Marriage Customs', *The Uganda Journal*, Vol. VII, No. 4, April 1940.)
Yat. Tree. See also Medicine. The word is used of all types of medicine, poison or substances having magical properties. Old men carry small pieces of wood hanging round their necks or with their hunting whistles. These are their fighting magic, hunting

Yat (*contd.*)

magic, or cures for sores, etc. A little of the wood is scraped off in a powder, which is rubbed into the sore or blown in the direction of the enemy. Perhaps this early use of roots and pieces of wood for medicinal and magical purposes is responsible for the use of the term *yat* to cover all types of medicine, poisons or magical substances, even though they may not be derived from any tree.

Yatchakdyang (p. 174). Plant.

Yat me dwar (p. 152). Hunting magic.

Yaws (p. 170).

Yeyo lyeto (pp. 81, 82, 87, 88–91, 93, 109, 140). Carrying the ornaments.

Yeyo moko me or (pp. 128, 129). Carrying flour for the mother-in-law.

Yiko dano ma to (pp. 106, 108, 111). Burying a dead man.

Yot kom (pp. 77, 128, 130). Good health.

Zebra (p. 67).